Threads
of History

TEACHER EDITION

A Thematic Approach
to Our Nation's Story
for AP* U.S. History

by Michael Henry, Ph.D.

SHERPALEARNING
GUIDING YOU TO EVEN GREATER HEIGHTS

To the Memory of My Parents:
Gleason and Dorothy Henry

Publisher: David Nazarian

Copy-Editor: Christine DeFranco

Cartographer: Sal Esposito

The publisher would like to thank Connie Hines, Susan Reeder, Mark DiGiacomo, and Joe Villano for their support and guidance in building the 3rd Edition.

The publisher also thanks Dan Frederiks and Dan Brown for their influence and support.

ISBN 978-1-948641-01-2

Copyright © 2019

Sherpa Learning, LLC.

West Milford, New Jersey

www.sherpalearning.com

SHERPALEARNING
GUIDING YOU TO EVEN GREATER HEIGHTS

10 9 8 7 6 5 4 3

Threads
of History

3rd Edition

Introduction to the Teacher Edition

Thematic Review & Source Analysis Activities   (★ *indicates lesson plan content*)

The Long Essay Questions and Suggested Responses

The Document-Based Questions and Suggested Responses

Appendices

Introduction to the Teacher Edition

To my Friends and Colleagues,

Thanks for purchasing the updated and revised 3rd Edition of *Threads of History*! This Teacher Edition is designed to help you evaluate and deepen your students' understanding of the thirty-seven charts that are the heart of *Threads of History*. I hope that these materials will prove to be effective instructional tools for you throughout the school year as you prepare your students for the challenge of the exam and for the demands of college.

How to Use This Book

The resources in this companion text are designed to make it as easy as possible for you to integrate *Threads* into your existing curriculum plan. What follows is a guide to the resources found within this text. After that, you will find a guide to the materials on the Teacher's Companion Website.

The Lessons

Each of the 37 lessons in *Threads of History* is divided into two parts:

Part 1 – Thematic Review Activities: This section includes the lesson introduction, the thematic chart, and several multiple-choice questions about the chart.

> While thinking skills will be important on the test, students must still have relevant historical knowledge to fuel their thinking. Students can only reason historically if they have facts and ideas with which to reason. Without specific information about America's past, students will fail to identify the relationships asked for by the multiple-choice questions and be reduced to vague generalities and misrepresentations on the short-answer and long essay questions. The thematic charts in the lessons of *Threads of History* will help your students develop the factual base necessary to succeed on the exam.

> For a more in-depth and rigorous review of the topic/theme, extend this section of the lesson by using the **Core Chart Worksheets** (see p. *x*).

> New to the 3rd Edition, each lesson will now explore one aspect of each topic in greater depth in a new feature called **Enhancing Understanding**. These terms (key figures, events, documents, ideas, etc.) will help to expand the meaning of the issues at hand.

Part 2 – Source Analysis Activities: This section includes a primary or secondary source with corresponding Multiple-Choice and Short-Answer Questions.

The Source Activities in each lesson will help students develop and improve historical "habits of the mind"—the dispositions that include generating a plan of action to solve problems, accessing reliability of information, identifying point-of-view, and recognizing the relationship between facts and larger historical contexts. These exercises, while not attempting to precisely replicate questions that appear on the test, do anticipate many of the reasoning skills that are needed for students to be successful in the course, on the exam, and beyond!

> The **Primary Source Worksheets** (see p. *xi*) may be useful to students in need of reinforcement of their source analysis skills.

The Lesson Plans

To help you get started using *Threads* in your classroom as soon as tomorrow, some of the lessons in this book (including the first 7) feature detailed lesson plans designed for a typical 50-minute class period. Even if you have used previous editions of *Threads*, these lesson plans should prove useful to you throughout the year as the topics are covered in your course.

Each lesson plan includes a set of **Objectives** to guide you and give you an overall sense of the lesson. Building on the introductory material and chart activity, an additional **primary source document** is presented on one aspect of the topic developed in the chart. A series of **Discussion Questions** about the document is provided to promote class discussion and encourage student inquiry into the issues raised by the chart. Answers to the Discussion Questions are available on the companion website (see page *x*).

You may photocopy the additional primary source documents in the lesson plans in this text, but they are also available on the website in PDF format so that you can easily project them in class or duplicate them for your students.

> Four of the lesson plans use longer forms of the same documents used in the Source Activities of the corresponding lessons. These lesson plans will deepen student interaction with those documents.

The Essay Questions and Suggested Responses

The next two sections of this guide offer detailed response guidelines for the 19 Long Essay Questions and the 3 Document-Based Questions found on the website. The long essay questions are designed to assess students' understanding of topics and themes presented in one or more of the charts. The document-based questions have the rare quality of having never been published on a past exam.

We intentionally withheld the LEQ and DBQ prompts from inclusion in the Student Edition because we felt (and our reviewers agreed) that teachers would want to use them in quizzes and tests. Therefore, it would be best if the students were not able to view them in advance. The questions are available on the Teacher Companion Website in PDF format so that you can easily print and distribute them to your students. They are also available in Microsoft Word format, should you want to copy/paste them into your own quizzes and tests.

The suggested response outlines identify themes, interpretations, and facts that students might include in a well-developed response. The outlines are very detailed, so it is extremely unlikely that students would include all of the themes and information listed. These outlines are offered as guidelines to help assist you as you construct your own classroom grading standards and hopefully make it easier for you to grade your students' essays.

The essay questions can be used in several ways in your APUSH class.

- You may wish to assign the questions during the year as either in-class or out-of-class writing activities when the topics are presented in your curriculum. In this format, the questions could serve as measures of current student learning. They would provide an index of how much students have understood about the historical period they have just studied.

- You might also use one or more essay questions on a midterm or final exam to determine how much knowledge and understanding students have retained throughout the semester or year.

- Finally, several of the questions, in conjunction with multiple-choice items from the online test bank, could be used as part of a practice exam that you design.

APPENDIX A – The Rubric Guides

The College Board rubrics for the LEQs and DBQs are somewhat complex and may require a period of adjustment for some teachers. In order to facilitate this, I have included simplified guides to aid in the successful utilization of the College Board rubrics in your assessment of student responses. These guides offer a quick summary of each component of the rubric, along with a basic, at-a-glance version of the rubric that can be used as a quick grading reference once the grading process is more comfortable.

APPENDIX B – The Distribution Charts

Four distribution charts have been provided to help you effectively utilize the wealth of practice items contained in *Threads of History* and the online test bank.

The first chart identifies practice items by the major **Historical Time Periods** of the APUSH course. This chart is designed to help you build quizzes and practice activities that perfectly sync with your curriculum plan.

The second and third charts identify practice items by the corresponding **Learning Objectives** and **Disciplinary Practices/Reasoning Skills** provided by the College Board in the APUSH course framework. These charts are designed to make it easy for you to identify and target areas where your students struggle to achieve the standards outlined by the College Board.

You'll notice that the questions that accompany the charts in each lesson are not correlated to the College Board's standards. These questions are designed to test specific knowledge and understandings directly related to the charts and, as such, do not cleanly align to the intents of the Learning Objectives and Practices/Skills. They do, however, provide students with some of the information they will need to answer the questions posed about the primary sources, so they play a vital role in classroom instruction and preparation for the new types of multiple-choice questions they will encounter on the redesigned exam.

Finally, the fourth chart has been included to offer an overview of how this new edition of *Threads of History* aligns to the **Common Core State Standards for History/Social Studies for grades 11-12**. *Threads* was not designed with the CCSS in mind, yet it does an excellent job of addressing all 10 of these standards, some in greater depths than others.

APPENDIX C – The Source Worksheets

A collection of basic worksheets to aid in the analysis of different types of historical documents has been provided in Appendix C of this Teacher Edition. You may photocopy the worksheets, or you may print them from the companion website. The same worksheets also appear in Appendix A of the Student Edition, but with notes and tips about the sections of each worksheet.

APPENDIX D – The Historical Document Index

You may wish to use the Historical Document Index to identify documents you might like to use in class or as part of your own quizzes or exams. This simple index will help you choose sources by time period and type, and provides page locations for the sources in the Student and Teacher Editions. Some of the visual documents are available on the companion site so you can print them or display them in class.

Guide to the Website Resources

In addition to the abundance of content found in this Teacher Edition, a substantial collection of valuable resources has been made available to you through the companion website. These items have been placed on the website because they are most useful in digital form; it will be easier for you to display with a projector, print and copy handouts, and copy/paste items for your custom tests and quizzes. [This also makes it easier for you to share and distribute these items with other teachers—your friends and colleagues. **PLEASE DON'T**—not only because it's against the law, but because we cannot continue to provide quality resources like this without paying customers.]

https://threads.sherpalearning.com

To access these resources on the companion website, please go to the address shown above and register your copy of the Teacher Edition of *Threads of History*.

Unique ID Code: Each copy of the TE includes a label on the inside front cover with your unique identification code. If you misplace your code, or if your book happened to come without this label, please contact us at hello@sherpalearning.com and we'll get you straightened out.

No ID Code: If you purchased your copy on Amazon or another online retailer, you book may have come without a label on the inside front cover with a unique ID code. You can still register for an account, but there will be a short delay while your account is approved.

Already Registered: If you already had an account from the 2*nd* Edition of *Threads of History*, your account is still valid and can still be used to access the site. If you can't find your login info, just use the Forgot Password option to reset it. Again, if you run into any issues at all, please drop us a line at hello@sherpalearning.com.

Core Chart Worksheets

To extend and enhance the thematic review portion of each lesson, use the Core Chart Worksheets found on the companion site. These are the same as the thematic charts found in the core lessons, however, all or most of the cells have been left blank. Have your students fill in the blank cells in the charts, either in groups or individually. This activity will require students to research various topics and themes presented in a chart, discuss these ideas, expand their meaning, and expand their understandings beyond the recall level.

Each chart is available in different formats—either completely blank or partially completed. You can print these and give them to your students to complete with or without the lists of chart contents.

HIPPO: Getting Ready for the DBQ

H.I.P.P.O. is a tool you can use at the beginning of the school year to help your students build document analysis and writing skills required to successfully answer the Document-Based Question. It focuses on the four components identified as necessary for the new DBQ. It also reminds students that they must do more than simply decode a document; they must apply it to a thesis or argument.

Worksheets and Document Handouts

Appendix A in the Student Edition introduces students to the three primary source worksheets that should be used in conjunction with the Source Activities in each lesson. The three worksheets are available for printing and duplication on the website. [They are also found in Appendix C of this text, along with a blank SAQ answer sheet, for photocopying.] These worksheets provide critical support as your students begin to develop document analysis skills.

Also available are printable versions of the additional primary source documents included with the lesson plans.

The Online Test Bank

The test bank of multiple-choice questions available on the companion website will help you determine if your students have mastered the information. If they have not, identify the gaps in their understanding and hone in on exactly where each individual student needs to improve. Answering these questions will help your students know if they clearly understand a topic and build confidence in their ability to think critically, comprehensively, and comparatively.

Closing Thoughts

Again, I hope that these materials are a great help to you as you adjust to the new course and exam. If you have any questions about the materials, please raise them in the community forum on the Teacher Companion Website. If *Threads* has been a help to you and your students, please let us know! If you'd like to reach me personally, you can email me at mikehenryhistory@gmail.com. I'd love to hear from you.

Sincerely,

Michael Henry

SHERPALEARNING
GUIDING YOU TO EVEN GREATER HEIGHTS

Our mission is to open doors for high-achieving learners through access to high-quality, skills-based instruction written by rock-star teachers. Here are some of the other new resources now available from Sherpa Learning:

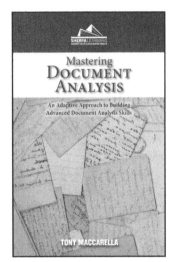

Mastering Document Analysis

A 3-Step Approach to Finding the Past

by Tony Maccarella

Analyzing primary sources vastly expands students' understanding of important historical events, while also promoting the development of high-level critical thinking skills. *MDA* presents students with a simple and effective 3-step approach to extract information from primary and secondary source documents so that they can make a deep and meaningful connection with the past.

(**isbn:** 978-0-9905471-7-4)

5-Minute Drill

A Simple Pre-Writing Process for Creating College-Level Essays

by Rich Mayorga

The 5-Minute Drill is an easy and effective way to answer challenging questions with an organized essay that a) makes an insightful interpretation and claim, b) contains evidence to support it, and c) provides an analytical explanation. With this prewriting activity, you can develop the major reasoning and organizational skills necessary for college-level thinking and writing. The 5-Minute Drill saves time, gets to the heart of the question's answer, and produces unparalleled success.

(**isbn:** 978-1-948641-17-3)

Go to www.sherpalearning.com for more information.

Thematic Review
& Source Analysis
Activities
with Suggested Responses

Lesson 1

The Atlantic World, 1492–1700

The exploration and settlement of the Western Hemisphere from 1492–1700 is often viewed through the prism of the Atlantic World concept. This construct analyzes the interactions, exchanges, and transmissions of trade, people, religion, diseases, and commodities among four areas: Western Europe, Western Africa, the Caribbean, and North/South America throughout the 16th, 17th, and 18th centuries. It examines how these regions that bordered the Atlantic Ocean were interconnected to define the age of exploration and settlement.

Motivated by the search for the "Northwest Passage," and the quest for riches, various European nations traveled the Atlantic Ocean as a highway that transported foods, plants, commodities, people, and diseases back and forth between the old world and the new. In addition, the ongoing rivalries and disputes that dominated Europe at the time were transferred to the Americas and the Caribbean.

The chart on the following page outlines the policies and programs of the four major colonial powers. As you study it, think of the concept of the Atlantic World as an organizing device for your analysis of this era.

Directions: Analyze the chart on the Atlantic World, and then answer the following questions.

1. In which pair of nations would colonists find the least amount of interference from the mother country?

    (A) Great Britain and the Netherlands

    (B) France and Spain

    (C) Spain and the Netherlands

    (D) Great Britain and France

OBJECTIVES

Have your students discuss how European racial attitudes affected the interaction with Native Americans during the period of colonialization. In their discussion, they should think about how a different set of attitudes might have changed the course of development in the Atlantic World.

After the class discussion on the Atlantic World and reading the Royal Order, students will be able to:

1. evaluate the goals the Spanish had in colonizing North America;

2. debate the benefits and costs colonization had on the lives of Native Americans in the 16th century;

3. analyze how the Spanish view of Native American culture impacted their colonization policies;

4. assess the role of religion played in Spanish goals for colonizing North America.

ADDITIONAL COMPONENTS

*   **Core Chart Worksheet:** "Lesson 1 – The Atlantic World" (website)

*   **Primary Source Handout:** "Royal Order from the King of Spain" (copy p. 5 or print from website)

*   **Document Source Worksheets:** "Worksheet for Document Source Analysis" (p. 246); "Worksheet for Map Analysis" (p. 248)

2. A common sequence for the use of forced labor among the colonizing nations was to utilize

   (A) the native population and then resort to African slavery

   (B) African slaves immediately upon founding the colony

   (C) indentured servants and then resort to African slaves

   (D) African slaves and then resort to indentured servants

3. In which colonial system was religion mostly likely to be used in controlling the native population?

   (A) France

   (B) Great Britain

   (C) Spain

   (D) the Netherlands

Enhancing Understanding

BLACK LEGEND — the charge that demonized Spanish exploration in the 15th, 16th, and 17th centuries as cruel and bigoted. While no longer universally accepted, the idea of Spain as a uniquely evil actor in exploration defined the historiography of the Atlantic World for many decades.

DISCUSSION QUESTIONS

Hand out or display the document, "Royal Order from the King of Spain," (shown on page 5) and ask the following:

1. How did the Spanish try to control Native Americans in the 16th century?

2. What racial and cultural attitudes did the Spanish display in the Royal Order?

3. What did the Spanish mean when they wrote that Native Americans must live "in a civilized manner?"

4. What benefits did the Spanish see for Native Americans in their policies of containing them in towns?

5. What was the cost to Native Americans in their interactions with the Spanish?

6. What were the pros and cons of the overall Spanish approach to Native Americans in North America?

Answers available on the companion website.

Four Major Colonial Powers of the Atlantic World

	Great Britain	France	Spain	Netherlands
Areas of exploration/ settlement	North American Seaboard Caribbean islands Later Canada	St. Lawrence river valley Great Lakes Lower Mississippi area West Indies	Mexico Peru Caribbean Southeast U.S.A.	Hudson River Valley New York New Jersey Delaware Pennsylvania Caribbean
Motivations for exploration	Acquire land/gold Reduce England's economic troubles Religious freedom	Acquire gold/silver Fur trade Sugar production	Sought Gold, God, and Glory Sought enrichment at expense of Native peoples	Fur trade Sugar Production Promote slave trade
Native American relations	Used "Irish model: suppressed/destroyed Indians/culture	Shared fur trade Respected culture— cooperated	Enslaved people Destroyed culture	More like French model of cooperation Respected Indian culture Shared fur trade
Religious Aspect	Domestic religious conflicts promoted migrations Many religions in colonies Little attempt to convert Indians	Jesuits attempted to convert Indians to Catholicism—mixed results	Tool of colonial control Church repressed Indians/ tried to convert to Catholicism	Little attempt at converting Indians Diverse population promoted many religions
System of Colonial Control	More decentralized than France/Spain Local authority established Royal, proprietary, self-governing colonies	Very loose Trading posts rather than settlements *Seigneurial system*: land to bring settlers to colonies	Strict direction from Spain Used forts/ missions *Encomiendas/Haciendas*: system of land control	Very autocratic Dutch East/West India Co. developed trade/ settlements *Patroons*: land distribution system
Labor System	Indian slaves, indentured servants, and African Slaves	Indians first then African slaves Black Code: some religious, economic freedom	Indians first, then African slaves Mainly in Caribbean for sugar production	Very active in slave trade Africans considered inferior, but freer than elsewhere
Comments	Religious struggles at home slowed exploration Plantations created: English system in America Farming became way of life	More interested in fur trade than farming New France always "provincial backward area	"Black Legend" of oppression established Intermarriage between Indians and Spanish common	Trade more important than colonization Migration sparse in North America Lost colony to British in 1664

Royal Order from the King of Spain

Juan de la Pena has reported to me saying that because the Indians of this province are not gathered into towns where they may be governed and controlled much harm is done... Moreover, the Indians resist the changes to their way of life. They assault, rob, and kill both Spaniards and peaceful Indians on the highways.... I have therefore approved it, and do now command you to issue orders and instructions for gathering the Indians of that province who are wandering in the mountains into towns. Here they may live in a civilized manner and be governed, may better communicate with each other, have order and system in their living, and be more easily taught the Catholic religion. They may also escape the dangers which result from living in the mountains and deserts....

SOURCE: King of Spain, May 1570

Directions: Using the map below and your knowledge of American history, answer the following questions. Use the Map Worksheet on page 158 (Student Edition) to guide your analysis of the source.

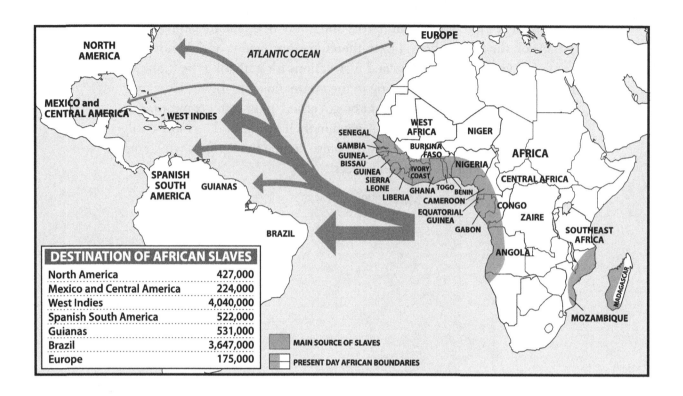

DESTINATION OF AFRICAN SLAVES	
North America	427,000
Mexico and Central America	224,000
West Indies	4,040,000
Spanish South America	522,000
Guianas	531,000
Brazil	3,647,000
Europe	175,000

MAIN SOURCE OF SLAVES

PRESENT DAY AFRICAN BOUNDARIES

Multiple-Choice

1. The development of the slave trade shown in the map led most directly to which of the following?

    (A) The British relied more on Indian slavery than did the Spanish and French.

    (B) Women increasingly made up a larger portion of the slave population in North America.

    (C) North American slaves work in the fur trade rather than in the production of cotton.

    (D) North American slaves were better educated and more docile than slaves elsewhere in the Atlantic World.

Because North American colonies were not primarily sugar producing areas, they had less need for direct importation of African slaves. Sugar was the money crop and the in the 17th and 18th centuries, male slaves were needed for its cultivation. The increase in the North American slave population was driven mainly by reproduction from existing slaves, of whom about 50% of the births were females, thus the portion of women slaves in North America was higher than in the Caribbean and South America.

(WXT-1, Causation)

2. Which of the following impacts did the slave trade have on the African continent?

(A) African peoples were gradually accepted as equals to their European counterparts.

(B) Africans encouraged Europeans to go into the interior areas of the continent to capture slaves.

(C) Africans unified to protect their people from European slave traders.

(D) Africans and Europeans developed commercial patterns that included trading goods for slaves.

> The Africans and Europeans developed trade patterns around the African's desire for commodities such as cloth, weapons, manufactured goods and the Europeans need for slave labor to cultivate sugar in the Caribbean and South America.
>
> *(WOR-1, Causation)*

Short-Answer

Using the information from the map, answer parts a, b, and c.

a) Briefly explain ONE important similarity in the treatment of African slaves in the Caribbean and North America.

b) Briefly explain ONE important difference in the treatment of African slaves in the Caribbean and North America.

c) Briefly explain ONE factor that accounts from the difference that you indicated in <u>part b</u>.

---

a) Answers will vary, but may include similarities in treatment such as:
- Both groups were beaten and tortured when they did not work
- Both groups resisted slavery.
- Both groups had their families broken up.
- Both groups had little control over their daily lives.
- Both groups were ripped from their homeland in Africa.

(WXT-1, Comparison)

b) Answers will vary, but may include differences in treatment:
- Caribbean slaves worked in sugar, which was more difficult than North American slaves.
- Caribbean slaves were preponderantly male and more rebellious than North American slaves.
- Caribbean slaves had a shorter life expectancy than North American slaves because of the harsher working conditions.

- North American slaves worked principally in tobacco, wheat and corn.

- North American slaves had more females in the populations.

- North American slaves were less likely to rebel than Caribbean slaves.

(WOR-1, Comparison)

c)   Answers will vary, but may include:

- There were fewer slaves imported directly to North America so it was more likely to see a large portion of females in the slave population.

- Working in sugar was more difficult and unhealthy than working in other crops and thus a short life expectancy in the Caribbean.

- More African males, who had not been born into slavery, were imported into the Caribbean and had experienced freedom and were more likely to rebel.

(WOR-1, Analyzing Historical Evidence)

Historical Periods

By the time you are ready to take the Advanced Placement (AP) test in May, you will have been bombarded by hundreds of facts and dates. In this blizzard of information, it is possible to lose track of the broad delineations of U.S. history. On the AP test, however, there will often be essay questions or multiple-choice questions that refer to a historical period rather than to a set of specific years. Unless you are familiar with the labels for these eras, you may misinterpret or incorrectly answer parts a question that you could otherwise easily master.

The following chart presents the major historical periods of U.S. history. In addition, it identifies events that roughly marked the beginning and ending of the era. You might review the chart by looking at a list of events (perhaps in the index of your primary textbook) and placing them in their appropriate historical period. This will help you develop a stronger chronological sense and decrease the likelihood of encountering unfamiliar time references on the AP test.

Directions: Analyze the chart on historical periods, and then answer the following questions.

1. Which one of the following events did NOT occur during the antebellum period?

    (A) the ratification of the Fourteenth Amendment

    (B) the development of the cotton gin

    (C) the dispute over slavery in Missouri

    (D) the dispute over the tariff in South Carolina

OBJECTIVES

Have your students discuss why historians use historical periods to categorize events. In their discussion they should examine specific periods and evaluate whether they are accurate means of sorting facts about America's past.

After the class discussion on historical periods and reading the two views on Reconstruction, which follow, students will be able to:

1. evaluate two contrasting views of Reconstruction;

2. assess differing views of the role of African Americans in Reconstruction governments;

3. debate the usefulness of 1877 as an end date for the Reconstruction period;

4. evaluate how a historian's background and point of view may affect their writing and sorting of historical facts.

ADDITIONAL COMPONENTS

- **Core Chart Worksheet**: "Lesson 2 – Historical Periods" (website)

- **Primary Source Handout**: "Two Views on the Period of Reconstruction" (p. 12 or website)

- **Document Source Worksheets**: "Worksheet for Document Source Analysis" (p. 246); "Worksheet for Map Analysis" (p. 248)

2. Federal government regulation of the meat industry and the beginnings of the Great War (World War I) occurred during

    (A) the Gilded Age

    (B) the Progressive Era

    (C) the New Deal Era

    (D) the Fair Deal Era

3. Which one of the following events occurred during the Gilded Age?

    (A) the end of the War of 1812

    (B) the election of Andrew Jackson as president

    (C) the end of World War II

    (D) the election of Ulysses Grant as president

Enhancing Understanding

PERIODIZATION OF HISTORY — a process used by historians of categorizing historical facts and data into blocks of time so they can be addressed more efficiently. This allows for a more systematic study of events, a clearer delineation in textbook chapters, and a spirited debate over what topics belong in a particular period.

DISCUSSION QUESTIONS

Hand out or display the set of documents, "Two Views on the Period of Reconstruction," (shown on page 12) and ask the following:

1. How did Randall and DuBois differ on the role of African Americans in Reconstruction governments?

2. How did the two historians differ on the role of white men in Reconstruction governments?

3. What does your textbook say about the motives of carpetbaggers and scalawags? Does it agree with Randall's assessment?

4. How does a historian's bias affect the writing of history?

5. What do you know about the author/authors of your textbook? How might their backgrounds affect their view of history?

Answers available on the companion website.

Major Historical Periods throughout U.S. History

Period	Date	Events marking beginnings and endings
Colonial Period	1607–1763	1. Jamestown founded 2. French and Indian War ended
Revolutionary Period	1763–1783	1. England ended salutary neglect 2. Treaty of Paris signed ending Revolution
Confederation Period	1781–1789	1. States surrender their western land claims 2. Constitution ratified
Era of Good Feelings	1815–1824	1. War of 1812 ended 2. Election of 1824
Jacksonian Era	1828–1848	1. Andrew Jackson elected president 2. Mexican War ended/James Polk leaves office
Antebellum Period (South before Civil War)	1793–1861	1. Cotton gin invented/rise of slavery 2. Civil War started
Reconstruction Era	1865–1877	1. Civil War ended 2. Compromise of 1877
Gilded Age	1868–1901	1. Ulysses Grant elected president 2. Assassination of William McKinley
Progressive Era	1901–1917	1. Square Deal began 2. America entered the Great War
New Deal Era	1933–1939	1. Franklin Roosevelt began his presidency 2. World War II began in Europe
Fair Deal Era	1945–1953	1. Truman became president/FDR died 2. Korean War divided nation/Truman retired
New Frontier/ Great Society Era	1961–1968	1. John Kennedy became president 2. Vietnam War divided nation

Two Views on the Period of Reconstruction

Document A

Coming south after the war to make money and seize political power, the Northern "carpetbagger" became the dominant figure in Southern politics for a decade. In collusion with the carpetbaggers were the "scalawags", native whites in the South who took advantage of the chance for aggrandizement which the postwar regime offered...As the process of carpetbag rule unfolded, and honest men in the South felt increasing disgust. Conservative editors referred to the fancy state conventions as "black and tan" gatherings, "ring-streaked and speckled" conventions, or assemble of "baboons" "ragamuffins" or jailbirds."

SOURCE: James G. Randall, *The Civil War and Reconstruction*, 1937

Document B

The whole history of Reconstruction has with few exceptions been written by passionate believers in the inferiority of the Negro. The whole body of facts concerning what the Negro actually said or did, how he worked, what he wanted, for whom he voted is masked in such a cloud of charges, exaggeration and biased testimony....Little effort has been make to preserve the records of Negro effort and speeches, actions, work and wages, home and families. Nearly all this has gone down beneath a mass of ridicule and caricature, deliberate omission and misstatement. No institution of learning has made any effort to explore or probe Reconstruction from the point of view of the laborer and most men have written to explain the excuse, the former slaveholder, ... the landholder...and the capitalist...

SOURCE: W.E.B. DuBois, *Black Reconstruction*, 1935

Directions: Using the map below and your knowledge of American history, answer the following questions. Use the Map Worksheet on page 158 (Student Edition) to guide your analysis of the source.

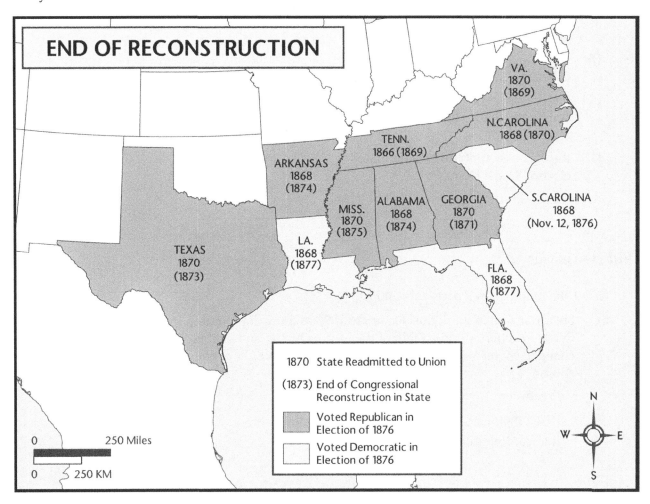

Multiple-Choice

1. The map best serves as evidence of which of the following?

- **(A)** that the Civil War resentments had been forgotten
- **(B)** that the Radical Republicans' plan for equality was in retreat
- **(C)** that the Republican Party had made lasting gains in the South
- **(D)** that a "Solid South" had formed in the former Confederacy

> As part of the deal to make Rutherford Hayes president, the last federal troops were withdrawn from the South. This symbolic gesture sent a message that Reconstruction was over and removed the last pressures on the South to abide by the Radical Republican program that had been assembled after the Civil War.
>
> *(Pol-3, Analyzing Historical Evidence)*

2. What Republican Party decision in 1876–1877 marked the end of Reconstruction?

   (A) the withdrawal of military support from several Reconstruction governments in the South

   (B) the suspension of tariff duties collection in the South for ten years

   (C) the exemption of several Southern states from enforcing the Fourteenth Amendment

   (D) the concession of the presidential election to the Democrats

> With three states (Florida, South Carolina, and Louisiana) in dispute in the election, neither candidate had a majority in the Electoral College. All the disputed votes were given to Hayes in return for the Republicans' agreement to pull the troops from the South. The Compromise marked the end of Reconstruction.
>
> *(Pol-3, Causation)*

Short-Answer

Using the map, answer parts a, b, and c.

a) Historians often mark the election of 1876 as a turning point in the history of Reconstruction. Choose ONE of the groups below and explain how their lives were most changed by the results of the election and cite ONE piece of evidence to support your choice:

- Freedmen
- Redeemers
- Radical Republicans

b) Contrast your choice with ONE of the other options above and explain why your selected group experienced the greater transformation in their lives.

c) Briefly explain ONE other event from 1876–1896 that marked a departure from Reconstruction Era ideals.

> **a)** Answers will vary. The Freedmen suffered greatly as a result of the election. The Redeemers were ex-Confederates who reasserted themselves when the troops were withdrawn and they proceeded to implement a Jim Crow system throughout the South. The Radical Republicans were in decline with less and less influence. The election punctuated their retreat. *(Pol-3, Causation, Analyzing Historical Evidence)*
>
> **b)** Answers will vary. *(NAT-4, Analyzing Historical Evidence)*
>
> **c)** Answers will vary. Students might explain the various Supreme Court Cases from the Slaughterhouse Cases to *Plessy v. Ferguson*. They might mention the two depressions of 1873 and 1893 as diverting attention away from civil rights. And they might mention the cultural impact of Thomas Dixon's books, which depicted the Ku Klux Klan in a heroic way and demeaned African Americans. *(POL-1, Argument Development)*

Lesson 3

Famous Rebellions

Several armed rebellions helped shape American development before the Civil War. Three early uprisings (Bacon's, Shays's, and Whiskey Rebellions) were sparked by economic and political grievances against authority that was perceived as arbitrary and distant. Each of the clashes played a transformational role in its era: Bacon's Rebellion helped weaken the indentured servant system; Shays's Rebellion undermined the already dwindling support for the Articles of Confederation; and the Whiskey Rebellion established the authority of the new national government and moved George Washington firmly into the Federalist Party camp. The chart on the next page will help you analyze these rebellions.

As you consider the chart, you may wish to evaluate whether these early dissenters were driven by their inherently rebellious nature, the rugged frontier environment, unfair government actions, or a combination of all these factors.

Nat Turner's revolt differed significantly from the previous rebellions. It epitomized the great nightmare of the antebellum slavocracy—a large-scale slave revolt. The uprising stands alone as the most dramatic and violent slave revolt in U.S. history. The Turner Rebellion also reinforced the South's commitment to slavery and made peaceful manumission almost impossible. Historians have speculated about why there were no other major slave uprisings. How would you explain this lack of large-scale slave resistance?

OBJECTIVES

Review the introductory material and the chart "Three Major Rebellions in Early U.S. History" (pages 10–11 in the Student Edition). Have your students discuss what these rebellions (other than Nat Turner's) suggest about the American character. Can your students identify any common traits that contributed to the three uprisings?

After the class discussion on rebellions and after reading "Nathaniel Bacon's Manifesto," students will be able to:

1. analyze the causes of Bacon's Rebellion;

2. compare the views of Bacon and governor Berkeley on the causes of the rebellion;

3. evaluate to what extent Bacon's Rebellion was a defense of colonial rights against insensitive British policies;

4. explain how the rebellion was viewed as a clash between the haves and the have-nots in Virginia.

ADDITIONAL COMPONENTS

- **Core Chart Worksheet**: "Lesson 3 – Famous Rebellions" (website)

- **Primary Source Handout**: "Nathaniel Brown's Manifesto" (copy p. 18 or print form website)

- **Document Source Worksheets**: "Worksheet for Document Source Analysis" (p. 246)

Directions: Analyze the chart on famous rebellions, and then answer the following questions.

1. The most significant result of Nat Turner's rebellion was

   (A) the South's intensified commitment to slavery

   (B) Abraham Lincoln's decision to emancipate the slaves

   (C) the formation of the American Colonization Society

   (D) the emancipation of most of the slaves in Virginia

2. Which of the following individuals would favor the actions taken by the national government during the Whiskey Rebellion?

   (A) a backcountry farmer who supported the Articles of Confederation

   (B) a states' rights supporter who feared a strong central government

   (C) a Quaker who opposed the use of force

   (D) a supporter of law and order

3. The common element of Bacon's, Shays's, and the Whiskey Rebellion was that

   (A) all resulted in changes in the economic conditions that caused them

   (B) all occurred before the American Revolution

   (C) all were challenges to perceived unfairness by a distant government

   (D) all resulted in widespread changes in American society

---

Enhancing Understanding

SOVEREIGNTY — the question of who will have power, rank, and authority over others. Ultimately, all rebellions are a struggle over sovereignty—who will rule and what system of control they will employ.

DISCUSSION QUESTIONS

Hand out or display the document, "Nathaniel Bacon's Manifesto," (shown on page 18) and ask the following:

1. How does Bacon view himself and his supporters?

2. What oppressive acts does Bacon charge Governor Berkeley with? How do you think the governor would answer these charges?

3. Whom does Bacon call "juggling parasites"?

4. From your knowledge of the rebellion, which of its elements are not mentioned in Bacon's Manifesto?

5. How does Bacon attempt to make the rebellion a political and economic protest?

6. From this document and your knowledge of the rebellion, was Bacon the first American revolutionary or simply a blood-thirsty Indian hater?

Answers available on the companion website.

Major Rebellions in Early U.S. History

	Date	Cause	Events	Significance
Nathaniel Bacon's Rebellion	1676	Virginia frontiersmen seeking land clashed with Indians Frontiersmen demanded help from government Jamestown refused aid, fearing Indian War	Bacon and his men lived on frontier Bacon and his men stormed Jamestown Burned Jamestown Bacon died of fever Rebellion collapsed	Colonial rebellion against government authority Clash between east/west, rich/poor Tidewater's discrimination against frontiersmen Revision of indentured servant system, greater reliance on slave labor
Daniel Shays's Rebellion	1786–1787	Unfair taxes in Massachusetts Farms foreclosed Farmers imprisoned as debtors	Shays/1,200 men attacked courts in western Massachusetts State militia put down rebellion	Uprising was a general threat to property Threat that rebellion could spread to other states Articles of Confederation viewed as too weak to maintain law and order Bolstered call for revisions of Articles (Constitutional Convention, 1787)
Whiskey Rebellion	1794–1795	Farmers in western Pennsylvania refused to pay federal excise tax on whiskey Attacked tax collectors Farmers compared tax to Stamp Act of 1765	Washington called for 13,000 troops to suppress the rebels Rebels dispersed, ceased rebellion	Put the force of the government behind the Constitution Government could enforce the law Constitution protected law/order Hamilton's idea of an energetic national government prevailed
Nat Turner's (slave) Rebellion	1831	Slaves wanted freedom Nat Turner saw "vision" and attacked whites in Southampton County, Virginia	Turner, 70 slaves, and 55 whites killed Turner caught; he was executed, and hundreds of slaves were punished	Frightened South Tightened slave codes Restricted freedom for all blacks in South South began to aggressively defend slavery as a "positive good"

Nathaniel Bacon's Manifesto

If virtue be a sin, if piety be guilt, all the principles of morality, goodness, and justice be perverted, we must confess that those who are now called rebels may be in danger of those high imputations. Those loud and several bulls [Governor Berkeley's declarations] would afright [sic] innocents and render the defense of our brethren, and the inquiry into our own sad and heavy oppressions, treason.

But if there be, as sure there is, a God to appeal to; if religion and justice be a sanctuary here; if to plead the cause of the oppressed; if sincerely to aim at this Majesty's honor and the public good without any reservation or by interest … [then] let God Almighty judge and let [the] guilty die.

But since we cannot in our hearts find one single spot of rebellion or treason, or that we have in any manner aimed at the subverting [of] the settled government, or attempting of the person of any either magistrate or private man, notwithstanding the several reproaches and threats of some who for sinister ends were disaffected to us and censured our innocent and honest designs; and since all people in all places where we have yet been can attest our civil, quiet and peaceable behavior, let truth be bold and all the world know the real foundation of pretended guilt …

But let us trace these men in authority and favor, to whose hands the dispensation of the country's wealth has been committed. Let us observe the sudden rise of their estates, composed [compared] with the quality in which they first entered this country, or the reputation they have held here amongst wise and discerning men. And let us see whether their extractions and educations have not been vile, and by what pretense of learning and virtue they could soon [enter] into employments of so great trust and consequences. Let us consider their sudden advancement and let us also consider whether any public work for our safety and defense … is here extant in any [way] adequate to our vast charge.

Now let us compare these things together and see what sponges have sucked up the public treasure, and whether it has not been privately contrived away by unworthy favorites and juggling parasites, whose tottering fortunes have been repaired and supported at the public charge.

Now if it be so, judge what greater guilt can be than to offer to pry into these and to unriddle [sic] the mysterious wiles of a powerful cabal. Let all people judge what can be of more dangerous import than to suspect the so long safe proceedings of some of our grandees, and whether people may with safety open their eyes in so nice a concern.

Source: Nathaniel Bacon, Rebel Leader

Directions: Using the excerpt below and your knowledge of American history, answer the following questions. Use the Document Source worksheet on page 156 (Student Edition) to guide your analysis of the source.

> "Without an alteration in our political creed, the superstructure we have been seven years in raising at the expense of so much treasure and blood, must fall. We are fast verging to anarchy and confusion…What stronger evidence can be given of the want of energy in our government, than these disorders?…Thirteen sovereignties pulling against each other, and all tugging at the federal head, will soon bring ruin on the whole…"

—Letter from George Washington to James Madison,
November 5, 1786

Multiple-Choice

1. Which of the following alterations in America's political creed would George Washington most likely support?

   (A) revising the governing principles of the American Revolution

   (B) promoting debt relief and currency reform

   (C) encouraging greater regional cooperation and trade

   (D) aligning America's creed more closely to that of Great Britain

> Shays's Rebellion showed that the emphasis on liberty and freedom expressed during the Revolution needed to be modified in the 1780s when liberty seemed to become license. A central government authority, which had been an anathema to revolutionaries, now seemed necessary.
>
> *(POL-1, Analyzing Historical Evidence)*

2. The sentiments expressed in the letter led most directly to late eighteenth-century political controversies over the issue of the

   (A) creation of the National Bank

   (B) ratification of the Jay Treaty

   (C) establishment of a presidential Cabinet

   (D) collection of excise taxes on whiskey

> The farmers of western Pennsylvania refused to pay their whiskey tax. The new government under Washington exercised "energy" by collecting the tax by force. Washington's forceful suppression of the protest caused controversy in his Cabinet (Jefferson) and in the nation.
>
> *(POL-2, Causation)*

Short-Answer

Using the excerpt, answer parts a and b.

a) Shays's Rebellion affected Washington's political thinking. Briefly explain how the disorder changed Washington's position on TWO of the following:

- Suppression of dissent in the mid-1780s
- The effectiveness of the Articles of Confederation
- Attendance at the Philadelphia meeting to amend the Articles of Confederation

b) Briefly explain how ONE of Washington's positions expressed in <u>part a</u> could be challenged in the mid- and late 1780s.

---

a. Answers will vary. Shays's Rebellion shook up Washington's political thinking because he feared the nation was coming apart. He accepted more power in a central government, a revision of the Articles of Confederation, and a willingness to attend the Constitutional Convention. His attendance at the meeting gave it importance and legitimacy in the eyes of many colonial citizens.

(POL-2, Continuity and Change over Time)

b. Answers will vary. Students might explain: that acceptance of suppression of dissent ran counter to the liberty achieved by the revolutionary leaders such as Washington; that the Articles overall provided a government supported by a majority of Americans and that they need only to be slightly changed; that attendance in Philadelphia raised questions about the motives and agenda of the participants who might replace the Articles with an oppressive government along the lines of England's.

(POL-2, Causation)

Religious Development, 1619-1740

Religion played an important role in the founding and development of the British colonies in North America. The English Reformation generated alienation and turmoil for many religious denominations in Great Britain. Catholics were upset when Henry VIII created the Anglican Church and displaced the Pope as the religious leader of England. Other groups such as the Congregational Church (Puritans) and the Society of Friends (Quakers) challenged the beliefs and powers exercised by the new state-sponsored church. These groups began to look to North America as a place to realize their dreams of religious freedom.

These dissenters founded several colonies in the New World. For example, in New England, the Puritans settled Massachusetts Bay in hopes of purifying their church. In Maryland, the Catholics sought a place of unfettered worship, and, in Pennsylvania, the Quakers hoped to find religious freedom and noninterference.

Most historians agree that religious freedom and tolerance were stronger in the British colonies than in the mother country. As you study the chart, consider what factors contributed to this freedom. Where was religious tolerance least likely to occur in the colonies during the 17th century?

Directions: Analyze the chart on religious development, and then answer the following questions.

1. Which area of the British colonies maintained state-supported, religious practices similar to those found in the mother country?

    (A) Massachusetts and Connecticut

    (B) Virginia and Maryland

    (C) the frontiers of Georgia and South Carolina

    (D) Pennsylvania and New York

OBJECTIVES

Review the introductory material and the chart "Religious Development in the Colonies" (p. 13–14 in the Student Edition). Have your students discuss why religion was such an important political issue during the colonization of North America. Also ask them whether the political component became more significant than the spiritual side of worship during this time and what it said about a developing colonial identity.

After the class discussion on religious development in the colonies and reading Roger Williams view on religion that follows, students will be able to:

1. state the main principles of Roger Williams' religious philosophy;

2. evaluate the religious role the government played in Williams' Rhode Island;

3. compare and contrast Williams' religious views with those of the Puritans;

4. explain why some groups would support Williams' views and others would oppose them.

ADDITIONAL COMPONENTS

- **Core Chart Worksheet**: "Lesson 4 – Religious Development" (website)

- **Primary Source Handout**: "The Bloody Tenent...1644" (p. 24/web)

- **Document Source Worksheets**: "Worksheet for Document Source Analysis" (p. 246)

2. Which religious group faced the greatest persecution in the colonies?

   (A) Congregational Church

   (B) Presbyterian Church

   (C) Society of Friends

   (D) Catholic Church

3. Which of the following groups was characterized by beliefs in innate depravity, predestination, and intolerance of other religions?

   (A) Anglicans

   (B) Catholics

   (C) Quakers

   (D) Puritans

DISCUSSION QUESTIONS

Hand out or display the document, "The Bloody Tenent of Persecution for Cause of Conscience, 1644," (shown on page 24) and ask the following:

1. What was Williams' position on settling religious disputes by force?

2. How did Williams' views on the role of government in religion differ from those of the Puritans?

3. In what ways did Williams' ideas in the 1640s anticipate the Bill of Rights of the 1790s?

4. How did Williams's position on religion influence the political structure of Rhode Island?

5. What groups would most likely be drawn to Rhode Island's religious policies? What groups would reject them?

Answers available on the companion website.

Religious Development in the Colonies

	Congregational Church (Puritans)	Anglican Church	Society of Friends (Quakers)	Catholic Church	Presbyterian Church
Leaders	John Cotton John Winthrop Cotton Mather	King or queen of England Bishop of London	George Fox William Penn	Pope in Rome Bishops Priests	Francis Makemie William Tennent
Areas of Influence	New England	Virginia Maryland	Pennsylvania Scattered in New England, New Jersey	Maryland (early) Scattered in parts of Pennsylvania	Frontier and backcountry; Pennsylvania, New Jersey
Beliefs	Man is depraved/sinful One is saved or damned at birth Wicked life was a sign of damnation Only "visible saints" were saved Intolerant of all other religions Coerced nonbelievers with force or banishment	King/queen headed church King's power came from God Used Book of Common Prayer Some Catholic liturgy and doctrine maintained	"Inner light" a guide to salvation Minimal church structure All people equal in God's eyes Pacifism Refused to take oaths Tolerant of other religions	Strict hierarchy with Pope at head Salvation earned by good works, faith, loyalty to church Priests were path to God No divorce allowed	Calvinism Split from Puritans over church governance Power lay with church elders Like other Protestants, accepted Jesus as savior Tolerant of other religions
Comment	By 1740 church represented largest denomination in colonies Lost much of their political influence in New England after 1700 Intolerance cost its support Hoped to create a religious "City Upon a Hill"	By 1740 had second-largest membership in colonies Much less influence in colonies than in England Being a member carried great status in colonies	Grew from Puritanism Clashed often with Puritans "Holy Experiment" in Pennsylvania	Maryland originally a Catholic haven Catholics very unpopular in other colonies, where they could not vote or hold office	By 1740 had third-largest membership in colonies Scotch/Irish immigrants changed church in early 1700s Split between New/Old Lights

The Bloody Tenent of Persecution
for Cause of Conscience, 1644

First, That the blood of so many hundred thousands of souls of Protestants and Papists, split in the wars of present and former ages, for their respective consciences, is not required nor accepted by Jesus Christ, the Prince of Peace.

Sixth, It is the will and command of God that (since the coming of his Son, the Lord Jesus) a permission of the most pagan, Jewish, Turkish, or anti-Christian consciences and worships be granted to all men in all nations and countries…

Eighth, God requires not uniformity of religion to be enacted and enforced in any civil state…enforced uniformity…is the greatest occasion of civil war, ravishing of conscience, persecution of Christ Jesus in his servants, and of the hypocrisy and destruction of millions of souls… [Twelfth] the government of the civil magistrate extends no further than over the bodies and goods of their subjects, not over their souls, and therefore they many not undertake to give laws unto the souls and consciences of men…the Church of Christ does not use the arm of secular power to compel men to the true profession of the truth, for this is to be done with spiritual weapons, whereby Christians are to be exhorted, not compelled.

SOURCE: Roger Williams, Founder of Rhode Island

Directions: Using the excerpt below and your knowledge of American history, answer the following questions. Use the Document Source worksheet on page 156 (Student Edition) to guide your analysis of the source.

"(1) The doors of the churches of Christ upon earth do not by God's appointment stand so wide open, that all sorts of people, good and bad, may freely enter therein at their pleasure, but such as are admitted thereto, as members, ought to be examined and tried first, whether they fit and meet to be received into church-society or not...

(6) ...The end of the magistrate's office is not only the quiet and peaceable life of the subject in matters of righteousness and honesty, but also in matters of godliness; yea, of all godliness...profanation of the Lord's Day,... disturbing the peaceable administration and exercise of the worship and holy things of God...and the like...are to be restrained and punished by civil authority."

—Platform of Church Discipline adopted by the
General Court of Massachusetts, 1649

Multiple-Choice

1. The authors of the Platform of Church Discipline would most likely oppose which of the following ideas?

   (A) punishment of religious dissenters

   (B) holding church services during periods of unrest

   (C) separating church and government functions

   (D) restricting church membership to a select few

   > The Puritans created a theocracy in Massachusetts. They believed the church and state should be united and that the church should govern the colonies as the civil authority.
   >
   > *(CUL-1, Analyzing Historical Evidence)*

2. In creating the new nation in the 1780s and 1790s, the Founding Fathers challenged the main idea of the passage above by prohibiting

   (A) regional church control of their membership

   (B) government establishment and support of churches

   (C) church members from serving in government

   (D) private cash donations to churches

   > When the Constitution was written, the authors made sure that there were no religious tests for office and that the church and state were separated. The First Amendment to the Constitution addressed this concern.
   >
   > *(CUL-1, Causation)*

Short-Answer

Using the excerpt, answer parts a, b, and c.

a)   Briefly explain the main points made in the Platform of Church Discipline.

b)   Briefly explain why the Massachusetts Court adopted the measures expressed in the excerpt.

c)   Briefly explain how the ideas expressed in the passage helped form a distinct New England identity from 1620–1660.

---

a)   Answers will vary. The platform stated that not everyone would be accepted in church; and that the church (civil authority) would enforce the rules of the colony.

(CUL-1, Analyzing Historical Evidence)

b)   Answers will vary.

(CUL-1, Analyzing Historical Evidence)

c)   The Puritans were known for their exclusivity, their intolerance, and their harsh suppression of dissent and "misbehavior."

(NAT-1, Causation)

Lesson 5

Presidents of the United States, 1789-2016

Most classes in U.S. history are taught chronologically and organized by presidential administrations. The charts on the following two pages are designed to help review the presidential chronology you learned this year and to examine four outstanding presidents.

Though it's not necessary to memorize the charts, you should study them carefully so you can associate major events, such as wars, depressions, and land acquisitions, with various presidents. As you study the presidential charts, also consider why there were periods of undistinguished presidents. The two eras of forgotten presidents were 1837–1861 and 1865–1901. Why do you think these two periods were characterized by presidential mediocrity?

The first chart summarizes the achievements of our four greatest presidents. In all cases, these leaders achieved major domestic successes and/ or promoted America's strength and security in foreign relations. In addition, each man changed American political thinking and transformed the office of president. Historians suggest that, in order to achieve presidential greatness, a president must make the office "a more splendid instrument of democracy." What do you think this means? Do you feel any other presidents deserve the label of greatness? Why?

Directions: Analyze the charts on the presidents, and then answer the following questions.

1. Between 1861 and 1889, a common element among the presidential administrations was that most presidents

   (A) were impeached

   (B) were from the Democratic Party

   (C) were from the Republican Party

   (D) had personal scandals in their administrations

OBJECTIVES

Review the introductory materials and the chart "The Four Great Presidents" (pages 16–17 in the Student Edition). Have your students discuss the four presidents identified as great. From the list of four, ask your students to select one president who stands out as the greatest of the great. Ask them to defend their answer.

After the class discussion on presidential greatness and reading James Bryce's "Why Great Men Are Not Chosen Presidents," which follows, students will be able to:

1. defend their choice of America's greatest president;

2. identify the characteristics of a great president;

3. list several limitations and/or hurdles that block great men from achieving the presidency;

4. apply these limitations specifically to the political circumstances that defined presidential politics from 1868–1900.

ADDITIONAL COMPONENTS

- **Core Chart Worksheet:** "Lesson 5 – Presidents of the U.S." (website)

- **Primary Source Handout:** "Why Great Men Are Not Chosen President" (copy p. 33 or website)

- **Document Source Worksheets:** "Worksheet for Document Source Analysis" (p. 246)

2. What common characteristic did the presidencies of Ulysses Grant, Warren Harding, and Richard Nixon have?

   (A) All had scandals during their administrations.

   (B) All were Democratic administrations.

   (C) All had wars begin during their administrations.

   (D) All were famous generals.

3. What characteristic did the great presidents of the United States share?

   (A) Each survived a political scandal during his presidency.

   (B) Each won a foreign war during his presidency.

   (C) Each dealt with an economic depression during his presidency.

   (D) Each had a major legislative success during his presidency.

Enhancing Understanding

IMPEACHMENT — the leveling of charges against a government official by a legislative body. A president or government official is impeached when charges are voted on by a majority of the House of Representatives. A trial in the Senate decides whether the official should be removed from office. Two presidents, Andrew Johnson and Bill Clinton were impeached, but not convicted, and both remained in office.

DISCUSSION QUESTIONS

Hand out or display the document, "Why Great Men Are Not Chosen President," (shown on page 33) and ask the following:

1. Is James Bryce an unbiased observer of American politics? (Focus on the statement, "Besides, most American voters do not object to ordinary candidates" in the article).

2. What factors did Bryce identify that restricted great men from achieving the presidency?

3. Examine the presidential greatness chart ("The Four Greatest Presidents") on page XX of the Student Edition. How did these men overcome the hurdles Bryce mentioned to become great presidents?

4. Can you think of examples in the years 1868–1900 of men who "would make a good president, but a very bad candidate"?

5. Is it true that "a president need not be brilliant"?

6. What qualities does Bryce think a great president needs? Do you agree?

Answers available on the companion website.

The Four Greatest Presidents

President	Domestic Success	Foreign Success	Lasting Impact on Country/Presidency
George Washington	Bill of Rights approved National Bank founded Established authority of federal government to tax citizens Government authority established by Whiskey Rebellion	Jay Treaty: British out of forts in Northwest Maintained neutrality in European war Farewell Address advocated no entangling alliances Treaty of San Lorenzo with Spain opened up the Mississippi River to American trade	Created/established dignity and power of president Sound financial footing established Isolationism toward Europe proposed Secured the "West" (area beyond the Appalachian Mountains)
Thomas Jefferson	Reduced size of government Abolished Whiskey Tax Reduced national debt Pardoned Sedition Act violators Enacted Judiciary Act to reform court system	Negotiated Louisiana Purchase Barbary pirate wars establish respect for U.S. Kept U.S. out of European war	Achieved peaceful transition of power between parties Doubled geographic size of U.S. Promoted rights rather than control of people by government
Abraham Lincoln	Preserved the Union Emancipation Proclamation and Thirteenth Amendment Passed the Homestead Act Reformed banking system	Kept Europe out of Civil War	Kept nation whole Gave nation a new birth of freedom Expanded president's war-making power
Franklin Roosevelt	Created New Deal reforms to combat Depression Established Social Security Assisted homeless and unemployed Federal Deposit Insurance Corp. established Security and Exchange Commission created Civil Conservation Corp. founded	Led U.S. through World War II Established United Nations Led U.S. from isolationism to internationalism	America became a superpower Government permanently expanded its role in society Focused attention and power in Oval Office

All Presidents with Administration Highlights

President	Term	Party	Major Events/Developments
George Washington	1789–1797	Federalist	Establishes new government; Whiskey Rebellion; Jay Treaty; Farewell Address
John Adams	1797–1801	Federalist	Undeclared war with France; XYZ affair; Alien and Sedition Acts
Thomas Jefferson	1801–1809	(Democratic) Republican	First Republican president; Executed Louisiana Purchase; Embargo Act of 1807
James Madison	1809–1817	(Democratic) Republican	War of 1812
James Monroe	1817–1825	(Democratic) Republican	Florida purchase; Era of Good Feelings; Executed the Missouri Compromise and the Monroe Doctrine
John Q. Adams	1825–1829	(National) Republican	Corrupt bargain
Andrew Jackson	1829–1837	Democrat	Expands presidential power; Bank battle; Tariff/Nullification Crisis; Indian removal
Martin Van Buren	1837–1841	Democrat	Panic of 1837; Trail of Tears
William H. Harrison	1841–1841	Whig	First Whig president; Died in office
John Tyler	1841–1845	Whig	Annexation of Texas
James K. Polk	1845–1849	Democrat	Mexican-American War; Mexican Cession
Zachary Taylor	1849–1850	Whig	Last Whig president elected; Died in office
Millard Fillmore	1850–1853	Whig	Compromise of 1850
Franklin Pierce	1853–1857	Democrat	Kansas-Nebraska Act; Ostend Manifesto
James Buchanan	1857–1861	Democrat	Dred Scott decision; John Brown's raid; Seven states leave Union
Abraham Lincoln	1861–1865	Republican	Civil War; Emancipation Proclamation; First president assassinated
Andrew Johnson	1865–1869	Republican	Reconstruction; First president impeached; Purchased Alaska

All Presidents with Administration Highlights

President	Term	Party	Major Events/Developments
Ulysses S. Grant	1869–1877	Republican	Reconstruction continued; Many scandals
Rutherford B. Hayes	1877–1881	Republican	Compromise of 1877; Reconstruction ended
James Garfield	1881–1881	Republican	Second president assassinated
Chester Arthur	1881–1885	Republican	Pendleton Act
Grover Cleveland	1885–1889	Democrat	First Democratic president since Civil War; Tariff battle with Congress
Benjamin Harrison	1889–1893	Republican	Built up navy; Grandson of William H. Harrison; McKinley Tariff
Grover Cleveland	1893–1897	Democrat	Only president to serve two nonconsecutive terms; Depression of 1893
William McKinley	1897–1901	Republican	Spanish-American War; Third president assassinated
Theodore Roosevelt	1901–1909	Republican	Trust buster; Square Deal reforms; "Big stick" in Caribbean
William Howard Taft	1909–1913	Republican	Dollar Diplomacy in Caribbean; Split with Theodore Roosevelt in 1912
Woodrow Wilson	1913–1921	Democrat	Progressive reforms; World War I; Fought for League of Nations
Warren Harding	1921–1923	Republican	Normalcy period; Political and personal scandals; Died in office
Calvin Coolidge	1923–1929	Republican	Pro-business, *laissez-faire* administration; Kellogg-Briand Pact
Herbert Hoover	1929–1933	Republican	Great Depression strikes; Promoted attitude of rugged individualism
Franklin D. Roosevelt	1933–1945	Democrat	New Deal reforms; World War II; Elected to four terms
Harry S. Truman	1945–1953	Democrat	Fair Deal reforms; Cold War begins; Upset victory in 1948; Korean War
Dwight Eisenhower	1953–1961	Republican	Ended Korean War; Maintained peaceful coexistence with USSR; Established modern Republicanism

Lesson 5: Presidents of the United States, 1789–2016 –

All Presidents with Administration Highlights

President	Term	Party	Major Events/Developments
John F. Kennedy	1961–1963	Democrat	New Frontier reforms; Bay of Pigs; Cuban Missile Crisis; Assassinated 1963
Lyndon B. Johnson	1963–1969	Democrat	Great Society reforms; Civil rights acts; Escalated Vietnam War
Richard Nixon	1969–1974	Republican	Ended Vietnam War; Recognized China; Watergate scandal; First president to resign
Gerald Ford	1974–1977	Republican	Took over when Nixon resigned; Pardoned Nixon for his crimes
Jimmy Carter	1977–1981	Democrat	Camp David Accords; Iran Hostage Crisis
Ronald Reagan	1981–1989	Republican	Supply-side economics; Military buildup; Soviet Union's Cold War decline began
George H. W. Bush	1989-1993	Republican	Collapse of Soviet Union; End of Cold War; First Gulf War
William (Bill) Clinton	1993-2001	Democrat	Dismantling of Soviet Empire; Welfare Reform; Impeachment
George W. Bush	2001-2009	Republican	2000 election decided by Supreme Court; attack on 9/11; Presidency mired by 2003 invasion of Iraq
Barack Obama	2009-2016	Democrat	First African American president; Recovery from Great Recession; Affordable Care Act passed

Why Great Men Are Not Chosen President

Europeans often ask, and Americans do not always explain, how it happens that this great office—to which any man can rise by his own merits—is not more frequently filled by great men … it might be expected that the presidency would always be won by a man of brilliant gifts. But since the heroes of the Revolution died out with Jefferson and Adams and Madison some sixty years ago, no person except General Grant has reached the office whose name would have been remembered if he had not been President. No President except Abraham Lincoln has shown rare or striking qualities in the office… .

Several reasons may be suggested for this fact, which Americans are themselves the first to admit.

One is that the number of people with great abilities drawn into politics is smaller in America than in most European countries. In France and Italy, half-revolutionary conditions have made public life exciting and easy to enter … In England, many persons of wealth and leisure seek to enter politics, while vital problems touch the interests of all classes and make people eager observers of the political scene. In America, many able men rush into a field which is comparatively small in Europe, the business of developing the material resources of the country.

Another reason is that the methods and habits of Congress and indeed of political life generally, seem to give fewer opportunities for personal distinction. There are fewer ways in which a man may win the admiration of his countrymen by outstanding thought, speech or ability in administration.

A third reason is that important men make more enemies than less well-known men do. They are therefore less admirable candidates … No man can be in public life for long and take part in great affairs without causing criticism….

… Besides, most American voters do not object to ordinary candidates. They have a lower idea of the qualities necessary for a statesman than those who direct public opinion in Europe … They do not value, because they see no need for, originality or profundity, a cultured background or great knowledge …

It must also be remembered that the merits of a President are one thing and those of a candidate another thing. An important American is reported to have said to friends … "Gentlemen, let there be no mistake. I would make a good President but a very bad candidate" … After all—and this is a point much less obvious to Europeans than to Americans—a President need not be brilliant … They forget that the President does not sit in Congress. His main duties are to promptly and effectively carry out the laws and maintain public order … Firmness, common sense, and, most of all, honesty are the qualities which the country needs in its chief executive.

SOURCE: James Bryce, English Scholar

Directions: Using the excerpt below and your knowledge of American history, answer the following questions. Use the Document Source Worksheet on page 156 (Student Edition) to guide your analysis of the source.

"...this [election] being now decided by the voice of the nation, announced according to the rules of the Constitution, all will, of course, arrange themselves under the will of the law, and unite in common efforts for the common good. All, too, will bear in mind this sacred principle, that through the will of the majority is in all cases to prevail, that will to be rightful must be reasonable; that the minority possess their equal rights, which equal law must protect, and to violate would be oppression...

We are all Republicans, we are all Federalists. If there be any among us who would wish to dissolve this Union or to change its republican form, let them stand undisturbed as monuments of the safety with which error of opinion may be tolerated where reason is left free to combat it..."

—Thomas Jefferson, March 4, 1801

Multiple-Choice

1. Based on Jefferson's speech of 1801, which one of the following governmental actions would he most likely support?

(A) accepting peaceful disunion

(B) suppressing dangerous dissent

(C) establishing bi-partisan relationships

(D) modifying the system of federalism

> Jefferson's statement that "We are all Republicans, we are all Federalists" was a call for national unity and bi-partisanship. He hoped to put the divisiveness of the past over foreign and domestic issues behind the nation. He did not succeed.
>
> *(POL-1, Analyzing Historical Evidence)*

2. The passage above was likely written in response to the earlier government attempts to

(A) add new territories without congressional approval

(B) limit political freedoms of expression and dissent

(C) enhance the power of the president through the veto

(D) alter international trade policies by treaties

> Jefferson was referring to the partisan debate that surrounded the rights of the people to protest taxes (Whiskey Rebellion) and to express their freedom of speech, which the Sedition Act severely restricted. Both actions were challenged by the Republicans, but they were unable to stop the Federalist majority from implementing them in the mid and late 1790s.
>
> *(POL-1, Comparison)*

Short-Answer

Using the excerpt, answer parts a, b, and c.

a) Identify the main points Thomas Jefferson outlined in his 1801 speech.

b) Briefly explain ONE action taken by President Jefferson that challenged the sentiment expressed in the excerpt.

c) Briefly discuss how ONE of these ideas was most important in explaining why historians ranked Jefferson as a great president.

---

a) Jefferson called on the nation to come together as one people and accept the verdict of the election. The people had spoken and must be obeyed. He also encouraged tolerance for legal dissent. He believed that protesters should be heard until they came to realize the errors of the views.

(POL-1, Causation)

b) Answers will vary. Students might note Jefferson's Judiciary Act of 1801, which challenged various judges, support for the Impeachment of Samuel Chase, the Purchase of Louisiana, and then enacted the Embargo Act of 1807. All actions occurred over the protest and opposition of the Federalists.

(POL-1, Analyzing Historical Evidence)

c) Jefferson showed the ability to lead the nation in the peaceful transfer of power from one political group to another. His measured response gave hope that America's republican experiment could work and survive.

(POL-1, Analyzing Historical Evidence)

Lesson 6

The First and Second Great Awakenings

American history has been marked by several religious, often evangelical, upheavals. Two of the most significant occurred in the mid-eighteenth and nineteenth centuries and were known as the First and Second Great Awakening. Neither developed as a tightly coordinated movement. Rather, these revivals were a series of local events linked together by "a religion of the heart." Both challenged their congregations to renounce sin, seek salvation, and reform their daily lives.

The First Great Awakening began in England and spread to the American colonies in the 1730s and 1740s. It presented a Calvinistic message of predestination, original sin, and a punishing God. The Second Great Awakening began in the 1790s on the American frontier and spread into New England and New York in the 1830s and 1840s. It attacked sinfulness, secularism (materialism), and offered salvation for both individuals and society. Although each movement presented unique messages, they both transformed the social, political, and religious thinking of their eras.

The chart on the following page compares and contrasts the two Awakenings. As you study it, think about the conditions that existed in mid-eighteenth and nineteenth century America that gave rise to these two revivals. In addition, contrast each movement's message, its approach to salvation, and how each transformed people's attitudes about themselves and society.

OBJECTIVES

Review the introductory material and the chart on "The Great Awakenings" (page 22–23 in the Student Edition). Have your students discuss how the societal conditions that precipitated both movements were different. In addition, your students should discuss whether the two movements made lasting changes in society, and if they did not, why were they only short lived events.

After the class discussion on the two Great Awakenings and reading Charles Finney's "A Christian's Duty," students will be able to:

1. state Finney's point of view about slavery;

2. evaluate his view on the role of the church in the secular world;

3. assess the effectiveness of churches in changing political and economic questions;

4. outline the basic principles of the Second Great Awakening.

ADDITIONAL COMPONENTS

- **Core Chart Worksheet:** "Lesson 6 – Great Awakenings" (website)

- **Primary Source Handout:** "A Christian's Duty, 1835" (copy p. 39 or website)

- **Document Source Worksheets:** "Worksheet for Document Source Analysis" (p. 246); "Worksheet for Visual Source Analysis" (p. 247)

Directions: Analyze the chart on the two Great Awakenings, and then answer the following questions.

1. Both the First and Second Great Awakening

   (A) presented a Calvinistic message of salvation

   (B) called for the abolition of slavery

   (C) appealed to many classes/levels of society

   (D) offered a less emotional form of worship

2. The First Great Awakening promoted which of the following ideas:

   (A) salvation at birth through God's grace

   (B) social reform before personal salvation

   (C) allowing only ordained, trained ministers to preach

   (D) political revolt against British rule

3. Members of both Awakenings would agree with which of the following statements?

   (A) "The world is too much with us… Getting and spending we lay waste our powers."

   (B) "Women are equal to men in both intellectual and moral attributes."

   (C) "Slavery must be abolished immediately without compensation."

   (D) "Man is always better whipped than damned."

Enhancing Understanding

CALVINISM — the ideas of John Calvin that people are predestined at birth to either salvation or damnation, and that only God's elect will be saved. To ensure divine acceptance, one must practice strict morality and work hard in life—this was a bedrock belief of the First Great Awakening.

DISCUSSION QUESTIONS

Hand out or display the document, "A Christian's Duty, 1835," (shown on page 39) and ask the following:

1. What audience was Finney trying to persuade in his article?

2. What advice was he offering to his audience in the article?

3. What groups did Finney criticize in the article? Do you think this was a fair criticism?

4. Do you think the churches were an effective vehicle for changing the political/economic questions around slavery?

5. As a leading voice of the Second Great Awakening, what principles and positions did Finney outline for the movement?

Answers available on the companion website.

The Great Awakenings

	First Great Awakening	Second Great Awakening
Background/ Causes	Began in England with John Wesley's, and George Whitefield's crusades Rise in secularism Met outdoors; often involved thousands Countered Enlightenment's rationalism Whitefield brought ideas to colonies	Rise in secularism Desire to strengthen public morality Met outdoors; often involved thousands Grew from "camp meetings" of 1790s (Cane Ridge, Kentucky) spread to "burned-over district" of New York
Participants	Lower classes: laborers, servants, small farmers Many women converts; free/enslaved blacks Many church denominations, but Baptists, Methodists, Presbyterians in forefront	Many women converts Evangelical Baptists, Methodists, Presbyterians in forefront Millennialists: second coming of Christ Some African Americans, Native Americans Reform groups: temperance, abolitionists
Ideas	Predestination: salvation by faith/grace not by good works (Calvinistic) Stressed universality of sin Repent sins; reaffirm faith Choose Christ or Hell Literal interpretation of Bible	Rejected Calvinism: salvation through good works/personal efforts Believed people are "free moral agents" Universal salvation Belief in personal/societal perfection Condemned greed/indifference to poor
Leaders	George Whitefield – main spokesman; emotional/spoke to throngs outdoors Jonathan Edwards – "Sinners in the Hands of an Angry God" William/Gilbert Tennent – Presbyterian ministers Theodore Frelinghuysen – Dutch Reform minister	Charles Grandison Finney – evangelical minister in the "burned-over district" James McGready – Presbyterian leader of camp meetings Peter Cartwright – Methodist circuit rider Timothy Dwight – spread ideas at Yale college and in New England
Impact	Challenged clergy: untutored ministers could preach Attacked status quo: egalitarian with universal salvation; challenged deference Spoke out against slaves' treatment, but did not support abolition of slavery Divided churches: "Old Light" / "New Light" Presbyterians; turmoil in Congregational and Dutch Reformed churches as well Promoted inter-colonial communication and cooperation	Energized reformers: abolition, temperance, peace movement, women's rights Promoted personal self improvement Individual could remake self and society Divided social classes/churches Increased membership in evangelical churches (Methodists/ Baptists) Rise of more emotional, personal approach to God and salvation

A Christian's Duty, 1835

Here the question arises, what is the right stand? First I state some things to be avoided.

1. A bad spirit should be avoided. Nothing will injure religion and the slaves themselves more than an angry controversy among Christians on the subject. Those proud professors of religion who think it is a shame to have a black skin may shut their ears because of their prejudices and be disposed to quarrel with those who urge the subject upon them. But I repeat, the subject of slavery is a subject upon which Christians need not and must not differ.

2. Another thing to be avoided is an attempt to be neutral on this subject. Christians can no more take a neutral stand on the subject of the sanctification of the Sabbath. It is a great national sin. It is a sin of the church. The churches by their silence, and by permitting slaveholders to belong to their religious group, have been consenting to it. They have virtually declared that it is lawful. Allowing slaveholders quietly to remain in good standing in their churches, is the strongest and most public expression of their views that slavery in not sin. For the church, therefore, to pretend to be neutral on the subject is perfectly absurd. The fact is that she is not on neutral ground at all. While she tolerates slaveholders in her communion, SHE JUSTIFIES THE PRACTICE.

...Church members are God's witnesses. The fact is that slavery is, pre-eminently, the sin of the church. It is the very fact that ministers and professors of religion of different denominations hold slaves, which sanctifies the whole abomination of slavery in the eyes of ungodly men.

...It is the church that mainly supports this sin. Her united testimony upon this subject would settle the question. Let Christians of all denominations meekly but firmly come forth, and pronounce their verdict; let them clear their communions, and wash their hands of this this; let them give forth and write on the head and front of his great abomination, SIN! In three years, a public sentiment would be formed that would carry slavery away. There would not be a shackled slave, not a bristling, cruel slave driver left in this land.

Source: Lecture by Charles Grandison Finney, American Minister

Directions: Using the illustration below and your knowledge of American history, answer the following questions. Use the Visual Source worksheet on page 157 (Student Edition) to guide your analysis of the source.

CAMP MEETING AT EASTHAM, MASS.

Multiple-Choice

1. Which of the following twentieth-century continuities most closely parallels the developments during the Second Great Awakening?

    (A) religious groups' support of "Born-Again Christians" in political races

    (B) religious groups' defense of creationism in the schools

    (C) religious groups' promotion of social and economic changes in society

    (D) religious groups' crusade for universal peace

Religious groups promoted social and economic agendas during many periods in the 20th century. For example, during the Progressive Era, the Social Gospel movement was active in encouraging government action to promote social justice. In the 1920s, evangelicals, while conservative in their beliefs, embraced certain policies such as Prohibition. In the 1930s, Father Charles Coughlin, a Catholic priest, endorsed free silver and criticized the New Deal for its lack of attention to the poor. And in the 1950s and 1960s, Martin Luther King used religion as a basis for civil rights reforms.

(CUL-1, Continuity and Change over Time)

2. Which of the following activities highlighted in the illustration made the Second Great Awakening controversial before the Civil War?

   (A) the movement's call for an end to slavery

   (B) the movement's rejection of the idea of progress in society

   (C) the movement's involvement of clergy in political reform

   (D) the movement's involvement of women in changing society

> Women were very active in the Second Great Awakening. Drawing inspiration from the religious ideas of salvation for themselves and others, they joined the abolitionist movement and sought equal rights for all people. These actions challenged the conventional thinking (cult of domesticity) of the era.
>
> *(CUL-1, Causation)*

Short-Answer

Using the illustration, answer parts a, b, and c.

a) Briefly explain how the principles of the Second Great Awakening transformed the group identity of ONE of the following:

- Women participants in the Great Awakening
- Clergy in the Great Awakening
- Male participants in the Great Awakening

b) Briefly explain how ONE development from 1820–1840 promoted the point of view expressed in the picture.

c) Briefly explain how ONE development from 1820–1840 challenged the point of view in the picture.

---

a) Answers will vary. Women took an active role in many aspects of the Second Great Awakening. These actions challenged the cult of domesticity as women took on duties outside of their normal sphere (the home). Clergy became active in the reforms of abolitionist and temperance and used their influence to change societal policies. They often traveled outside of their churches to spread the word of God and change. Male participants in the Second Great Awakening were challenged to broaden the concept of democracy to include the disadvantages and the oppressed.
(NAT-1, CUL-1, Causation)

b) Answers will vary. Students might explain the general spirit of reform in the era. They might mention the rise of abolition and other movements. They might also credit reformers such as Charles Finney and William Garrison with creating a spirit of reform. Also the Panic of 1837 shook up the country. *(NAT-1, Causation)*

c) Answers will vary. Many political and social conservatives pushed back against the various reforms and reformers. Andrew Jackson and Catherine Beecher were not sympathetic to many of the reformers with abolitionists and women's suffrage supporters under great stress. *(NAT-1, Causation)*

Lesson 7

Coming of the American Revolution

Although the first shots of the American Revolution were fired in 1775, trouble between England and its colonies had been building for many years. During the 1740s, European conflicts spilled into the colonies, creating continuous trouble over issues of economic, military, and political sovereignty. Some historians believe that the British policy of "salutary neglect" ended as early as 1748, at the conclusion of King George's War. Others suggest it didn't end until 1763, when British policy toward the colonies changed drastically following the French and Indian War. At that time, England sought to raise revenue in America to pay down its national debt and to provide for colonial defenses. Britain proposed to do this through a series of revenue acts and policies designed to tighten its system of mercantilism.

The chart on the next page traces the British attempt to bring the American colonies closer to the empire after 1763. As you study it, consider whether, given the British mercantilist system and the colonial mind-set of the 1760s and 1770s, the American Revolution could have been avoided.

Directions: Analyze the chart on the acts and reactions leading up to the American Revolution, and then answer the following questions.

1. From 1764 to 1773, the principal British method of raising revenue in the colonies was to

   (A) tax the trade and commerce of the colonies

   (B) tax the income of individual colonists

   (C) permit colonial legislatures to raise money for their own needs

   (D) sell land in the West

OBJECTIVES

Review the introductory material and the chart "Acts, Actions, and Reactions Leading Up to American Revolution" (pages 26–27 in the Student Edition). Have your students discuss whether the American Revolution was inevitable, given the English mercantile system and the colonial attitudes in 1776.

After the class discussion on the inevitability of the Revolution and reading Charles Inglis's "The True Interest of America Impartially Stated, 1776," students will be able to:

1. outline the Loyalists' reasons for supporting British control of the colonies;

2. evaluate the economic basis for the Loyalists' position;

3. analyze why the Loyalists' point of view did not have more support in the colonies.

ADDITIONAL COMPONENTS

- **Core Chart Worksheet:** "Lesson 7 – Coming of the Revolution"

- **Primary Source Handout:** "The True Interest ... Stated" (copy p. 45 or website)

- **Document Source Worksheets:** "Worksheet for Document Source Analysis" (p. 246)

2. What was the colonists' most common method of protesting British taxation policy from 1764 to 1773?

    (A) to complain but to pay the taxes

    (B) to offer Britain an alternative means of raising revenue

    (C) to refuse to import or use British products/goods

    (D) to deal with Britain on a colony-by-colony basis

3. The most common British reaction to colonial resistance from 1764 to 1773 was to pass a tax or take an action, experience colonial resistance, and then

    (A) strongly confront the colonials

    (B) back away from the tax or action

    (C) appeal to the churches for help with enforcement

    (D) use foreign troops to overcome it

Enhancing Understanding

VIRTUAL REPRESENTATION — the British answer to the American cry of "no taxation without representation." The colonists demanded to be taxed only by their local representatives. The British countered that Englishmen sat in Parliament and represented all Englishmen around the world; thus, the colonists were represented in London. This idea was rejected in America.

DISCUSSION QUESTIONS

Hand out or display the document, "The True Interest of America Impartially Stated," (shown on page 45) and ask the following:

1. How does Inglis attempt to appeal to national pride in making the case for staying with England?

2. What advantages does he see in the colonies remaining in the British Empire?

3. How do you think the colonial rebels countered these arguments?

4. Why do you think Inglis believed "a republican form of government would neither suit the spirit of the people, nor the size of America?

5. According to Inglis, what part of colonial life would be most affected by independence from England?

6. Why do you think the Loyalist's position had limited appeal in the colonies?

Answers available on the companion website.

Acts, Actions, and Reactions Leading Up to American Revolution

Act or Action	Purpose	Provisions of Act	Colonial Reaction	British Reaction
Proclamation Line of 1763	British hoped to pacify Indians in West Pacification would reduce need for troops to battle Indians on frontier	Forbade settlement west of Appalachian Mountains Everyone in the western region must return to the East	Anger; colonists had fought French and Indian War to gain access to western region Colonists continued to settle in the area	British modified law with Treaty of Fort Stanwix, 1768 Moved line of permitted settlement farther to west
Sugar Act 1764	Act passed to raise money for colonial defense	Duty on foreign molasses had been reduced but now would be enforced	Anger Smuggling	Attempted to enforce tax
Stamp Act 1765	Passed to raise money Same tax existed in Great Britain	Taxed dice, playing cards, newspapers, marriage licenses Total of 50 items taxed	Convened Stamp Act Congress Petitioned the King Urban riots Boycotted goods Viewed as an internal tax	Repealed law Little money raised
Declaratory Act 1766	When Stamp Act repealed, British needed to save face	England could pass any laws for the colonies	Ignored it	British attempt to assert their dwindling authority
Townshend Act 1767	Passed to raise money and regulate trade External tax	Taxed imports: glass, paint, lead, paper, tea	Boycott of British goods Urban riots	Repealed taxes on everything but tea in 1770
Boston Massacre 1770	British troops in city to enforce laws	n/a	Confronted soldiers	Opened fire on mob, five colonists killed
Boston Tea Party 1773	Colonists protested tea tax	Tax on tea from 1770 remained	Sons of Liberty threw 342 cases of tea into Boston Harbor	Intolerable or Coercive Acts passed
First Continental Congress 1774	Met to decide how to help Massachusetts resist Intolerable Acts	n/a	Pleaded to King to repeal the Intolerable Acts Boycotted taxed goods Called another Congress in 1775	Put troops in cities Decided to hold firm

The True Interest of America Impartially Stated

By a settling of differences with Britain an end would be put to the present terrible war, by which so many lives have been lost, and so many more must be lost, if it continues. This alone is an advantage devoutly to be wished for. [Thomas] Paine says—"The blood of the slain, the weeping voice of nature cries. 'Tis time to part." I think they cry just the reverse. The blood of the slain, the weeping voice of nature cries—it is time to be reconciled.

By a connection with Great Britain, our trade would still have the protection of the greatest naval power in the world. The protection of our trade, while connected with Britain, will not cost us a fiftieth part of what it must cost, were we ourselves to raise a naval force sufficient for this purpose. The manufactures of Great Britain confessedly surpass any in the world… .

The advantages are not imaginary but real. They are such as we have already experienced; and such as we may derive from a connection with Great Britain for ages to come.

Suppose we were to revolt from Great Britain, declare ourselves Independent, and set up a Republic of our own—what would be the consequence?—I stand aghast at the prospect—my blood runs chill when I think of the calamities, the complicated evils that must follow… .

What a horrid situation would thousands be reduced to who have taken the oath of allegiance to the King. They must renounce that allegiance, or abandon all their property in America! By a Declaration of Independency, every avenue to a compromise with Great Britain would be closed. The sword only could decide the quarrel. And the sword would not be sheathed till one had conquered the other.

Devastation and ruin must mark the progress of this war along the sea coast of America. Hitherto, Britain has not exerted her power. Her number of troops and ships of war here at present, is very little more than she judged necessary in time of peace. The troops amount to no more than 12,000 men. The ships to no more than 40, including frigates. Both Great Britain and the colonies hoped for and expected compromise. Neither of them has lost sight of that desirable object.

But supposing once more that we were able to cut off every regiment that Britain can spare or hire, and to destroy every ship she can send. Suppose we could beat off any other European power that would presume to invade this continent. Yet, a republican form of government would neither suit the spirit of the people, nor the size of America.

Source: Essay by Charles Inglis, Anglican clergyman

Directions: Using the excerpt below and your knowledge of American history, answer the following questions.

> "Suppose we were to revolt from Great Britain, declare ourselves independent, and set up a Republic of our own—what would be the consequences? —I stand aghast at the prospect—my blood runs chill while I think of the calamities, the complicated evils that must follow…
>
> What a horrid situation would thousands be reduced to who have taken the oath of allegiance to the King. They must renounce that allegiance, or abandon all their property in America! By a Declaration of Independency, every avenue to a compromise with Great Britain would be closed. The sword only could decide the quarrel…
>
> Devastation and ruin must mark the progress of this war along the sea coast of America. …But supposing once more that we were able to cut off every regiment that Britain can spare or hire, and to destroy every ship she can send. Suppose we could beat off any other European power that would presume to invade this continent. Yet, a republican form of government would neither suit the spirit of the people, nor the size of America."

—Charles Inglis, "The True Interest of America Impartially Stated," 1776

Multiple-Choice

1. Which of the following groups would most directly challenge the ideas expressed in "The True Interest of America Impartially Stated?"

(A) ministers of King George in the southern colonies

(B) members of the Free African Society

(C) merchants with trade relations with Great Britain

(D) members of the Sons of Liberty

> The Sons of Liberty were opposed to the ideas of remaining in the Empire. They could not see any real advantage for continuing with the colonial relationship that seemed to be enslaving the Americans.
>
> *(NAT-1, Analyzing Historical Evidence)*

2. Which of the following controversies after the American Revolution most directly developed from the clash of national identity suggested in the excerpt above?

(A) disputes over compensation for confiscated property

(B) disputes over Native American land claims

(C) disputes over ending the slave trade

(D) disputes over trade relations with Great Britain

> After the Revolution, the Loyalists tried to get compensation for the property that they abandoned when tens of thousands Tories left America for England and Canada. The British occupied forts on American soil until the mid 1790s when the Jay Treaty resolved most of the disputes.
>
> *(NAT-1, Contextualization)*

Short-Answer

Using the excerpt, answer parts a, b, and c.

a) From 1765–1776, a new American identity emerged in the British colonies. Select ONE of the events below and briefly explain how it contributed to this emerging national identity:

- The Stamp Act Congress (1765)
- The Boston Massacre (1770)
- The Boston Tea Party (1773)

b) Briefly analyze ONE other element of the emerging American identity that was not discussed in <u>part a</u>.

c) Briefly explain ONE attempt by the British government to suppress the emerging American identity from 1765–1776.

---

a. Answers will vary. The Stamp Act gave the colonists a new sense of unity as 9 of 13 colonies joined in New York to protest the Stamp Act. The Boston Massacre helped heightened the colonial outrage against Great Britain as five colonials were shot and killed in Boston. It was another stepping stone to an emerging national unity. The Tea Party promoted a final unification of the colonies as 12 of 13 met in Philadelphia to decide how to help Massachusetts resist the Intolerable Acts.

(NAT-1, Analyzing Historical Evidence)

b. Answers will vary.

(NAT-1, Analyzing Historical Evidence)

c. Answers will vary. Students might explain that the British:

(1) sent troops to colonies

(2) offered colonists representation in Parliament

(3) proposed the concept of virtual representation

(4) repealed the Stamp Act, Townshend Acts

(5) reminded colonists that Parliament was superior to colonial assemblies

(6) appealed to colonists' loyalty as Englishmen abroad

(NAT-1, Analyzing Historical Evidence)

Lesson 8

The National Banks

The National Banks of the United States dominated American economic history from 1791 to 1845. No issue was more contentious between Federalists and Republicans as these two parties established the financial foundation of the nation. In the early years of the Republic, Alexander Hamilton's supporters clashed with Thomas Jefferson's supporters over the Bank's constitutionality and its alleged unfairness to the poor.

Later, the rechartering of the Bank sparked a raging controversy between the Jacksonian Democrats and Henry Clay's Whigs. Further, it divided the country geographically as western farmers blamed the Bank for their economic woes and saw it as a symbol of eastern financial elitism and dominance.

The following chart summarizes the First and Second Banks of the United States. It can be used in conjunction with the chart on political parties (Lesson 11). As you study the Bank, consider why it was so controversial. Can you think of any other economic issue that so dominated United States history?

Directions: Analyze the chart on the National Banks, and then answer the following questions.

1. A primary reason for opposition to the National Banks was that these banks

    (A) failed to provide sound economic services to the country

    (B) contributed to foreign speculation in the American economy

    (C) promoted speculation and risk-taking in banking

    (D) were not authorized by the Constitution

2. The person most likely to support the First National Bank would be someone who

    (A) farmed in the frontier regions of Tennessee

    (B) voted for Thomas Jefferson in the presidential election of 1796

    (C) lived in Philadelphia and was involved in commerce and trade

    (D) feared the rapid expansion of government power in the 1790s

---

Enhancing Understanding

LOOSE CONSTRUCTION — An interpretation of the "elastic clause" (Article 1, Section 8, Clause 18) that allows Congress to make all laws that "shall be necessary and proper for carrying into execution the foregoing powers...." This expanded the powers of the central government and was the basis for the creation of the National Bank in 1791. Its interpretation was an ongoing dispute in the early days of the Republic.

---

3. The main argument for rechartering the National Bank in 1816 was that

    (A) England had a national bank and America must remain competitive

    (B) the Bank would prevent falling land prices from hurting economic growth

    (C) the Constitution had been amended and Congress now had the power to create a Bank

    (D) the Bank could restore economic stability after the War of 1812

The National Banks

	First Bank	Second Bank
Years	1791–1811	1816–1836
Reasons for Creation	Hamilton modeled it after Bank of England Paid dividends and interest to government, which was the source of revenue	1811–1816 country in economic chaos following War of 1812 Explosion in number of unstable state banks
Function	Provided flexible currency Created adequate credit for business Generated revenue for national government	Controlled state banks Provided flexible currency Controlled inflation Restrained land speculation
Supporters	Alexander Hamilton's supporters Members of the Federalist Party Mercantile, eastern groups Friends of strong central government	Madison signed recharter National Republicans/Whigs Henry Clay/Nicholas Biddle Mercantile, eastern groups
Opponents	Thomas Jefferson's supporters (Democratic) Republicans Backcountry farmers States' rights supporters	Old Jeffersonians Andrew Jackson—Democrats Western farmers Small banking interests Land speculators
Reasons for Demise	Republicans gain political power and, by 1811, control Washington Madison's government did not renew charter	Andrew Jackson's veto Became a cause célèbre for opponents of Jackson Appeared undemocratic/elitist in the egalitarian 1830s
Constitutional Issue	Federalists: Bank was "necessary and proper" under "elastic clause" in Constitution Republicans: Bank violated the Constitution—establishing Bank was not enumerated as a power of Congress in Article 1, Section 8 Great struggle of loose vs. strict interpretation of the Constitution	1819 *McCulloch v. Maryland* declared the Bank constitutional 1832 Jackson declared the Bank unconstitutional in his veto message Part of an ongoing debate between the loose/strict interpretations of Constitution and the strong/weak views of federal government

Directions: Using the excerpt below and your knowledge of American history, answer the following questions.

> "It is to be regretted, that the rich and powerful too often bend the acts of government to their selfish purposes. Distinctions in society will always exist under every just government. Equality of talents, or education, or of wealth can not be produced by human institutions. In the full enjoyment of the gifts of Heaven and the fruits of superior industry, economy, and virtue, every man is equally entitled to protection by law; but when the laws undertake to add to these natural and just advantages artificial distinctions…to make the rich richer and the potent more powerful, the humble members of society—the farmers, mechanics, and laborers—who have neither the time nor the means of securing like favors to themselves, have a right to complain of the injustice of their Government."

—Andrew Jackson's veto message of the
National Bank Bill, July 1832

Multiple-Choice

1. Which of the following continuities from 1865–1900 most directly reflects the sentiment expressed in the passage?

(A) farmers' attempts to institute currency reform

(B) industrialists' attempts to raise protective tariff duties

(C) Southern Redeemers attempts to expand states' rights

(D) Eastern European immigrants' attempts to gain citizenship status

> After the Civil War, the issue of the type and amount of currency in circulation dominated the economic and political debate. Farmers wanted silver and/or paper money added to the gold in circulation to inflate the money supply and to aid debtors. The issue was comparable to the pre-Civil War debate over the National Bank. Both controversies revolved around the advantages economic policies gave to the rich and the elites in society and to wealthy easterners in particular.
>
> *(POL-3, Continuity and Change over Time)*

2. The ideas expressed in the passage above most closely resemble an earlier political debate over the

(A) passage of the Sedition Act of 1798

(B) approval of Alexander Hamilton's financial plan

(C) ratification of the Jay Treaty

(D) passage of the Tariff of 1816

> Alexander Hamilton's financial plan was seen as benefiting the elite in society. Similar charges were made against both the First and Second National Banks. Also his plan called for an expansion of the central government's economic reach in a fashion that was similar to the increased governmental role that went along with the creation of the National Banks.
>
> *(POL-3, Continuity and Change over Time)*

Short-Answer

Using the excerpt, answer parts a, b, and c.

a) Briefly explain how ONE of the following actions was both a validation and a repudiation of President Jackson's economic program and philosophy:

- the veto of the National Bank
- the passage of the Specie Circular
- the creation of "pet" banks

b) Briefly explain how Jackson's Bank veto challenged past government economic policy from 1815–1829.

c) The National Bank was a source of political division in both the years 1791–1811 and 1816–1836. Briefly explain ONE important similarity in the opposition to its creation in both eras.

---

a) Answers will vary. Jackson's constituents (western and southern farmers) supported the veto of the Bank, but its elimination had an adverse impact on the American economy. The Specie Circular curtailed land speculation by requiring land purchases to be made in gold or silver. This requirement tamed inflation, but it helped to cause the Panic of 1837. The pet banks made credit more available, especially in the South and the West, but they also made risky investments that generated speculation and inflation.

(POL-3, Analyzing Historical Evidence)

b) Jackson attempted to reduce the federal government's reach in the economy. He sought to curtail the growth of federal power that occurred after the War of 1812 as the government increased the tariff; reconstituted the National Bank; and embarked on an expanded internal improvements program.

(POL-3, Analyzing Historical Evidence)

c) Answers will vary. Students might explain opposition to both Banks revolved around:

(1) the government had no business in the Banking industry;

(2) the Bank was a tool of the rich;

(3) the Bank favored one class of Americans over another;

(4) general tax receipts were used to promote a private business;

(5) the Bank was foreign owned.

(POL-3, Continuity and Change over Time)

Lesson 9

Liberal and *Conservative*
in United States History, 1790–1940

Two of the most misunderstood political terms in any U.S. history course are *liberal* and *conservative*. In general, liberals examine and challenge the existing attitudes and behaviors of their society and seek to change them. Conservatives, on the other hand, embrace the conventional wisdom of their times, accept the status quo, and support only small, incremental changes. These fundamental beliefs shaped the specific policies that liberals and conservatives endorsed during each era of U.S. history.

However, the two terms have a perplexing way of confusing students. Part of the difficulty is that their meanings have flip-flopped throughout the decades. For example, the liberal idea of early nineteenth-century Jeffersonians that government's involvement in society should be limited became a conservative belief during the twentieth century. And Alexander Hamilton's conservative idea of expanding the government's role in society during the 1790s to promote public interest was warmly endorsed by the liberals of the 1930s.

The chart on the next page will help you understand the shifting nature of liberal and conservative labels from 1790 to 1940. (The next section will examine the idea from 1940 to 1985). As you study the chart, try to formulate clearer definitions of *liberal* and *conservative*. Also, consider why the meaning of the terms changed so often during the course of U. S. history.

Directions: Analyze the chart on *liberal* and *conservative*, and then answer the following questions.

1. From 1790 to 1840 a liberal would have supported

    (A) the National Bank

    (B) limiting the power of governments

    (C) secession

    (D) a strong central government

2. A similarity between the conservatives of the 1790s and the liberals in the twentieth century was that both favored

    (A) government use of the spoils system

    (B) expanding the money supply by coining silver

    (C) an agrarian (farming) way of life

    (D) an active government involved in society

3. Which pair of issues divided liberals and conservatives from 1865 to 1900?

    (A) civil rights and the tariff issue

    (B) expansion of slavery and the National Bank

    (C) business regulation and road/canal construction

    (D) the money supply and business regulation

Dates	Liberal	Conservative
1790–1824	Thomas Jefferson spokesman Favored farmers Best government is the least government Advocated states' rights Opposed National Bank Supported low taxes/tariffs Supported reduced army and navy *Laissez-faire*	Alexander Hamilton spokesman Favored commercial, mercantile groups Government should be strong Wanted centralized government power Favored National Bank Believed that tariffs were necessary Strong national defense
1824–1840	Personal liberty, weak government Free competition, egalitarian opportunity Anti-National Bank, anti-tariffs States should fund roads, canals Supported Andrew Jackson	Supported compact theory of government Weak presidents Pro-National Bank National government should fund roads, canals Whigs—opponents of Andrew Jackson Supported Henry Clay
1840–1865	Pro-union Anti-slavery Favored national program of roads/canals Opposed westward expansion Opposed extending slavery into territories Opposed secession	States' rights Pro-slavery Opposed national program of roads/canals Favored westward expansion Favored extending slavery into territories Supported secession
1865–1900	Supported Radical Reconstruction Wanted honesty in government Supported Reform Darwinism Anti-imperialist Expanded money supply (paper, silver) Supported government regulation of business Wanted low tariffs	Resisted Radical Reconstruction Tolerated spoils system Supported Social Darwinism Expansionist Supported gold standard *Laissez-faire* High tariffs Gospel of Wealth
1900–1940	Government intervention in society Progressive social and labor reforms Regulations and limitations of trusts Collective security (League of Nations) Promoted consumer protection Presidents: T. Roosevelt, W. Wilson, and FDR Direct government relief/welfare in 1930s Square Deal, New Deal Low tariffs	Old Guard Republicans Extremely favorable to business interests Isolationism Leaders: Taft, Lodge, Harding, Coolidge, Hoover Rugged Individualism Normalcy in 1920s Best government is least government No direct relief or welfare High tariffs

Directions: Using the excerpt below and your knowledge of American history, answer the following questions.

> "There is a widespread belief among the American people that the great corporations known as trusts are harmful to the general welfare... It [the danger of corporations] is based upon the sincere belief that combination and concentration should be, not forbidden, but supervised and within reasonable limits controlled. In my judgment this belief is right.
>
> It is no limitation upon property rights or freedom of contract to require that when people receive from the government the privilege of doing business under corporate form, they should be truthful as to the value of the property in which capital is to be invested. Great corporations exist only because they are created and safeguarded by our institutions. It is therefore our right and our duty to see that they work in harmony with these institutions...In the interest of the public, the government should have the right to inspect and examine the workings of the great corporations engaged in interstate business..."

—Theodore Roosevelt on Trusts and Business Reform, 1901

Multiple-Choice

1. Which one of the following would most likely support the perspective expressed in the passage?

   (A) a member of the Social Gospel movement

   (B) a disciple of Herbert Spencer

   (C) an advocate of *laissez-faire* Capitalism

   (D) an opponent of Socialism in the United States

> The members of the Social Gospel movement believe the churches should encourage the government to take responsibility to defend people's welfare and opportunities. Roosevelt supported this concept as he believed government regulation of trusts (monopolies) would provide a "Square Deal" for the less powerful in society and giving them a better chance to succeed in life.
>
> *(POL-2, Analyzing Historical Evidence)*

2. In their efforts to address the challenges noted above by President Roosevelt, progressive reformers

   (A) nationalized many businesses and corporations

   (B) asked corporations to downside voluntarily

   (C) curtailed consolidation of corporations

   (D) supported corporations in labor disputes

> The progressives, led by presidents Theodore Roosevelt, William Taft, and Woodrow Wilson used the Sherman Anti-Trust Act over two hundred times to reign in the power of large corporations and trusts. While never attempting to take over the businesses or to restore old-fashion competition, the progressives hoped to regulate corporations and protect the public interest. *(POL-2, Causation)*

Short-Answer

Using the excerpt, answer parts a, b, and c.

a) Historians have discovered the roots of the Progressive Movement in the political developments after the Civil War. Briefly explain which ONE of the groups listed below contributed most to progressive thought from 1901–1917.

- Populist Party
- Greenback Labor Party
- Women's Christian Temperance Union

b) Contrast your choice against ONE of the other options, demonstrating why that option is not as good as your choice.

c) Both the years 1901–1917 and 1933–1941 saw an increase in government intervention in the economy. Briefly explain ONE important reason for a more active government response to economic problems in both time periods.

---

a) Answers will vary. Each of the three groups called on the government to alleviate the suffering of the poor. The Populist Party with its Omaha Platform probably had the greatest influence on the Progressive Movement among the three. The Greenback Labor Party called for the government to reform the currency and to help debtors. And the Women's Christian Temperance Union anticipated the Prohibition movement with their drive to restrict the use of alcohol. (Some historians view the 18th Amendment as one of the last gasps of progressive reform.)

(POL-2, Causation, Continuity and Change over Time)

b) Answers will vary.

(POL-2, Causation)

c) Answers will vary. Students might explain that both the years 1901–1917 and 1933–1941 shared some common characteristics:

(1) strong executive leadership in the White House;

(2) followed an era of reduced government activities;

(3) saw a popular belief that businesses had grown too large and were somewhat abusive to the general welfare;

(4) followed economic downturns (Depressions of 1893–1897 and 1929–1933)

(POL-3, Causation)

Lesson 10

Liberal and *Conservative* in United States History, 1940–1985

The division between liberals and conservatives continued after 1940. Liberals maintained their desire to promote change and to challenge the conventional thinking and behavior of their times. Conservatives adhered to their beliefs in protecting current societal norms and resisting sweeping, dramatic changes.

The post-World War II world presented the United States with a host of new challenges. The New Deal, while not ending the Depression, had transformed thinking about governmental domestic policy. The wartime alliance of England, the Soviet Union, and the United States collapsed quickly into a new East-West ideological rivalry. Liberals and conservatives divided over the best ways for the nation to address these foreign and domestic changes. Both groups grappled with the role of the United States in confronting the rising communist threat, the role of the government in regulating the economic life in the nation, and the pace of advancement for women and blacks in society. These issues would shape the postwar liberal-conservative debate.

The chart on the following page outlines the differences between liberal and conservative beliefs from 1940 to 1985. As you study it, look for consistent patterns of beliefs that each group held throughout the post-World War II years. Was one philosophy more consistent than the other? Also, was there a belief that conservatives embraced in one time period that became the liberal position in another? And vice versa?

Directions: Analyze the chart on *liberal* and *conservative*, and then answer the following questions.

1. From 1940 to 1985, conservatives consistently believed that

   (A) civil rights are a national priority

   (B) the role of the government in society should be limited

   (C) the New Deal should become a permanent part of American society

   (D) the Soviet Union is a trustworthy and dependable ally

2. A liberal in the 1960s would have supported

   (A) a declaration of war against North Vietnam

   (B) Mississippi's right to handle its own racial problems

Enhancing Understanding

SILENT MAJORITY — a reference to the white, working-class Americans who were alarmed with the permissiveness and direction of American society in the late 1960s and early 1970s. They opposed many Great Society programs as wrongheaded and too slanted toward minorities. President Nixon cited this group as supporters of both his domestic and foreign policy initiatives.

   (C) a federal law protecting park lands

   (D) the use of federal troops to curb civil rights protest marches

3. A conservative during the 1980s would have supported a law that

   (A) raised income taxes by 20%

   (B) reduced the defense budget by 20%

   (C) increased research on alternative sources of energy

   (D) reduced taxes for married people

Dates	Liberal	Conservative
1940–1960	Government should regulate economy Government responsible for people's welfare Deficit spending acceptable U.S. accepts international role Communism a challenge at home and abroad Supported organized labor Embraced federal support of racial justice and equality Encouraged flexible military response	Government should be limited in society Promoted individual responsibility for welfare Wanted a balanced budget Communism was a great domestic threat Limited overseas involvement but contained Communism with force Reconsidered much of the New Deal States should handle their racial issues Encouraged massive retaliation
1960–1968	Expanded role of government in society Wanted Vietnam to be a limited war Racial justice was national priority Protected the environment Women's rights important U.S. should end domestic poverty Youth culture tolerated and celebrated	Government should be limited in society Total military victory in Vietnam States handle racial problems Wanted to restore law and order in cities Upheld sexual/gender roles Defended traditional family values Youth culture deplored
1968–1975	Withdraw from Vietnam Promoted Equal Rights Amendment for women Richard Nixon and Watergate a threat to liberty Great Society must be maintained Blacks' gains must expand with busing and affirmative action Nixon should be impeached	Wanted limited government in society Peace with honor in Vietnam Maintained traditional gender roles 'Silent Majority' should be heard Watergate not that important Repealed much of Great Society No special treatment for minorities to achieve equality Maintained that Nixon was no more corrupt than earlier presidents
1975–1985	Maintain Great Society Insisted on human rights in foreign policy Avoid future "Vietnams" Détente with USSR Promoted affirmative action Supported Equal Rights Amendment Supported conservation of energy Supported abortion rights (*Roe v. Wade*)	Wanted limited government in society Cut taxes Increased defense spending Acted aggressively overseas USSR viewed as an "evil empire" Limited federal role in civil rights Maintained family values Stressed finding new sources of oil Pro Life (anti-abortion)

Directions: Using the excerpt below and your knowledge of American history, answer the following questions.

"During four futile years, the Administration…has talked and talked and talked the words of freedom, but it has failed and failed and failed in the works of freedom…failures mark the slow death of freedom in Laos; failure infest the jungles of Vietnam, and failure haunt the houses of our once great alliances…

Rather than useful jobs in our country, our people have been offered bureaucratic "make work"; rather than moral leadership, they have been given bread and circuses. …today in our beloved country we have an Administration which seems eager to deal with the Communism in every coin known—from gold to wheat, from consulates to confidences, and even human freedom itself.

…And I want to make this abundantly clear—I don't intend to let peace or freedom be torn from our grasp because of lack of strength or lack of will…"

—Barry Goldwater at the Republican Convention, 1964

Multiple-Choice

1. The ideas expressed in the passage most directly contributed to which of the following trends from 1980–1992?

(A) the call for expanded civil rights for African Americans

(B) a drive to balance the federal budget

(C) a military buildup and challenge to the Soviet Union

(D) the flow of political power from the President to Congress

> The conservative movement spearheaded by Barry Goldwater believed that the nation became weak after the debacle of Vietnam. America's retreat in the 1970s led many to believe American security and place in the world had slipped. The Reagan presidency from 1981-1989 reversed this trend with expansion of military spending and a more confrontational approach to the Soviet Union. *(POL-1, Causation)*

2. Which of the following movements in the first half of the twentieth century would most directly support the argument made in the excerpt?

(A) the movement to restrict the formation of trusts

(B) the movement to limit the hours of women in factories

(C) the movement to make the world safe for democracy

(D) the movement to reduce government regulation and taxation

> The conservative movement, especially in the 1920s, sought to lessen the role of government in society as it reacted to the progressive reforms of the early 20th century. The policies of Harding and Coolidge in particular cut regulations and taxation from the pre- Great War era.
>
> *(POL-1, Continuity and Change over Time)*

Short-Answer

Using the excerpt, answer parts a and b.

a) Historians have proposed that Barry Goldwater was influential in the conservative revival in the United States from 1975–1992. Briefly explain how TWO of the ideas expressed in the passage were translated into public policy in the last quarter of the twentieth century.

b) Briefly explain how ONE development from 1960–1964 that is *not* mentioned in the excerpt supported the author's argument.

---

a) Answers will vary. Goldwater suggested the following in his speech: American foreign policy was weak and adrift in the mid-1960s; the federal government did not promote job growth, rather it expanded its bureaucracy and stifled economic growth; freedom was endangered by the current administration's attempts to cooperate with the communists.

(POL-1, Continuity and Change over Time)

b) Answers will vary. Students might explain:

(1) the United States had setbacks in fighting Communism (Castro in Cuba);

(2) the U-2 episode ruined peaceful coexistence and the Cold War had deepened;

(3) the U.S. and Soviet Union signed a Nuclear Test Ban Treaty, which many saw as favorable to the U.S.S.R.;

(4) the Soviets made inroads in the Middle East, Africa, and space.

(POL-1, Analyzing Historical Evidence)

Lesson 11

Political Parties in the Nineteenth Century

The founding fathers dreaded the formation of political parties in America. They feared that factions would corrupt and compromise the integrity of the government. Men such as James Madison and George Washington believed that political parties would undermine the foundation of a successful republic—the virtue of the people.

Nevertheless, parties formed quickly. Disagreements over Hamilton's financial plan, the nature of the Constitution, and the French-English conflict of the 1790s gave rise to the Federalist and Republican Parties. Thus, despite the fears of some leaders, by 1800 the United States had developed a full-fledged political party system.

The charts on the following two pages trace the evolution of the political parties during the nineteenth century and present their principles. Because the parties divided themselves into conservative and liberal positions, these materials should be used in conjunction with the chart on liberal and conservative beliefs from 1790 to 1940. As you study these materials, think about the political issues that have consistently divided Americans over the years, and consider whether parties serve any useful function in our political system.

Directions: Analyze the charts on political parties, and then answer the following questions.

1. A farmer who opposed the creation of the National Bank in the 1790s would likely join the

   (A) Democratic Republican Party

   (B) Democratic Party

   (C) Free Soil Party

   (D) Whig Party

2. The Federalist Party, the Whig Party, and the Republican Party of the 1850s all supported

   (A) government assistance to end slavery

   (B) government assistance to business interests

   (C) strict construction of the Constitution

   (D) an expansionistic foreign policy

3. A businessman in the 1840s who sought government assistance in building a road through his state would support the policies of the

   (A) Democratic Republican Party

   (B) Federalist Party

   (C) Populist Party

   (D) Whig Party

Enhancing Understanding

STRICT CONSTRUCTION — the view of the "necessary and proper" clause of the Constitution that challenged a loose interpretation of the clause (*see LOOSE CONSTRUCTION on p. 30*). Rather than expanding the elasticity of government power, this position said that if a power was not explicitly stated in the document, Congress was prohibited from using it.

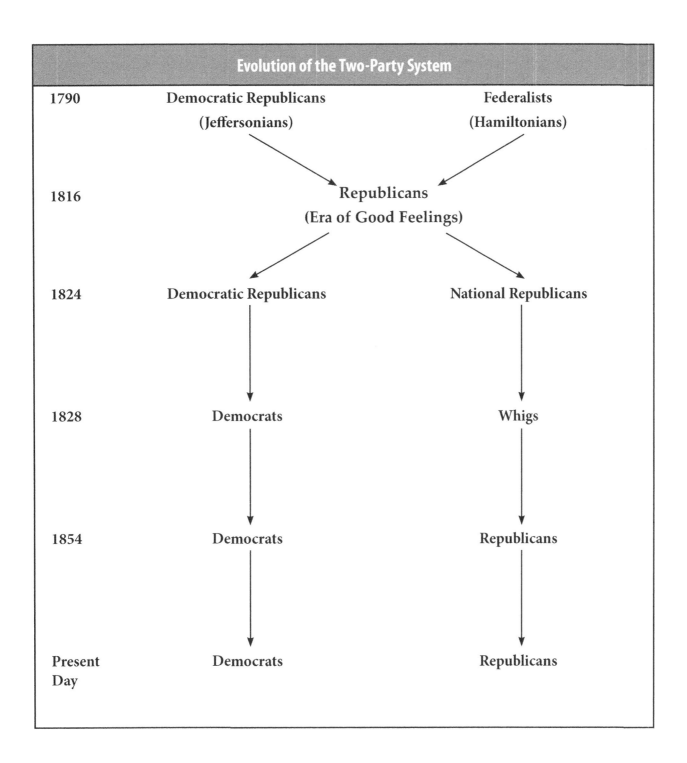

Evolution of the Two-Party System

1790	Democratic Republicans (Jeffersonians)		Federalists (Hamiltonians)
1816		Republicans (Era of Good Feelings)	
1824	Democratic Republicans		National Republicans
1828	Democrats		Whigs
1854	Democrats		Republicans
Present Day	Democrats		Republicans

Principles of the Political Parties, 1790–1900

Democratic Republicans (1790–1810)	Federalists (1790–1810)
Leader: Thomas Jefferson	Leader: Alexander Hamilton
Weak central government	Strong central government
Protect states' rights	Reduce states' rights
Strict view of Constitution	Loose view of Constitution
Agrarian oriented (pro-farmer)	Business and commerce oriented
Low taxes	High taxes
Weak military	Strong military
Anti-National Bank	Pro-National Bank
Pro-French	Pro-British

Jacksonian Democrats (1828–1848)	Whigs (1832–1852)
Jeffersonian traditions/ideas	Hamiltonian traditions/ideas
Supporters: small farmers and mechanics	Mercantile/business interests
Anti-National Bank	Pro-National Bank
States control/building of roads and canals	National government control/building of roads and canals (American System)
Pro-slavery	Opposed spread of slavery
Pro-Mexican War	Anti-Mexican War
Strong executive	Weak executive
Laissez-faire	Energetic national government

Democrats (1850–1900)	Republicans (1854–1900)
Proslavery	Opposed the spread of slavery
Favored secession from Union	Opposed secession
Blamed for Civil War (Bloody Shirt Issue)	Whig influence/pro-business
States' rights (especially on civil rights)	Briefly championed civil rights
Agrarian oriented	Business oriented
Feared strong central government	Supported active national government
Opposed gold standard (usually)	Supported gold standard
Used Spoils System	Used Spoils System but made some reforms
Supported lowering tariffs (1887)	Supported high tariffs
Reduced government role in railroad building	Government support in building railroads
In 1890s opposed Imperialism	In 1890s favored Imperialism

Directions: Using the excerpt below and your knowledge of American history, answer the following questions.

> "…The great object of the institution of civil government is the improvement of the condition of those who are parties to the social compact. …For the fulfillment of those duties governments are invested with power, and to the attainment of the end—the progressive improvement of the conditions of the governed. …I would suggest the expediency of connecting the equipment of a public ship for the exploration of the whole northwest coast of this continent. …Connected with the establishment of a university, or separate from it, might be undertaken the erection of an astronomical observatory…
>
> But…if these powers and others enumerated in the Constitution may be effectually brought into action by laws promoting the improvement of agriculture, commerce, and manufactures, the cultivation and encouragement of the mechanic and of the elegant arts, the advancement of literature, and the progress of the sciences, …to refrain from exercising them for the benefit of the people themselves…would be treachery to the most sacred of trusts…"

—John Quincy Adams, Message to Congress,
December 6, 1825

Multiple-Choice

1. For a supporter of the excerpt above, what change in America's political identity in the 1820s would be necessary to improve "the social compact?"

   (A) broadening suffrage by eliminating property requirements in order to vote

   (B) reducing the reach of the federal government in economic matters

   (C) limiting the power of the judicial branch of government

   (D) accepting an expansion of the elastic clause of the Constitution

   > Adams called for the government to expand its role in society. His activism was based on the elastic clause that called on Congress to take "necessary and proper" actions (in Adams' thinking) and make improvements in agriculture, commerce, and advancements in the arts. Adams proposed this expansion, but the Jacksonians blocked his endeavors.
   >
   > *(POL-1, Continuity and Change over Time)*

2. The ideas expressed in the excerpt were later reflected in the political platform of the

(A) Democratic Party

(B) Anti-Masonic Party

(C) Whig Party

(D) Liberty Party

> The Whig Party grew from the National Republicans, which Adams briefly headed. The Whigs called for the government to be beneficent and paternal in its policies. The party supported building roads, canals, and a new National Bank. The party was significant politically from 1832-1852.
>
> *(POL-1, Contextualization)*

Short-Answer

Using the excerpt, answer parts a and b.

a) Briefly explain how TWO of the following events gave rise to the political beliefs expressed in the excerpt:

- The conclusion of the War of 1812
- The promulgation of the Henry Clay's American System
- The recharter of the Bank of the United States

b) Briefly explain ONE political development from 1824–1840 that challenged the point of view expressed in the excerpt.

---

a) Answers will vary. The end of the War of 1812 marked a new era of government activism, which Adams supports in the passage. The government raised the tariff, re-chartered the Bank, and began a limited program of road and canal building. The American System supported internal improvements, the National Bank, and higher tariffs. The re-charter of the National Bank in 1816 supported the idea that the federal government should play an active role in the financial and economic development of the nation.

(POL-1, Causation)

b) Answers will vary. The rise of Jacksonian democracy after the election of 1824 challenged the agenda of the National Republicans and later the Whigs as they tried to expand the power of the federal government. Jackson's veto of the Maysville Road and the National Bank demonstrated his commitment to reducing the power of the government. Martin Van Buren continued Jackson's policies in his term from 1837-1841.

(POL-2, Analyzing Historical Evidence)

Lesson 12

Third Parties in United States History

Third parties have played a peripheral, but important, role in the American political process. Although no third party has ever come close to winning the White House, some have played the role of spoiler. For example, in 1844, the Liberty Party won enough votes in New York State to cost Henry Clay the presidency. And in 1912, the Progressive Party (Bull Moose Party) split the Republican vote and assured Woodrow Wilson's election.

A more common role for third parties has been as a vehicle for groups to vent their anger and opposition to the political status quo. In many cases, third parties have introduced ideas that eventually gained acceptance by the two major parties. And once they delivered their message, these third parties faded away. Specifically, the Free Soil Party's opposition to the spread of slavery in the 1840s influenced the Republican Party's platform in the 1850s, and the Populist Party platform of the 1890s was a preview of the progressive Republican and Democratic Parties' agendas of the early nineteenth century. Similarly, both Democrats and Republicans embraced the American Independent Party's law-and-order message in the late 1960s and early 1970s. In many ways, the historian Richard Hofstadter was right when he suggested that third parties are like bees: once they sting, they die.

The charts on the following two pages look at the most influential third parties of the nineteenth and twentieth centuries. As you review them, think about ways the American political system has limited the role of third parties, yet has also created conditions that promote their formation.

Directions: Analyze the charts on third parties in United States history, and then answer the following questions.

Enhancing Understanding

NATIVISM — a term associated with anti-immigration feelings, often expressed by promoting the interest of native-born inhabitants over non-native people trying to gain admissions to the United States. It has been an attitude of varying intensity from the beginning of the Republic in the 1790s to the present day.

---

1. The third party that provided the greatest influence on the progressive reformers of the early twentieth century was the

    (A) American Independent Party

    (B) Liberty/Free Soil Party

    (C) Populist Party

    (D) States' Rights Party (Dixiecrats)

2. Which of the following pairs of third parties represented an attempt to prevent changes in the racial policies of their times?

    (A) the States' Rights Party (Dixiecrats) and the Populist Party

    (B) the Liberty/Free Soil Party and the Populist Party

    (C) the Progressive Party (Bull Moose) and the States' Rights Party (Dixiecrats)

    (D) the American Independent Party and the States' Rights Party (Dixiecrats)

3. A factory worker in the 1840s who hoped to become a farmer in the non-slave territories of the West would likely support the ideas of the

    (A) Populist Party

    (B) Progressive Party (Bull Moose)

    (C) States' Rights Party (Dixiecrats)

    (D) Liberty/Free Soil Party

Third Parties in United States History

	Liberal Party, 1840–1848; Free Soil Party, 1848–1852	American Party (Know-Nothings), 1849–1856	People's Party (Populist), 1892–1903
Background	Grew out of split in abolitionist movement in late 1830s Liberty party merged into the Free Soil party in 1848	Grew out of nativist sentiment of the 1830s and 1840s Started as the "Supreme Order of Star-Spangled Banner"	Grew from farmer grievances against railroads and banks after the Civil War
Candidates	James Birney John P. Hale Martin Van Buren	Millard Fillmore	James B. Weaver William J. Bryan Tom Watson
Principles	Opposed the spread of slavery into territories Motto: "Free soil, free speech, free labor and free men" Free homesteads Repeal of Fugitive Slave Law End slavery in Washington, D.C.	Secrecy surrounded policies and members Immigration restrictions Anti-Catholic Literacy test to vote Tried to avoid a position on slavery (failed) Opposed Kansas-Nebraska Act	Free coinage of silver Public ownership of railroads/communications systems Income tax Eight-hour work day Immigration restrictions Direct election of U.S. senators
Impact	First political parties to oppose spread of slavery into territories Forerunners of the Republican Party of 1850s May have cost Henry Clay the 1844 election when Birney ran strong in New York State	Focused anti-immigrant, anti-Catholic resentment that had been building for years Briefly poised to replace Whigs as second national party Strong in Pennsylvania, New York, Massachusetts Eventually split over slavery	Omaha Platform of 1891 became blueprint for progressive reforms of twentieth century 1892 won 22 electoral votes Silver issue had little appeal to non-farmers Failed to gain support of urban laborers

Third Parties in United States History

	Progressive Party (Bull Moose, 1912), 1912–1924	States' Rights Party (Dixiecrats), 1948	American Independent Party, 1968–1972
Background	Grew from split between William Taft and Theodore Roosevelt in 1912	Grew from Democratic platform plank in 1948 that endorsed a modest civil rights program	Grew from civil rights revolution in 1960s Reaction to urban, racial unrest and rioting in mid-1960s
Candidates	Theodore Roosevelt Robert M. LaFollette	Strom Thurmond	George Wallace
Principles	Antitrust action Regulation of business Conservation of natural resources Women's suffrage Lower tariffs Direct democracy—recall, initiative, referendum	States should control civil rights Retain segregation of the races Maintain Jim Crow system in South Strict interpretation of Constitution	Law and order States should control civil rights Maintain racial segregation Reduce government power in Washington Repeal much of the Great Society's War on Poverty All-out victory in Vietnam
Impact	Split Republican vote in 1912 elected Woodrow Wilson president Roosevelt rejoined the Republican Party; Progressive Party faded after election of 1924	Expected to cost Truman and Democrats the election but Truman won Carried four southern states with 39 electoral votes Beginning of decline of Democratic Party in South	Won 46 electoral votes Made both Republicans and Democrats toughen their law-and-order stands Gave voice to a "white backlash" against integration Anti-Washington message adopted by other conservatives

Directions: Using the illustration below and your knowledge of American history, answer the following questions.

"The Grange Awakening the Sleepers," 1873

Multiple-Choice

1. The sentiment expressed in the cartoon most directly contributed to which of the following activities?

    (A) farmers' attempts to de-regulate the railroads

    (B) farmers' attempts to move to eastern cities

    (C) farmers' attempts to break national railroad strikes

    (D) farmers' attempts to challenge the economic status quo

The Grange and other farmers' organizations hoped to reverse the declining economic and political power of agrarian interests after the Civil War. Although the absolute numbers of farmers increased during these years, the percentage of farmers in the workforce declined. In addition, farm prices tumbled by 1/3 from 1868–1896.

(WXT-2, Continuity and Change over Time)

2. The ideas expressed in the cartoon most directly reflect which of the following continuities in United States history?

(A) an attempt to reduce the declining status of farmers in America

(B) an attempt to increase the use of civil disobedience protest in America

(C) an attempt to reduce the power of trusts in America

(D) an attempt to increase the price of farm products in America

> The cartoon depicts the attempt by the Grange to regulate railroads. The railroads had a monopoly in many parts of the West and abused farmers with rates that were unfair and capricious. The farmers hoped to change the dominance of railroads through government regulation of rates and policies.
>
> *(WXT-2, Causation)*

Short-Answer

Using the illustration, answer parts a, b, and c.

a) Explain the point of view reflected in the cartoon regarding ONE of the following:

- An American farmer
- A railroad executive
- A passenger on the train

b) Explain how the point of view you explained in <u>part a</u> might conflict with ONE of the other two groups.

c) Cite and explain ONE political development in the last quarter of the nineteenth century that supported the action depicted in the cartoon.

a) Answers will vary. The farmers needed to become active and defend themselves against railroad abuses. Farm organizations attempted to unite farmers and to fight the railroads. The railroad executives disliked agrarian groups attempting to reduce their profits and interfering with their consolidation of power in the west. Passengers on the train, representing the general public, did not want their lives disrupted by protests nor did they support farmers' attempt to raise food prices.

(WXT-2, Analyzing Historical Evidence)

b) Answers will vary. *(WXT-2, Analyzing Historical Evidence)*

c) Answers will vary. Students might explain the Grange Laws, the creation of the Interstate Commerce Commission, the Greenback Labor Party, and the Populists. All of which tried to reign in the power of the railroads before the turn of the century.

(WXT-2, Analyzing Historical Evidence)

Lesson 13

Freedom of the Seas and Wars with Europe

The United States has always defended its right to sail the seas. In exercising this right, however, America has periodically encountered difficulty, especially when its claims to maritime freedom intruded into general wars on the European continent. In 1793 and 1796, President George Washington proclaimed that, during European conflicts, the United States would avoid political and military alliances but would continue sailing the seas and maintaining commercial relations with all nations (see also Lesson 16, "Cornerstones of United States Foreign Policy").

This policy, while prudent and in the national interest, led to war on two occasions. In 1812 and 1917, events forced the United States to abandon its neutrality (so-called "isolationism") and to use force to defend its rights to freedom of the seas.

The chart on the following page outlines the background and events that led to America's entry into war in 1812 and 1917. As you review it and the chart on "Cornerstones of U.S. Foreign Policy" in Lesson 16, assess the wisdom of America's decision to remain neutral while asserting its right to sail into the European war zone. What factors did our leaders consider when they formulated and followed this policy? How did they define our national interests in 1812 and 1917?

Directions: Analyze the chart on wars with Europe, and then answer the following questions.

1. The United States' neutrality (isolationism) during the two European wars meant that America would

   (A) maintain commercial ties with Europe, but would not join military alliances

   (B) assist France, because such help was in America's national interest

   (C) join the side most likely to win the war

   (D) cease all connections with Europe until the war was over

2. The principal impact of the War of 1812 within the United States was the

   (A) quick uniting of the nation around the policies of President Madison

   (B) repudiation of the War Hawks in Congress

   (C) triumph of the Federalist Party in the election of 1812

   (D) division of the country along regional lines

3. In declaring war in 1917, the United States hoped to

   (A) eliminate Germany as a commercial rival

   (B) promote democracy in Europe

   (C) make a permanent alliance with France and England

   (D) eliminate Mexico as a threat to America's security

Enhancing Understanding

IMPRESSMENT — the forceful drafting of men into the armed forces, as employed by England prior to the War of 1812. The British came aboard American ships and removed both British deserters *and* American sailors. This practice was a major cause of the conflict between the two nations in 1812.

Wars with Europe

	War of 1812	The Great War (WWI) 1917
Background	France and England went to war in 1793 over European rivalries Both countries asked U.S. for assistance Both countries prohibited U.S. trade with the other U.S. refused and both countries seized American ships and cargoes England seized American men as well (impressment)	War began in Europe in July 1914 Central powers (Germany et al.) fought against Allied powers (France, England et al.) Both Germany and England blockaded their enemies German submarines sank shipping vessels without warning England searched American ships
President(s)	Thomas Jefferson James Madison	Woodrow Wilson
Action to Stay Neutral	Withheld trade by: • Embargo Act, 1807 • Nonintercourse Act, 1809 • Macon's Bill Number 2, 1810	Neutrality proclamation *Lusitania* protest *Sussex* pledge to stop the use of submarines against neutral shipping
Major Events	*Chesapeake-Leopard* clash in 1807 Thousands of men seized by British (1803–1812) Hundreds of American ships searched and seized by British and French	*Lusitania* sunk May 1915 (1,400 killed) *Sussex* pledge issued in 1916 Zimmerman note, 1917 (Germany proposed an alliance with Mexico against U.S.)
Outcome	War declared against England in June 1812	War declared against Germany in April 1917
Comments	War supported by South and West "War Hawks" like Henry Clay, John C. Calhoun, and Felix Grundy pushed the president into war, had hopes U.S. would gain Canada by victory New England shippers opposed war, calling it "Mr. Madison's War" War divided the country, yet Madison won re-election in 1812	Germany's unrestricted submarine warfare led to war with Germany England seized many ships but did not take lives U.S. waged war "to make world safe for democracy" U.S. did not formally join military alliance with England and France

Directions: Using the excerpt below and your knowledge of American history, answer the following questions.

"The true question in controversy…involves the interest of the whole nation. It is the right of exporting the production of our own soil and industry to foreign markets. Sir, our vessels are now captured…and condemned by the British Courts of Admiralty, without event the pretext of having on board contraband of war…

…For my part I am not prepared to say that this country shall submit to have her commerce interdicted or regulated by any foreign nation. Sir, I prefer war to submission.

Over and above these unjust pretensions of the British Government, for many years past they have been in the practice of impressing our seamen, for merchant vessels; this unjust and lawless invasion of personal liberty, calls loudly for the interposition of this Government."

—Felix Grundy, December 9, 1811

Multiple-Choice

1. The controversy highlighted in the passage developed, in part, because of the ideas expressed in
    (A) Thomas Jefferson's Declaration of Independence
    (B) George Washington's farewell address
    (C) James Madison's war message
    (D) John C. Calhoun's *Exposition and Protest*

In his Farewell Address, Washington called for the United States to avoid "entangling alliances" in Europe. When the nation tried to stay out of the conflict between England and France in the 1790s and early 1800s, both nations attacked our ships. Great Britain, however, also began to impress our sailors. This slap at our honor and trade eventually led to war in 1812.

(WOR-1, Causation)

2. The sentiment expressed in the passage would most likely be opposed by a
    (A) Southern slaveholder
    (B) Mid-Atlantic banker
    (C) New England shipper
    (D) Western farmer

New England shippers, while the victims of much of England's trade interdiction and loss of seamen, still were realizing great profits. As the most important neutral trading partner, the New Englanders (and the United States in general) saw their shipping interests flourish during the European conflict. With war, all trade ceased between England and depression replaced prosperity in the Northeast.

(WXT-2, Analyzing Historical Evidence)

Short-Answer

Using the excerpt, answer parts a and b.

a) Briefly explain how TWO of the following measures attempted to avoid both war and submission to Great Britain from 1807–1810:

- The Embargo Act (1807)
- The Non-Intercourse Act (1809)
- The Macon's Bill Number 2 (1810)

b) In the years 1803–1812 and 1914–1917, the United States faced challenges to its rights on the sea. Briefly explain ONE important similarity in the United States' response to challenges in both eras.

---

a) Answers will vary. The Embargo Act of 1807 was a total stoppage of trade with all countries. The act took American shipping off the seas until American rights on the seas were recognized by England and France. The Non Intercourse Act was a partial embargo with the United States trading with all countries except England and France. Macon Bill No. 2 was another partial embargo with a different wrinkle. It said the United States would trade with all countries, but if either Great Britain or France agreed to stop interfering with our shipping, America would stop trading with that countries' enemy. All three actions tried to avoid both war and submission, but war came in 1812 with England.

(NAT-1, Analyzing Historical Evidence)

b) Answers will vary. Students might explain:

(1) Presidents Jefferson, Madison, and Wilson all tried to avoid war;

(2) all followed Washington's advice to avoid entangling the United States in European conflicts;

(3) all used diplomacy and the threat of economic retaliation to avoid war;

(4) Madison and Wilson reluctantly asked for a declaration of war.

(WOR-1, Comparison)

Lesson 14

Compromises and the Union

Compromise was an essential element in the creation and maintenance of American democracy during the nation's first century of existence. On four different occasions, the political process reached a critical impasse, and only through compromise was a serious crisis avoided. The issues of congressional representation, the extension of slavery, and the settlement of Reconstruction all threatened the nation's domestic tranquility and the Union itself. In each instance, however, a compromise was reached that defused the crisis and restored some measure of domestic harmony.

The chart on the next page offers an overview of the four major compromises in U. S. history through the era of Reconstruction. As you review the chart, consider whether the compromises and the temporary solutions they provided were really in the national interest at the time or whether it would have been better for the country to confront the issues directly at that moment. Also consider whether a democratic republic is more dependent on compromises than other forms of government.

Directions: Analyze the chart on compromises in American history, and then answer the following questions.

1. The Great Compromise of 1787 resulted in

   (A) a legislative branch just like the one created by the Articles of Confederation

   (B) agreement on representation and taxes that counted slaves as 3/5 of a person

   (C) a national government with a two-house legislative branch

   (D) a government that gave disproportionate power to the small states

OBJECTIVES

Review the introductory material and the chart "Four Major Compromises in U.S. History" (pages 56–57 in the Student Edition). Have your students discuss whether compromise is a positive or negative process in a republic. Focus on whether postponing the issue of slavery and its future was beneficial to the nation's well-being.

After the class discussion on compromises and reading John C. Calhoun's March 4, 1850 speech, which follows, students will be able to:

1. outline the southern position on slavery and its spread in the 1850s;

2. describe the South's view of the Union in 1850;

3. evaluate the role of the abolitionists in bringing on the sectional crisis in antebellum America;

4. assess whether Calhoun's position in 1850 could forge the basis for a compromise over slavery.

ADDITIONAL COMPONENTS

- **Core Chart Worksheet:** "Lesson 14 – Compromises and the Union"

- **Primary Source Handout:** "John C. Calhoun's Speech" (copy p. 77 or print from website)

- **Document Source Worksheets:** "Worksheet for Document Source Analysis" (p. 246)

2. A common element in the Compromises of 1820 and 1850 was that both

(A) dealt with land areas acquired by war

(B) were followed by three decades of domestic peace

(C) combined earlier proposals to end the domestic slave trade

(D) dealt with the extension of slavery into the territories

3. The Compromise of 1877 marked the end of

(A) northern military occupation of the South

(B) deep resentments over the Civil War

(C) Republican presidential dominance

(D) sectional discord over race issues

Enhancing Understanding

POPULAR SOVEREIGNTY — a proposal to allow the citizens of a territory a vote to determine the status of slavery within that territory's boundaries. Settlers could vote to include or exclude the institution by majority vote. It was an attempted solution to the question of where slavery could expand in the 1850s, and was supported by Stephen Douglas.

DISCUSSION QUESTIONS

Hand out or display the document, "John C. Calhoun's Speech, March 4, 1850," (shown on page 77) and ask the following:

1. Whom does John Calhoun blame for most of the sectional troubles from 1830–1850? Do you agree with this view?

2. How does Calhoun explain the relative political strengths of the two sections? Do you agree with this view?

3. What is Calhoun's solution for solving the crisis in 1850?

4. From what you already know about Calhoun, is this consistent with his earlier views?

5. Given Calhoun's position, is compromise likely in 1850?

6. What events and developments from 1830–1850 brought John Calhoun to his point of view?

Answers available on the companion website.

Four Major Compromises in U.S. History

	Great Compromise 1787	Missouri Compromise 1820	Compromise of 1850	Compromise of 1877
Issue	Representation in Congress	Admission of Missouri would disrupt Senate balance between free and slave states Should slavery extend into new territories?	Admission of California to Union Disposition of the territory acquired from Mexican War	Who won the presidency in the election of 1876?
Background	Congress was expected to be dominating branch of government Virginia Plan called for representation by population New Jersey Plan proposed equal representation	Missouri wanted to become the 12th slave state (11 free) Should slavery extend north of Ohio River line? What would happen regarding slavery in rest of Louisiana Territory?	Should slavery extend into the Mexican Cession? Should D.C. outlaw slavery and/or slave trade? Should the Fugitive Slave Law be strengthened? Should California be admitted as a free state? What should be done about Texas's disputed boundaries?	Three states sent two sets of election returns Democrat Samuel Tilden needed only one electoral vote to win Commission gave all 20 disputed votes to Republican Rutherford Hayes South threatened new rebellion
Resolution	Two houses of Congress House based on population Senate has two senators from each state Combined the Virginia and New Jersey Plans	Missouri became slave state Maine became free state No slavery north of 36 degrees/ 30 minutes in Louisiana Territory	California became free state Utah/New Mexico Territory organized by popular sovereignty Stronger Fugitive Slave Law Slave trade ended in D.C. Texas's land claims denied, but U.S. will pay Texas' debt	Hayes given presidency Removal of troops from South Aid for Southern railroads Two Southerners in Cabinet Patronage jobs given to Southerners
Significance	Allowed Constitution to be written and approved	Postponed debate over spread of slavery for 30 years	Postponed the Civil War for ten years	Ended Radical/ Congressional Reconstruction

John C. Calhoun's Speech, March 4, 1850

A single section, governed by the will of the numerical majority, now controls the government [in] its entire powers. The North has absolute control over the government. It is clear, therefore, that on all questions between it and the South, where there are different interests, the interests of the South will be sacrificed to the North, no matter how oppressive the effects may be. The South possesses no political means by which it can resist.

Northern hostility towards the social organization of the South lay dormant a long time. The first organized movement against it began in 1835. Then, for the first time, antislavery societies were organized, presses established, lecturers sent forth to excite the people of the North, and incendiary publications were scattered over the whole South, through the mail… .

With the increase of their influence, the abolitionists extended the sphere of their action. In a short time, they had sufficient influence to get the legislatures of most of the northern states to pass acts which in effect repealed the provision of the Constitution that provides for the return of fugitive slaves. This was followed by petitions and resolutions of legislatures of the northern states and popular meetings, to exclude the southern states from all territories acquired or to be acquired, and to prevent the admission of any state into the Union which, by its constitution, does not prohibit slavery.

How can the Union be saved? There is but one way by which it can with any certainty; and that is, by a full and final settlement, on the principle of justice, of all the questions at issue between the two sections. The South asks for justice, simple justice, and less she ought not to take. She has no compromise to offer but the Constitution, and no concession or surrender to make. She has already surrendered so much that she has little left to surrender …

But can this be done? Yes, easily; not by the weaker party, for it can of itself do nothing—not even protect itself—but by the stronger. The North has only to do justice by conceding to the South an equal right in the acquired territory to do her duty by causing the constitutional provisions related to fugitive slaves to be faithfully fulfilled, to cease the agitation of the slave question, and to provide for an amendment to the Constitution. Such an amendment should restore to the South the power she possessed to protect herself, before the balance between the section [sic] was destroyed by this government.

But will the North agree to this? It is for her to answer this question. But, I will say, she cannot refuse, if she has half the love of the Union which she professes to have, or without justly exposing herself to the charge that her love of power is far greater than her love of the Union. At all events, the responsibility of saving the Union rests on the North, and not the South.

Source: **John C. Calhoun, U.S. Senator**

Directions: Using the excerpt below and your knowledge of American history, answer the following questions.

"I return to the question with which I began: How can the Union be saved? There is only one way. That is by a full and final settlement based on the principle of justice, of all the disputes between the two sections. The South asks for justice, simple justice. Less it ought not to accept. It has no compromise to offer but the Constitution, and no concession or surrender to make. It has already surrendered so much that it has little left to surrender.

Such a settlement would remove all the causes of dissatisfaction. It would satisfy the South that it could remain honorably and safely in the Union. It would bring back the harmony and good feelings between the sections that existed before the Missouri question. Nothing else can finally and forever settle the questions at issue, end agitation, and save the Union."

—John C. Calhoun, March 4, 1850

Multiple-Choice

1. The ideas expressed in the excerpt reflect a continuing controversy over

  (A) the place of slavery in the Constitution

  (B) the ability of the South to recover fugitive slaves

  (C) the abolitionist movement's right to free speech

  (D) the extension of slavery into the territories

> Calhoun spoke for the right of southerners to own slaves and to take them into the territories. He opposed the series of legislative proposals known as the Compromise of 1850. These bills included the concept of popular sovereignty, which allowed the people of a territory to decide whether to permit slavery or not. Calhoun believed slavery could not be excluded in the territories under any circumstances.
>
> *(WXT-1, Continuity and Change over Time)*

2. A proponent of the ideas expressed in the passage would likely believe that

  (A) the Constitution must be strictly interpreted

  (B) the Constitution is an evolving document

  (C) the Constitution is perpetual and could not be dissolved

  (D) the Constitution supports the regulation of slavery

> Calhoun was a strict constructionist. He believed the South had a constitutional right to hold slaves and to expand the institution westward. He cited the Fifth Amendment as support that property (slaves included) could not be taken without just compensation or due process. He also called attention to the fugitive slave provision and the 3/5 Compromise as evidence of constitutional support of the peculiar institution.
>
> *(POL-3, Analyzing Historical Evidence)*

Short-Answer

Using the excerpt, answer parts a, b, and c.

a) Briefly explain how ONE of the following compromises was most effective in preventing a break-up of the Union:

- The 3/5 Compromise
- The Missouri Compromise
- The Compromise of 1833

b) Contrast your choice from <u>part a</u> against ONE of the remaining options by demonstrating why your choice is the best.

c) Briefly explain one other instance in United States history when a compromise (other than the three mentioned in <u>part a</u>) was necessary to achieve a political settlement.

---

a) Answers will vary. The 3/5 Compromise addressed the conflict over how to count slaves for taxation and representation purposes at the Constitutional Convention. Both the North and South thought it fair at the time, but later the North complained the South got an unfair advantage in Congress and in presidential elections. The Missouri Compromise provided a thirty year truce over the question of the slavery's expansion. When it was repealed in the 1850s, it set off a political firestorm. The Compromise of 1833 solved the nullification dispute of the 1830s. South Carolina refused to pay the tariff and civil war seemed possible. While the compromise restored peace, many historians viewed the dispute as a preview of the South's growing concern over an increasing intrusive government that triggered the Civil War in the 1860s.

(POL-3, Analyzing Historical Evidence)

b) Answers will vary. *(POL-3, Analyzing Historical Evidence)*

c) Answers will vary. Students might cite the Great Compromise at the Constitutional Convention, the Compromise of 1850 or the Compromise of 1877. Each provide a political settlement that prevented a crisis.

(POL-3, Analyzing Historical Evidence)

Lesson 15

Judicial Nationalism, 1819–1824

The Federalists' political influence declined after the election of 1796. The party lost the White House in 1800 when Thomas Jefferson defeated John Adams. The War of 1812 further eroded Federalist political strength until, by 1818, Federalists represented less than one third of the Senate and House. Finally, by the election of 1820, there was no Federalist candidate to challenge James Monroe for the presidency. Thus, during the Era of Good Feelings (a.k.a. the National Period), the Federalists ceased to be a political force.

However, the Federalists' political ideology reached beyond 1820. The judiciary branch became a Federalist stronghold from 1801 to 1835, largely because of John Marshall. Appointed to the Supreme Court in 1801 by John Adams, Marshall served as Chief Justice until 1835. Throughout this time, he championed the twin Federalist goals of strengthening the central government and promoting business interests.

The Federalist philosophy was alive and well on the Supreme Court during the Era of Good Feelings (1816–1824). Three decisions in particular demonstrated how the Court strengthened the national government and encouraged business development. The chart on the following page summarizes these three important cases. As you study the chart, think about how Marshall, the lone Federalist on the Supreme Court for most of his tenure, could exert such influence in this era of Republican Party dominance. Further, how did the Supreme Court reflect the election returns from 1816–1824?

Directions: Analyze the chart on judicial nationalism, and then answer the following questions.

1. A significant impact of the Marshall Court decisions was to

  (A) expand the power of state governments at the expense of the national government

  (B) establish a confederation system of government where the states controlled the national political agenda

  (C) expand the powers of the national government at the expense of state governments' powers

  (D) promote economic conditions that benefited agrarian interests at the expense of mercantile interests

2. From 1819 to 1824, the Marshall Court favored business development with rulings that

  (A) put regulations into the hands of business-friendly state governments

  (B) restrained the restrictive regulations of the federal government

  (C) lowered property and corporate taxes

  (D) strengthened the partnership between financial interests and the federal government

3. The Marshall Court supported American nationalism from 1819 to 1824 by

   (A) eliminating the property requirement for voting

   (B) strengthening the central government's ability to direct and standardize economic policy

   (C) making American business competitive with other nations around the world

   (D) providing financial support for the "American System" of internal improvements

---

Enhancing Understanding

JUDICIAL REVIEW — the process by which the Supreme Court measures state and federal laws against the Constitution. The Court decides if laws are compatible with the powers set forth in the founding document. This is a fundamental function of the Court that was established in the case of *Marbury v. Madison* (1803).

Influential Cases for Judicial Nationalism

	Dartmouth College v. Woodward, 1819	McCulloch v. Maryland, 1819	Gibbons v. Ogden, 1824
Background	New Hampshire Republicans wanted to rid Dartmouth College of its Federalist influence Changed charter and fired president of college	Maryland wanted to regulate a branch of National Bank within its borders Placed a tax on all banks in state not chartered by the legislature Bank refused to pay tax	New York granted a monopoly on ferry boat service between New York and New Jersey to Robert Fulton's steamboat company Others challenged the monopoly New York courts upheld the monopoly
Question(s) to be decided	Could a state change a private college into a public university by revoking its charter?	Could Maryland tax a branch of National Bank? Was Bank constitutional?	Was monopoly legal? What powers to regulate interstate commerce did federal government have?
Ruling	New Hampshire could not revoke Dartmouth's charter because it was a form of contract	Maryland could not tax bank because state power was subordinate to Constitution Court said "power to tax involves the power to destroy" Bank constitutional under necessary-and-proper clause	A federal coastal license nullified New York's grant of monopoly Congress had power to regulate interstate commerce Commerce was more than exchange of goods; it included transportation and other types of commercial endeavors
Business Interest Promoted	Contract law strengthened by extending contract clause to corporate charter Sanctity of contracts encourages commercial growth	Upheld National Bank, which was very popular among mercantile groups National Bank encourages commerce, business growth	Struck down monopolies, encouraging business competition Strengthened federal government's power over interstate commerce (more business friendly than states)
States' Rights Diminished	New Hampshire could not change college from private to public	Maryland's taxing power reduced	New York's power to regulate trade reduced

Directions: Using the excerpt below and your knowledge of American history, answer the following questions.

> "…[the] mass of evidence stands opposed to those constructions which are laboring to invest the federal government with powers to abridge the state right of taxation; to control states by a power to legislate for ten miles square; to expend money belonging to the United States without control; to enrich a local capitalist interest at the expense of the people; to create corporations for abridging state rights; to make roads and canals; and finally to empower a complete negative over state laws and judgments, and an affirmative power as to federal laws."

—John Taylor's *New Views of the Constitution of the United States*, 1823

Multiple-Choice

1. In their efforts to address the challenges noted in the excerpt, the Jacksonians of the 1830s

   (A) supported the Supreme Court's use of judicial review

   (B) restricted states in developing internal improvements

   (C) restricted the government's role in the economy

   (D) supported the removal of Native Americans westward

2. Which of the following twentieth-century issues most closely parallels the controversy described in the passage?

   (A) the question of protecting African-American civil rights

   (B) the question of protecting the national environment

   (C) the question of ownership of natural resources off of the Continental Shelf

   (D) the question of where to store nuclear waste from power plants

The Jacksonians endorsed the ideas expressed in the passage that the federal government was growing too powerful and intruding on states' rights. In the 1830s, Jackson and his allies attempted to restrict the government's role in the economy by destroying the National Bank, and, at least, temporarily cutting back on federal sponsorship of internal improvements.

(POL-2, Causation, Contextualization)

The passage raised the issue of federal versus states rights. This was the core question that arose during the civil rights movement of the 1950s and 1960s. The southern states claimed they were solely responsible for their citizens' rights and welfare.

(NAT-1, POL-3, Continuity and Change over Time)

Short-Answer

Using the excerpt, answer parts a, b, and c.

a) Briefly explain the main points made in the passage.

b) Briefly explain how ONE of the decisions of John Marshall's court in the 1820s reinforced many of the concerns about the role of the federal government expressed in the passage.

c) The Supreme Court often issued controversial rulings concerning the role of the federal government in American society. Briefly explain ONE decision that caused controversy and debate from 1856–1896.

---

a) Answers will vary. The passage expresses fears of the growth of a central government at the expense of the states. The federal government encroached on the states with its taxing power, its support of business interests, and promotion of internal improvements.

(POL-1, Analyzing Historical Evidence)

b) The Marshall Court in the decisions of *Dartmouth College v. Woodward*, *McCulloch v. Maryland*, and *Gibbons v. Ogden* expanded the power of the federal government and promoted business interests and commerce. The overall effect of the rulings was to extend the power of the central government into states' rights. And this was exactly the fear expressed in the passage.

(POL-3, Analyzing Historical Evidence)

c) Answers will vary. The cases most likely to be cited are *Dred Scott v. Sandford* and *Plessy v. Ferguson*. Students might also mention The Slaughterhouse Cases, The Civil Rights Cases, *Ex parte Milligan*, *Ex parte Merryman*, or *U.S. v. Cruikshank*.

(POL-3, Continuity and Change over Time)

Lesson 16

Cornerstones of United States Foreign Policy

Throughout its existence, the United States has established consistent principles of behavior toward various parts of the world. This consistency has been shaped by geography, domestic politics, and the unique features of each overseas region. During its first 150 years, America built three distinct foreign policies in Europe, Asia, and South America.

The chart on the following page provides an overview of the cornerstones of U. S. foreign policy: isolationism in Europe, the Monroe Doctrine in South America, and the Open Door in Asia. Each of these policies changed in some ways during the second half of the twentieth century as America emerged from World War II as a superpower with a dedication to containing Soviet Communism. This chart should be used in conjunction with the charts on containment of Communism in Lesson 34, America's role in Vietnam in Lesson 35, and the chart of famous doctrines in Lesson 36. Together, these charts review both the continuity and change in America's basic foreign-policy principles.

As you study this chart, consider several questions. How did the United States define its national interest in each of the three areas of the world? What specific regional and cultural conditions shaped America's foreign-policy response in each area? Are there consistent threads of interest that run through all aspects of U.S. foreign policy?

Directions: Analyze the chart on cornerstones of American foreign policy, and then answer the following questions.

1. One consequence of the Monroe Doctrine was that
   (A) Russia decided to ally with the United States to keep other European nations out of South America
   (B) England and America clashed repeatedly over their foreign interests during the nineteenth century
   (C) the doctrine forced America into unwanted European alliances
   (D) America became increasingly aggressive in enforcing the doctrine in the Western Hemisphere

2. The United States believed its Open Door Policy was threatened when countries tried to
   (A) achieve exclusive trading rights in various regions of China
   (B) spread foreign ideologies among the Chinese people
   (C) establish multilateral trade arrangements in China
   (D) spread Christianity among the Chinese people

3. A common characteristic of the three American foreign policy cornerstones was that all of them

    (A) promoted friendships with European powers

    (B) resulted in large territorial acquisitions for the United States

    (C) were issued to protect American interests

    (D) were directed toward American interests in Asia

Cornerstones of U.S. Foreign Policy

	Isolationism	Monroe Doctrine	Open Door
Area of World	Europe	Western Hemisphere	Asia
Year Established	1793, 1796	1823	1899–1900
Author(s)	George Washington	James Monroe John Quincy Adams	John Hay
Background	Proposed when England and France went to war 1793 Both countries expected our help U.S. had an alliance with France from Revolution	U.S. feared Spanish recolonization in South America U.S. feared Russian colonies on west coast of U.S. England wanted to be a partner in issuance; U.S. said no to dual authorship	After Spanish War (1898) U.S. became interested in China Europeans were already in China and had created trading spheres of influence that could exclude U.S.
Elements	Neutrality in European affairs No entangling military or political alliances for U.S. Europe/U.S. have separate spheres of interest Commercial relations maintained	No new colonies in Western Hemisphere. Existing colonies left alone by U.S. Isolationism from Europe reinforced from earlier foreign policy pronouncements Discouraged extension of monarchies into Americas	All nations share equal trading rights in China All countries must guarantee China's territorial integrity
Comments	Washington's Farewell Address in 1796 reinforced ideas Resulted in war in 1812, 1917 Established a policy that lasted until 1949 when U.S. joined NATO Cited as reason to oppose League of Nations in 1919	England enforced doctrine for 70 years Roosevelt Corollary (1904) strengthened it U.S. became policeman of Caribbean "Big Stick" to keep down "chronic wrongdoing" Later became "Dollar Diplomacy" to control of the Caribbean region U.S. aggressiveness alienated many South American countries	U.S. became protector of China, but mainly sought trade access Boxer Rebellion (1900) frightened U.S. because China's territory might be divided by European powers Japan became greatest threat to Open Door When U.S. challenged Japan's violation of Open Door, Japan attacked Pearl Harbor

Directions: Using the cartoon below and your knowledge of American history, answer the following questions.

MONROE DOCTRINE

CLAIMS

U.S.

REPUBLIC OF SANTO DOMINGO

EUROPE

Dalrymple.

HANDS OFF!

" This in reality entails no new obligation upon us, for the Monroe Doctrine means precisely such a guarantee on our part."—*President Roosevelt.*

Puck Magazine, 1906

Multiple-Choice

1. The attitude expressed in the cartoon was most directly caused by the

   (A) closing of the frontier in the late nineteenth century

   (B) imperialist spirit in the late nineteenth century

   (C) economic turmoil in the late nineteenth century

   (D) debate over free silver in the late nineteenth century

America's Imperialism in the 1890s reflected both domestic and foreign pressures to look outward. Officials at home hoped to solve the domestic and social problems that arose during the Depression of 1893 by expanded overseas. Many Americans also realized that the "race of empire" was a world-wide competition and that the United States must compete with other nations for possessions around the globe.

(WOR-2, Causation)

2. The sentiment expressed in the cartoon most directly contributed to which of the following?

   (A) United States activism in the South American/Caribbean regions

   (B) United States acceptance of international cooperation in the South American/Caribbean region

   (C) United States involvement in European affairs rather than the South American/Caribbean region

   (D) United States withdrawal of aid to the South American/Caribbean region

> The cartoon reflected America's expanding interest in the Caribbean and its willingness to use force if necessary to protect the Panama Canal, and establish American hegemony in the Caribbean and South America.
>
> *(WOR-2, Causation)*

Short-Answer

Using the cartoon, answer parts a, b, and c.

a) Explain how ONE of the following individuals or groups in the early twentieth century would respond to the sentiment expressed in the cartoon:

   • An American President from 1898–1920

   • A European Head of State from 1898–1920

   • The Native populations of South and Central America from 1898–1920

b) Briefly explain how ONE of the remaining individuals or groups not selected would counter the sentiment you selected in <u>part a</u>.

c) Briefly explain how ONE development in the years 1930–1965 challenged the point of view expressed in the cartoon.

> **a)** Answers will vary. *(WOR-2, Analyzing Historical Evidence)*
>
> **b)** Answers will vary. *(WOR-2, Analyzing Historical Evidence)*
>
> **c)** Answers will vary. Students might explain that in the years 1930-1965, the United States tried to reverse the Big Stick, aggressive policies of the early twentieth century and embarked on The Good Neighbor Policy in the 1930s and the Alliance for Progress in the 1960s. Both eras emphasized cooperation and some multi-lateral solutions to the hemisphere's problems.
>
> *(WOR-2, Analyzing Historical Evidence)*

Lesson 17

Expansion of the United States, 1783–1853

One of the dominant forces of American history during the first half of the nineteenth century was the nation's relentless march westward. Nearly every president from George Washington to Franklin Pierce promoted and encouraged geographic expansion. The United States sought to expand its borders through purchase and treaties, but when countries would not relinquish territory peacefully, armed force was often deployed.

Although these acquisitions were intended to strengthen and unite the nation, the new territories eventually disrupted the political process and divided the nation. By the 1840s and 1850s, "Manifest Destiny," with its call for an empire from the Atlantic to the Pacific Oceans, became intertwined with the expansion of slavery, and this issue tore the country apart and brought on the Civil War.

As you examine the chart and map of U.S. expansion on the next two pages, think about the factors that propelled American expansion. Try to list them in order of importance and defend the hierarchy you have established. Also, consider why the United States, a country that believed in self-determination, imposed its will on areas where other governments and cultures were already established?

Directions: Analyze the chart and the map on American expansion, and then answer the following questions.

1. Which pair of acquisitions completed America's Manifest Destiny?

   (A) Louisiana Purchase and Florida Purchase

   (B) Mexican Cession and Oregon Treaty

   (C) Treaty of Paris and Oregon Treaty

   (D) Florida Purchase Treaty and Mexican Cession

2. A common characteristic of the Treaty of 1783 and the Louisiana Purchase Treaty was that both

   (A) resulted in land losses for Great Britain

   (B) cost the United States no money

   (C) led to war with France

   (D) helped secure control of the Mississippi River

3. In terms of cost per square mile, which of the following acquisitions was America's poorest land deal?

   (A) Louisiana Purchase Treaty

   (B) Florida Purchase Treaty

   (C) Gadsden Purchase Treaty

   (D) Oregon Treaty

Enhancing Understanding

54/40 OR FIGHT — a popular slogan of the Democrats and expansionists in the dispute with Great Britain over the Oregon Country in the mid-1840s. It called for the United States to threaten war unless Britain agreed to the southern boundary of Alaska as part of the Oregon Territory. The rhetoric gave way to the United States negotiating and agreeing to the current 49 degree boundary.

U.S. Expansion

Land Area	Date	Means of Acquisition	Cost	Significance
Original thirteen states and area east of Mississippi River	1783	Treaty of Paris with England to conclude the American Revolution	$0	U.S. gained trans-Appalachian empire Gateway to land beyond Mississippi River Led to Northwest Ordinance
Louisiana Territory	1803	Treaty with Napoleon in France	$15 million	Doubled the size of the U.S. Gave United States control of Mississippi River (New Orleans) Eliminated Napoleon as threat to American security Led to conflicts over status of slavery in new territories
Florida	1819	Adams-Onís Treaty with Spain (Transcontinental Treaty)	$5 million	Set Sabine River as southern boundary of U.S. Established boundary between New Spain and Louisiana Territory Spain recognized U.S. claims to Oregon U.S. surrendered its claims to Texas
Oregon	1846	Treaty with England	$0	Prevented war with England by splitting Oregon Territory at 49th parallel Gave U.S. clear claim to land on the Pacific Coast U.S. now stretched from ocean to ocean
Mexican Cession	1848	Treaty of Guadalupe Hidalgo settled Mexican-American War	$15 million	U.S. acquired California and large portions of southwest North America Completed Manifest Destiny Led to conflict over status of slavery in territory won from Mexico
Gadsden Purchase	1853	Treaty with Mexican government	$10 million	Bought with the hope of building a transcontinental railroad across the southern U.S. Instead, transcontinental railroad went through middle of the nation in 1860s

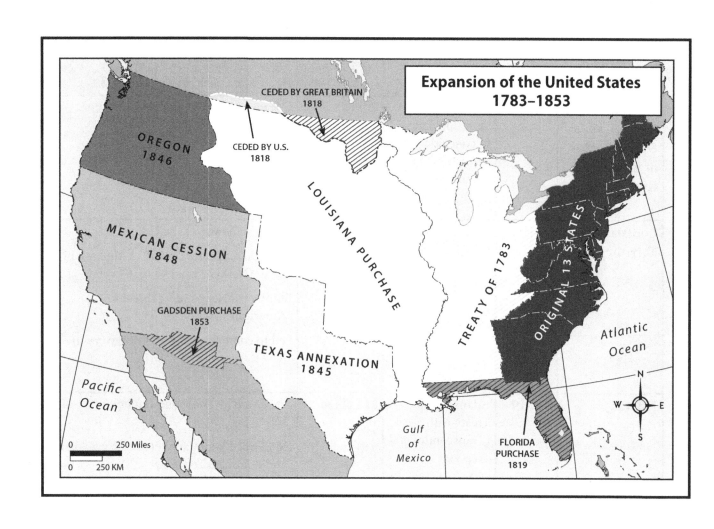

**Expansion of the United States
1783–1853**

CEDED BY GREAT BRITAIN
1818

CEDED BY U.S.
1818

OREGON
1846

LOUISIANA PURCHASE

MEXICAN CESSION
1848

TREATY OF 1783

ORIGINAL 13 STATES

GADSDEN PURCHASE
1853

Atlantic
Ocean

TEXAS ANNEXATION
1845

N
W   E
S

Pacific
Ocean

0   250 Miles
0   250 KM

Gulf
of
Mexico

FLORIDA
PURCHASE
1819

Directions: Using the excerpt below and your knowledge of American history, answer the following questions.

> "It is time now for opposition to the annexation of Texas to end. It is time for the common duty of patriotism to the country to take over. …The sweep of our eagle's wing already includes its fair and fertile land.
>
> If we needed a reason for taking Texas into the Union, it surely is to be found in the manner in which other nations have interfered in the matter. Their object is to oppose our policy and hold back our power, to limit our greatness, and to check the fulfillment of our manifest destiny to spread over the continent…
>
> The independence of Texas was complete and absolute. And these people will have a right to independence—to self government, to possession of homes conquered from the wilderness by their own labors and dangers, sufferings, and sacrifices…"

—John L. O'Sullivan, "Annexation,"
<u>Democratic Review</u>, July–August 1845

Multiple-Choice

1. The ideas expressed in the passage reflect earlier debate over how to

(A) preserve United States neutrality in European wars

(B) avoid the waning of patriotism during the War of 1812

(C) protect the Western Hemisphere from foreign countries

(D) justify the acquisition of Louisiana and Florida

The passage suggested that other nations were trying to influence events in Texas. The idea of European meddling in the affairs of the Western Hemisphere had been a concern going back to 1823 and the issuance of the Monroe Doctrine.

(NAT-1, Continuity and Change over Time)

---

2. The ideas expressed in the excerpt most closely show the influence of which of the following beliefs?

(A) that America had purchased the territory in question

(B) that America had a Constitutional right to expand

(C) that America was better suited than Europe to rule others

(D) that America had a divine right to expand

The passage, written in the mid-1840s, reflected the spirit of Manifest Destiny. In fact, O'Sullivan coined the phrase. A major component of this expansionistic concept was that God approved of American expansion and its acquisition of Texas.

(WOR-2, Causation)

Short-Answer

Using the excerpt, answer parts a, b, and c.

a)   Briefly summarize the main points of the passage.

b)   Briefly explain how ONE of the following resulted from the Mexican-American War and how it helped divide the nation in the 1850s:

- The Wilmot Proviso
- The Compromise of 1850
- The rise of "Slave Power"

c)   Briefly explain how the sentiments expressed in the passage are similar to the point of view adopted by the United States in world affairs from 1890–1910.

---

a)   Answers will vary. Students might explain that the author was calling for the annexation of Texas. Based on America's national security needs and the Monroe Doctrine, O'Sullivan suggested that America should not allow European countries to restrict our expansion. He also noted that Texas was an independent nation that sought union with the United States.

(WOR-1, Analyzing Historical Evidence)

b)   Answers will vary. The Wilmot Proviso was added to a money bill during the early stages of the Mexican American war. It became a divisive rallying point for opponents of the expansion of slavery in the 1850s. The Compromise of 1850 was necessary when the Utah and New Mexico territories were organized. These lands were part of the Mexican Cession and raised sectional debate about the expansion of slavery. The "Slave Power" was an ephemeral construct embraced by many Northerners after the Mexican War. The conflict seemed to embolden the South as they pushed to undermine the Missouri Compromise with the Kansas-Nebraska Act, which gave further credence to the "Slave Power" existence and reach.

(NAT-1, Causation)

c)   Answers will vary. The idea that the United States had a right to expand its territory was expressed in the late nineteenth century and early twentieth century. The nation also put military might behind the Monroe Doctrine and expanded its meaning beyond prohibiting colonization to restricting almost all European political and economic action in Latin America.

(WOR-2, Continuity and Change over Time, Contextualization)

Lesson 18

Wars in United States History

Although the United States has professed its dedication to peace, much of its history has been shaped by armed conflicts with other countries. Most of the nineteenth-century clashes resulted from America's attempt to establish and enhance its place in the world. On the other hand, as it matured in the twentieth century, the United States fought principally to maintain its position in the world community and to defend its many overseas interests.

The charts on the following two pages present the eight wars in which the United States was involved in the 163 years between 1812 and 1975. The chart should be studied in conjunction with the materials on "Freedom of the Seas" in Lesson 13, "Expansion of the United States" in Lesson 17, and "Major Treaties in United States History" in Lesson 23. As you study the two charts of warfare, compare the conflicts of the nineteenth century with those of the twentieth century. What similarities do you see in them? What differences do you notice? How did America's opponents change in the two centuries? How did the causes of the conflicts change? Would you have difficulty defending the proposition that Americans are a peaceful people?

Directions: Analyze the charts on the wars in American history, and then answer the following questions.

1. Both the Mexican War and Spanish-American War resulted in

   (A) little territory lost or gained by the belligerents

   (B) completion of America's drive for Manifest Destiny

   (C) stopping European aggression in the Caribbean and South America

   (D) the United States gaining significant territorial acquisitions

2. In terms of objective and outcome, the war that most resembled the Korean War was

   (A) Vietnam

   (B) World War II

   (C) the Spanish-American War

   (D) World War I

3. The War of 1812, the Spanish-American War, and World War I all involved

   (A) disputes over land claims in the Western Hemisphere

   (B) toppling foreign leaders who threatened United States security

   (C) maritime incidents that led to war

   (D) border incidents that started the conflicts

Enhancing Understanding

WAR HAWKS — a group of Congressmen from the West and South who pushed for war against England in 1812. Henry Clay (Kentucky), John C. Calhoun (South Carolina), and Felix Grundy (Tennessee) pressured President Madison to enact a more aggressive response to the British violation of American neutral rights on the seas.

	War of 1812	Mexican War	Civil War	Spanish-American War
Dates	1812–1814	1846–1848	1861–1865	1898
President(s)	James Madison	James K. Polk	Abraham Lincoln	William McKinley
Causes	Impressment Freedom of the seas threatened U.S. hoped to gain Canada from England War Hawks' pressure	Manifest Destiny Texas boundary dispute South's desire for new slave territory	Slavery States' rights Eleven southern states withdrew from Union to start their own country	Oppression of Cubans by Spain sparks revolt U.S. business interests threatened in Cuba by the fighting between the rebels and Spanish Battleship Maine blown up Yellow press strengthened anti-Spanish sentiment Pressures of new Manifest Destiny
Important Military Events	England burned Washington Battle of Plattsburgh Battle of the Thames Siege of Baltimore New Orleans	Buena Vista Siege of Veracruz Mexico City	Antietam Fredericksburg Chancellorsville Gettysburg Vicksburg Sherman's march to sea	Manila Bay San Juan Hill
Treaty	Ghent	Guadalupe Hidalgo	Appomattox	Paris
Terms	No resolution of original disputes No territory gained for either side	U.S. got Mexican Cession Agreement on Texas border	South rejoined the Union, but without slavery	Cuba freed from Spain U.S. got Guam, Puerto Rico, Philippines
Importance	War promoted American nationalism and patriotism Crushed Indian resistance in South and West Federalist Party died Industrialization began in New England Era of Good Feelings began	Fulfilled Manifest Destiny Re-opened debate over expansion of slavery (Wilmot Proviso) Led to Compromise of 1850	Union saved Ended slavery in the U. S. Bloodiest war in American history Difficult and divisive Era of Reconstruction left bitter feelings on both sides for decades	U.S. acquires foreign territory and becomes world power U.S. enforced Monroe Doctrine with aggressiveness

	World War I	World War II	Korean War	Vietnam
Dates	1917–1918	1941–1945	1950–1953	1950–1975
President(s)	Woodrow Wilson	Franklin D. Roosevelt Harry Truman	Harry Truman Dwight Eisenhower	Harry Truman to Gerald Ford
Causes	German submarine attacks Sinking of the *Lusitania* Zimmerman Note Trade, cultural ties with Britain Make "world safe for democracy"	Japan closed Open Door in China Japanese expansion in Asia and Pacific Pearl Harbor attacked Germany declared war on U.S.	Communist North Korea attacked South Korea and the United States sent troops to contain communism	Failure to hold Geneva Accords' elections in 1956 caused communist insurgency in South Vietnam and attacks by North Vietnamese forces
Important Military Events	Belleau Wood Chateau Thierry Second Battle of the Marne Meuse-Argonne	Guadalcanal Midway Leyte Gulf El Alamein Stalingrad Normandy Invasion Battle of the Bulge	Pusan siege Inchon landing Chinese communist intervention	Gulf of Tonkin Pleiku Tet Attacks Invasion of Cambodia
Treaty	Versailles	Accords with the Axis powers	Panmunjom Accords	Paris Accords
Terms	Germany surrendered, punished for war League of Nations created European boundaries redrawn to create new nations	Unconditional surrender Germany, Italy and Japan gave up Fascist philosophies and methods Japan and Germany occupied by Allied forces	South Korea remained free of Communism Communism remained in the North	Cease fire Communist troops remained in South Americans withdrew South Vietnam temporarily remained free of Communism
Importance	Four empires destroyed Communists took over in Russia U.S. rejected membership in League of Nations Harsh treatment of Germany leads to rise of Hitler	Atomic age began at Hiroshima USSR/U.S. began Cold War United Nations founded U.S. became international superpower	First test of military containment First limited war Hardened relations between the U.S. and Communist China	Six U.S. presidents tried to contain Communism War divided nation, left legacy of distrust of government and foreign intervention In 1975 North conquered South and Communism triumphed

Directions: Using the excerpt below and your knowledge of American history, answer the following questions.

> "...In my generation, this was not the first occasion when the strong had attacked the weak. I recalled some early instances: [Japan in] Manchuria, [Italy in] Ethiopia, [Germany in] Austria. I remembered how each time that the democracies failed to act it had encouraged the aggressors to keep going ahead.
>
> Communism was acting in Korea just as Hitler, Mussolini, and the Japanese had acted ten, fifteen, and twenty years earlier. I felt certain that if South Korea was allowed to fall, Communist leaders would be emboldened to override nations closer to our shores. If the Communists were permitted to force their way into the Republic of Korea without opposition from the free world, no small nation would have the courage to resist threats and aggression. ...If this was allowed to go unchallenged it would mean a third world war, just as similar incidents had brought on the second world war..."

—*Memoirs of Harry S. Truman: 1946–52,*
Years of Trial and Hope, 1956

Multiple-Choice

1. Which of the following individuals would be most likely to support the perspective of the excerpt?

(A) an opponent of foreign aid

(B) a proponent of massive retaliation

(C) an opponent of the United Nations

(D) a proponent of collective security

> The supporters of collective security believed that stopping aggression in one country before it grew too powerful would, in the long run, be in America's national interest. Building on the pre-World War lessons against appeasing aggressor nations, and the ideals of Woodrow Wilson, they called for the United States to help other nations maintain their independence and freedom.
>
> *(WOR-2, Analyzing Historical Evidence)*

2. The sentiment expressed in the passage led the United States in the 1950s and 1960s to

(A) acquire overseas areas that provided vital natural resources

(B) withdraw military assistance from non-democratic countries

(C) send military aid and forces overseas

(D) exploit political unrest within the Soviet bloc countries

> The United States was very active in Europe and Asia in resisting Communism by sending military aid and forces to Korea and Vietnam. In Europe, the U.S. strengthened the resistance to Communism through the North Atlantic Treaty Organization.
>
> *(WOR-2, Causation)*

Short-Answer

Using the excerpt, answer parts a, b, and c.

a) Briefly explain how ONE of the following actions was most effective in implementing George Kennan's ideas of containment:

- The Truman Doctrine
- The Marshall Plan
- The North Atlantic Treaty Organization

b) Briefly explain ONE development in the period 1945–1950 that is not included in the passage, and explain how it supported President Truman's point of view.

c) Briefly explain ONE criticism of United States policy toward the Soviet Union from 1945–1950.

---

a) Answers will vary. The Truman Doctrine was the first implementation of Kennan's ideas in 1947. It called for economic assistance to Greece and Turkey to block communist (U.S.S.R.) expansion into the Balkans. The Marshall Plan expanded the Truman Doctrine to most of Western Europe to help countries resist Communism. NATO was a military alliance formed in 1949 to protect Western Europe from Soviet military attack. All these actions were designed to contain the spread of Communism from 1947-1954.

(WOR-2, Analyzing Historical Evidence)

b) Answers will vary. The Soviet Union took a series of actions from 1945-1950 that gave the United States concern and triggered the containment of Communism. Students might mention:

(1) Soviet support of Greek rebels;

(2) U.S.S.R. refusal to evacuate northern Iran;

(3) a communist coup in Czechoslovakia;

(4) the erection of an "Iron Curtain" in Eastern Europe;

(5) Soviet support for Mao Tse Tung in the Chinese Civil War.

(WOR-2, Analyzing Historical Evidence)

c) Critics of containment such as Henry Wallace called for a more conciliatory policy toward the U.S.S.R. They reminded that the Soviets were a wartime ally that had fought heroically against the Nazis, suffered enormous losses in the war, did not want to conquer the world, sought only to protect their borders, and were reacting to aggressive attempts by the U.S.A. to spread Capitalism and democracy in Eastern Europe.

(WOR-2, Analyzing Historical Evidence)

Lesson 19

Amendments to the Constitution

The amendments to the Constitution are an important but sometimes overlooked aspect of the United States history survey course. Usually students examine the first ten amendments in conjunction with the struggle over the ratification of the Constitution between 1787 and 1788. The opponents of the Constitution (anti-Federalists) complained that the document lacked a Bill of Rights and demanded this omission be corrected in order for ratification to proceed. Amendments also figured prominently in events during Reconstruction (1865–1877) and the early 1920s.

The chart on the next page is a quick summary of the twenty-seven amendments to the Constitution. As you study them, consider several questions. First, how did the first ten amendments reflect America's anxieties about government that developed during the colonial and revolutionary periods? Secondly, why were the Thirteenth, Fourteenth, and Fifteenth Amendments the most revolutionary of all the changes to the Constitution? Finally, how did the Eighteenth and Nineteenth Amendments represent both an extension and a termination of progressive reforms?

Directions: Analyze the chart on amendments to the Constitution, and then answer the following questions.

1. The first ten amendments to the Constitution were intended to
   (A) protect rights that were perceived as threatened during the colonial period
   (B) reestablish a republican form of government in the United States
   (C) strengthen the national government's ability to protect law and order
   (D) restore the national government's control over the economy

2. As a result of the Fifteenth, Nineteenth, and Twenty-sixth Amendments, the United States government
   (A) limited suffrage to white, native-born citizens
   (B) strengthened its commitment to the ideals of the Declaration of Independence
   (C) tried to increase suffrage for literate citizens
   (D) drew closer to the original intent of the Constitution regarding suffrage

3. During the 1950s and 1960s, which of the following amendments provided the basis for court action to expand and protect civil rights for African-Americans?
   (A) Thirteenth Amendment
   (B) Twenty-fourth Amendment
   (C) Eighteenth Amendment
   (D) Fourteenth Amendment

Enhancing Understanding

DUE PROCESS — the legal concept included in the 5th and 14th Amendments that require governments to follow the exact course of a law. It prohibits the governments from denying individuals their life, liberty, and property unless proper legal procedures are clear and followed to the precise letter of the law.

Amendments to the Constitution	
1	Prohibits federal government from restricting religion, speech, assembly, petition, press
2	Gives citizens right to bear arms
3	Prohibits federal government from housing troops in private homes during peacetime
4	Prohibits federal government from making unreasonable searches and seizures
5	Prohibits double jeopardy, self-incrimination, seizing property without due process, and just compensation
6	Citizens have right to speedy and public trial, be informed of charges against them, impartial jury, legal counsel
7	Citizens have right to a jury trial
8	Prohibits excessive bail or fines and cruel or unusual punishment
9	Rights not enumerated in Constitution remain in people's hands
10	Powers not delegated to federal government are reserved to the state or people
11	Federal courts have no authority in suits by citizens against another state or foreign states
12	Provides for separate electoral voting for president and vice president
13	Abolished slavery in the United States
14	Blacks given citizenship; all citizens guaranteed due process of law and equal protection of the law; federal government would protect rights if states failed to do so
15	Black men given the right to vote
16	Federal government allowed to tax incomes
17	Direct popular election of United States senators
18	Prohibited the manufacture, sale, and transportation of alcoholic beverages
19	Women given the right to vote
20	Congress begins new term on January 3; president and vice president begin terms on January 20 of year following their election
21	Repealed Eighteenth Amendment
22	Limited the president to two terms or ten years in office
23	District of Columbia given three electoral votes in presidential elections
24	Abolished poll taxes in the voting process
25	When president dies or is disabled, vice president becomes president and new vice president is appointed; established procedures in case of presidential disability
26	All citizens eighteen years of age and older given right to vote
27	Congress prohibited from changing its pay for the current congressional term

Directions: Using the excerpt below and your knowledge of American history, answer the following questions.

> "All persons born or naturalized in the United States, and subject to the jurisdiction thereof, are citizens of the United States and the State wherein they reside. No State shall make or enforce any law which shall abridge the privileges or immunities of citizens of the United States; nor shall any State deprive any person of life, liberty, or property, without due process of law, nor deny any person within its jurisdiction the equal protection of the laws."

—The Fourteenth Amendment, Section 1, 1868

Multiple-Choice

1. The principles expressed in the Fourteenth Amendment led most directly to which of the following continuities in the twentieth century?

  (A) recognition of group identities and rights in society

  (B) recognition of the superiority of one group over another

  (C) recognition that only native born groups had equal legal protection

  (D) recognition that group identities should be discounted in all cases

2. The ideas expressed in the Amendment most clearly reflect the influence of which of the following?

  (A) earlier judicial decisions that restricted suffrage

  (B) earlier judicial decisions that stated that only white people had legal rights

  (C) earlier judicial decisions that restricted self incrimination

  (D) earlier judicial decisions that stated that citizenship alone conferred suffrage

---

The Fourteenth Amendment became the foundation of much of the civil rights legislation of the 1960s and 1970s. The Court interpreted "due process and equal protection" to justify expanding social justices for many groups including women and African Americans.

(NAT-2, POL-1, Continuity and Change over Time)

The Fourteenth Amendment was a direct response to the Dred Scott decision of 1857. This infamous ruling denied citizenship to all African Americans, both free and enslaved. The amendment clearly defined citizenship and made the federal government ultimately responsible of protecting people's rights within the various states.

(POL-1, Causation)

Short-Answer

Using the excerpt, answer parts a and b.

a) Select TWO amendments to the United States Constitution and explain how collectively they helped form and strengthen an American identity.

b) Briefly explain why the amendments selected are a better choice than ONE of the other options available in the Constitution.

---

a) Answers will vary depending on the amendments selected.

b) Answers will vary depending on the amendments selected.

Lesson 20

Utopian Societies in the 1830s and 1840s

In the 1830s and 1840s, a number of experimental communities arose in the United States. Historians have often labeled these societies "utopian" because of their goals and practices, and their hopes to create perfect social, political, and economic relationships among their members. Some groups drew their inspiration from the secular philosophies of Robert Owen and Charles Fourier or from the writings of the Transcendentalists. Other groups followed strict religious principles and beliefs. All, however, attempted to find an alternative to the competitive, socially flawed (as they viewed it) world of the 1830s and 1840s.

By the early 1840s, over eighty communal experiments existed in the United States. Fueled by the Panic of 1837, and a general spirit of reform, these societies tended to feature rural, communal living, egalitarian gender relations, and cooperative, rather than competitive, economic systems. Some also embraced innovative and occasionally shocking family and sexual practices. Only a few lasted into the 1850s and 1860s, as their ideals conflicted with the economic and social realities of day-to-day living.

The chart on the following two pages outlines five of the most prominent utopian societies. As you study it, think about the conditions in America in the 1830s and 1840s that gave rise to disillusionment with mainstream society. Also, consider why the groups failed to sustain their living experiments over a long period of time.

Directions: Analyze the chart on utopian societies, and then answer the following questions.

1. One common principle shared by all the societies in the 1830s and 1840s was their

   (A) support of complex marriages

   (B) rejection of capitalism and private property

   (C) support of the ideas of Charles Fourier

   (D) dedication to improving both the mind and body

2. If a person put diet and food at the center of his or her reform ideals, he or she would be most comfortable joining

   (A) New Harmony

   (B) Brook Farm

   (C) Oneida

   (D) Fruitland

Enhancing Understanding

TRANSCENDENTALISM — an influential intellectual force in ante-bellum America. Ralph Waldo Emerson spoke for the movement as he asserted the primacy of the spiritual over the material and empirical. The movement called for people to rise above the limits of reason, and to recognize individualism and the power of nature.

---

3. The most common reason for the decline of these societies was their

   (A) inability to overcome internal conflicts and dissension

   (B) refusal to set up any type of economic planning

   (C) unpatriotic behavior as America expanded westward

   (D) unorthodox sexual ideas and practices

Five Prominent Utopian Societies

	Founders	Location/Background	Principles/Practices	Reasons for Decline
New Harmony **1825-1828**	Robert Owen	Harmonie, Indiana Former site of George Rapp's Harmonie Society.	Hoped to create "new moral world" Organized "phalanxes" Employed industrial Socialism Advocated communal living/ child rearing Defended women's rights	Intense infighting Insolvency No clear lines of authority Area was prone to flooding.
Brook Farm **1841-1847**	George Ripley Sophia Ripley	Concord, Massachusetts Attracted literary figures: Nathaniel Hawthorne, Margaret Fuller, Bronson Alcott Hawthorne wrote about it in *The Blithedale Romance* (1852)	Based on Transcendentalism Daily life consisted of manual labor combined with intellectual seminars Advocated "high thinking /plain living" In 1845 embraced Fourierism: created "phalanxes" (community property and living)	Intellectuals disliked farm work Fire destroyed Phalanstery (meeting house) in 1846 Series of illnesses ravaged community in 1845-1846
Fruitland **1843-1844**	Bronson Alcott Charles Lane	Harvard, Massachusetts Lasted from June 1843–January 1844 Never more than 30 members	Followed transcendental principles—commune with nature Believed that diet is key to a good life: ate no animal substances, milk, honey, cheese, coffee, or tea Lived on fruit, bread, water Rejected Capitalism	Failed to establish agricultural self-sufficiency Alcott and Lane were poor leaders Coming winter ended the experiment

Five Prominent Utopian Societies

	Founders	Location/ Background	Principles/ Practices	Reasons for Decline
Shakers Communities 1830-1860 (peak years)	Mother Ann Lee *(later)* Joseph Meacham Lucy Wright	Originated in England	God was both Father/ Mother	Reached peak membership in 1840
		In the U.S., established in Lebanon, NY	Both men and women equal in the eyes of God	Did not grow internally through live births
		By 1840s, settlements stretched from Maine to Kentucky	Celibacy was ideal; men and women lived apart, but could eat together	Gained new members only through conversion, indenturing children, adoption
		At peak had 6,000 members	Rejected accumulation of private property	
			Ann Lee was the daughter of God	
			Women had leadership roles in communities	
			Marketed vegetables, flower seeds, and fine furniture	
Oneida 1848-1880	John H. Noyes	Central New York State	Banned private property	Noyes fled to Canada, charged with adultery
		Grew to about 300 members	Communal property holdings	1879: stopped practicing complex marriages
		An economic success produced silk products, steel traps, silverware	Practiced "mutual criticism" of members	1881: became a joint stock company
			Practiced a form of eugenics	
			Enacted "complex marriages"—multiple sexual partners	

Directions: Using the excerpt below and your knowledge of American history, answer the following questions.

> In order more effectually to promote the great purposes of human culture; to establish the external relations of life on a basis of wisdom and purity; ... we the undersigned do unite in a voluntary Association...
>
> Article I. Name and Membership
>
> Sec. 2. No member of the Association shall ever be subjected to any religious test; nor shall any authority be assumed over individual freedom of opinion by Association, nor by one member over another; ...
>
> Article III. Guarantees.
>
> Sec. 1. The Association shall provide such employment for all its members as shall be adapted to their capacities, habits, and tastes; and each member shall select and perform operations of labor...as shall be deemed suited to his own endowments...
>
> Sec. 2. The Association guarantees to all its members, their children and family dependents, house-rent, fuel, food, and clothing, and the other necessaries of life, without charge, ...
>
> Article V. Government.
>
> Sec. 2. The General Direction and Direction of Education shall be chosen annually, by the vote of the majority. ...The Direction of Finance shall be chosen annually, by the vote of the majority of the share-holders and members of the Association...

> —The Constitution of the Brook
> Farm Association, 1841

Multiple-Choice

1. Which of the following twentieth-century developments most closely paralleled the interpersonal relationships proposed in the excerpt?

   (A) 1960s experiments in communal living

   (B) 1930s government attempts to promote racial understanding

   (C) 1920s efforts to promote self-help and personal advancement

   (D) 1950s attempts to reduce gender differences

> The communes of the 1960s were an attempt by "Hippies" and the counterculture to drop out of the competitive, capitalistic society that had grown up after World War II in the United States. Like the members of the utopian societies of the 19th century, these young people rejected traditional social, political, and economic ideas and tried to create living arrangements that emphasized individual freedom and cooperation rather than aggressive competition with each other.
>
> *(NAT-1, Continuity and Change over Time)*

2. The ideas expressed in the passage most closely show the influence of which of the following?

   (A) beliefs in America's destiny to expand

   (B) beliefs in self-government and liberty

   (C) beliefs in limitations on religious freedom

   (D) beliefs in checks and balances to maintain liberty

> The utopian societies reflected deeply held views that society should emphasize the principles of individualism and freedom. Part of the difficulty in maintaining these various experiments was that there tended to be too much freedom in the community and too little focused direction in making a living.
>
> *(POL-1, Causation)*

Short-Answer

Using the excerpt, answer parts a, b, and c.

a) Briefly explain why ONE of the following sets of writings would have been out of place in the library at Brook Farm:

- Joseph Smith's *Book of Mormon*
- Adam Smith's *The Wealth of Nations*
- Benjamin Rush's *Thoughts Upon Female Education*

b) Briefly explain ONE element of life at Brook Farm that was different from mainstream society in the 1840s.

c) Briefly explain ONE economic development from 1815–1845 that may have promoted the formation of societies such as Brook Farm.

---

a) Answers will vary. The *Book of Mormon*, which promoted a singular religion, would fly in the face of Brook Farm's promotion of religious freedom and diversity. *The Wealth of Nations*, which promoted unbridled capitalism, would not fit the philosophy of Brook Farm's collective, cooperative economic model. *Thoughts Upon Female Education*, which called for a specific educational experience for women that was distinct from men, would run counter to Brook Farm's support of gender equality.

(CUL-1, Analyzing Historical Evidence)

b) Answers will vary. With its support of freedom of religion, gender equality, direct democracy, and a benevolent form of socialism in economics, Brook Farm represented a stark alternative to the values and institutions of mainstream society.

(CUL-1, Analyzing Historical Evidence)

c) Answers will vary. The growing Market Revolution that developed after the War of 1812 saw the growth of more manufacturing and commerce in the United States. Often these developments came at enormous social and economic costs. The Panic of 1837 made many people question the capitalist system of *laissez-faire* and rampant competition. Also widespread poverty among immigrants troubled many Americans.

(WXT-2, Causation, Analyzing Historical Evidence)

Lesson 21

Expanding Democracy—
The Abolitionist Movement

The period from 1830 to 1860 was a time of social and political reform in the United States. Reformers such as Dorothea Dix, Horace Mann, and Elizabeth Cady Stanton attempted to change the way the country treated the mentally ill, educated its children, and viewed women. All these efforts, however, were dwarfed by the attempt to end slavery. Prodded by the British anti-slavery movement and the Second Great Awakening, Americans began establishing abolitionist societies during the early 1830s. The American abolitionist movement was united for a brief period of time, but, by the early 1840s, fissures had appeared in its leadership and tactics.

The chart on the next page outlines the three distinct strands of the abolitionist crusade. As you look at the chart, consider how the abolitionists found common areas of agreement with one another, yet disagreed over the means to achieve their goal of ending slavery in America.

Directions: Analyze the chart on abolitionist movements in America, and then answer the following questions.

1. Many abolitionists challenged the goals of the American Colonization Society because the organization

(A) had the support of most freed blacks and reduced their loyalty to other abolitionist groups

(B) was deeply religious, while most abolitionists were nonbelievers

(C) attempted to eliminate the free black population rather than end slavery itself

(D) called for penal and temperance reform, which detracted from abolitionism

OBJECTIVES

Review the introductory materials and the chart "Strands of the Abolitionist Crusade" (pages 86–87 of the Student Edition). Have your students discuss why the colonization movement had support in the South but was an anathema to the northern abolitionists.

After the class discussion on the colonization movement and reading Lydia Maria Child's "Colonization Society and Anti-Slavery Society," which follows, students will be able to:

1. explain the goals and methods of the abolitionists in the mid 1830s;

2. compare the ideas of the American Colonization Society to the anti-slavery ideas of William Lloyd Garrison and his supporters;

3. summarize the assumptions and beliefs of the abolitionists about race and the origins of slavery in America;

4. evaluate the overall impact of the abolitionists on America from 1830–1850.

ADDITIONAL COMPONENTS

- **Core Chart Worksheet**: "Lesson 21 – Expanding Democracy"

- **Primary Source Handout:** "Colonization Society" (p. 112/web)

- **Document Source Worksheets:** "Worksheet for Document Source Analysis" (p. 246)

2. William Lloyd Garrison clashed with the American and Foreign Anti-Slavery Society because he

(A) supported forming a political party to end slavery

(B) was very religious and sought close ties to the churches to end slavery

(C) was too timid in his methods to end slavery

(D) supported full participation for women in the crusade against slavery

3. An abolitionist in the 1840s who sought to end slavery by political means and supported paying slaveholders for their lost property would join the

(A) American Colonization Society

(B) American and Foreign Anti-Slavery Society

(C) American Antislavery Society

(D) American Bible and Temperance Society

DISCUSSION QUESTIONS

Hand out or display the document, "Colonization Society and Anti-Slavery Society," (shown on page 112) and ask the following:

1. What was the objective of the abolitionists according to Child?

2. How did the abolitionists propose to reach this objective?

3. Why did the abolitionists oppose the colonization movement?

4. According to Child, what was the origin of racial prejudice in America? Do you agree with this interpretation?

5. What attitudes or assumptions about African Americans did the abolitionists profess to have?

6. Were the abolitionists a positive or negative force in America during the antebellum period?

Answers available on the companion website.

Strands of the Abolitionist Crusade

	American Colonization Society	American Anti-Slavery Society	American/Foreign Antislavery Society
Year Started	1817	1833	1840
Leader(s)	Robert Finley Henry Clay James Madison	William Lloyd Garrison	Theodore Weld Lewis and Arthur Tappan
Goals	Voluntary emancipation and colonization Colonize free blacks in Africa Establish a colony in Africa for freed people	Immediate emancipation of all slaves in America No compensation to the slave holders	Gradual emancipation of all slaves in America Compensation to the owners for the loss of their slaves
Means	Lobbied Congress for support Gained $100,000 from Congress to establish Liberia Published appeals for freed people to colonize in Africa	Moral persuasion Paid agents to lecture on the evils of slavery Publication of an antislavery paper, *The Liberator* Opposed political action	Moral persuasion Paid agents and published a newspaper to rally support Worked with churches Political action—close to the Liberty Party
Women's Role	Not an issue	Full, equal participation Women should address both men and women at meetings	Limited role, mostly behind the scenes Feared male backlash if women were too prominent in meetings
Summary/ Comments	Established Liberia in 1823 Congress mandated that all captured slave ships return Africans to Liberia About 15,000 free black people colonized in Liberia 1817–1870 Most free blacks opposed organization and its efforts	Garrison's radicalism made him controversial and divisive Challenged the churches to attack slavery from pulpit Condemned Constitution because it condoned slavery Challenged the Union itself Involved in many reforms besides slavery	Moderate approach; viewed Garrison as too radical, split with him in 1840 Attracted older members Tried to use Liberty and Free Soil Parties to gain members Declined in late 1840s and disbanded in 1855

Colonization Society and Anti-Slavery Society

The Colonization Society has fallen into the habit of glossing over the enormities of the slave system ... they have pledged themselves not to speak, write, or do anything to offend the Southerners, and as there is no possible way of making the truth pleasant to those who do not love it, the Society must perforce keep the truth out of sight... .

But so long as the South insists that slavery is unavoidable, and say they will not tolerate any schemes tending to its abolition—and so long as the North take [sic] the necessity of slavery for an unalterable truth, and put [sic] down any discussions, however mild and candid, which tend to show that it may be done away with safely—so long as we thus strengthen each other's hand in evil, what remote hope is there of emancipation? ... To enlighten public opinion is the best way that has been discovered for the removal of national evils, and slavery is certainly a national evil... .

My ... greatest objection to the Colonization Society is, that its members write and speak, both in public and private, as if the prejudice against skins darker colored than their own, was a fixed and unalterable law of our nature, which cannot possibly be changed ... we are constantly told ... that people of color ... never can have all the rights and privileges of citizens ... because the prejudice is so great...

This is shaking hands with iniquity, and covering sin with a silver veil. Our prejudice against the blacks is founded in sheer pride ... We made slavery, and slavery makes the prejudice. No Christian, who questions his own conscience, can justify himself in indulging the feeling. The removal of this prejudice is not a matter of opinion—it is a matter of duty... .

[We] lay it down as a maxim that immediate emancipation is the only just course, and the only safe policy ... no other course can be pursued which does not ... involve a constant violation of the laws of God... .

The Colonization Society are [sic] always reminding us that the master has rights as well as the slave; The Anti-Slavery Society urge [sic] us to remember that the slave has rights as well as the master. I leave it for somber sense to determine which of these claims is in the greatest danger of being forgotten.

SOURCE: Lydia Maria Child, Abolitionist Activist

Directions: Using the excerpt below and your knowledge of American history, answer the following questions.

> "…The corner-stone upon which they founded the Temple of Freedom was broadly this— 'that all men are created equal; that they are endowed by their Creator with certain inalienable rights; that among these are life, LIBERTY, and the pursuit of happiness…'
>
> …those, for whose emancipation we are striving—constituting at the present time at least one-sixth of our countrymen, —are recognized by the laws, and treated by their fellow beings, as marketable commodities— as goods and chattels—as brute beasts; —are plundered daily of the fruits of their toil without redress; —really enjoy no constitutional nor legal protection from licentious and murderous outrages upon their persons; …
>
> We…maintain—That no man has a right to enslave or imbrute his brother— to hold or acknowledge him, for one moment, as a piece of merchandise…"

—William Lloyd Garrison, "Declaration of Sentiments of the American Anti-Slavery Convention," December 1833

Multiple-Choice

1. What direct action did the abolitionists take to try to correct the wrongs outlined in the excerpt?

(A) They established newspapers and made speeches against slavery.

(B) They elected anti-slavery senators to Congress.

(C) They worked to change the membership of the Supreme Court.

(D) They worked to create Jim Crow laws to protect African-American rights.

2. The sentiment expressed in the passage clearly shows the influence of earlier religious beliefs that

(A) religion had little impact on changing society

(B) the Declaration of Independence and religion were connected

(C) personal and societal salvation were connected

(D) personal and societal salvation were pre-determined

> The abolitionists sought to expand freedom for all people by forming newspapers such as The Liberator and The North Star. They also created organizations such as the American Anti-Slavery society that traveled around and made speeches against slavery in the North.
>
> *(POL-2, Analyzing Historical Evidence)*

> The abolitionists drew heavily from the spiritual and intellectual messages of the Second Great Awakening, which advocated the ideal that people, should strive not only for personal salvation, but also work to achieve social justice in society at large.
>
> *(POL-2, Causation)*

Short-Answer

Using the excerpt, answer parts a, b, and c.

a) Select ONE of the individuals below and explain how he might oppose the ideas expressed by William Lloyd Garrison:

- John Calhoun
- David Walker
- Lewis Tappan

b) Defend your choice from <u>part a</u> by contrasting it with ONE of the two remaining individuals.

c) Americans sought to expand freedom and equality in the years 1830–1865 and 1950–1970. Briefly explain ONE important similarity in the reasons why this quest emerged in both of these time periods.

---

a) Answers will vary. John Calhoun opposed the idea that equality for all Americans was a God given right. His racism was deeply felt and widely shared in the South. David Walker opposed Garrison non-violent approach to abolition. He believed Blacks should take direct action to gain their freedom even to the point of rebellion. Lewis Tappan opposed Garrison's moral approach to abolition. He also opposed his position attacking the Constitution and the churches.

(POL-2, Analyzing Historical Evidence)

b) Answers will vary. *(POL-2, Analyzing Historical Evidence)*

c) Answers will vary. Students might explain that both time periods had religious developments that supported reform (The Second Great Awakening in the 1830s/1840s and Martin Luther King's church based movement in the 1950s); both eras had strong leaders (William Lloyd Garrison, Frederick Douglass, Abraham Lincoln, Martin Luther King Jr., Earl Warren, Lyndon Johnson); and both the 1840s and 1960s were a time when the reform spirit was abroad in the nation (women's movement, temperance in 1840s, protest against Vietnam, drive for gender equality, civil rights in the 1960s).

(POL-2, Comparison, Analyzing Historical Evidence)

Lesson 22

Women's Movement during the 19th Century

The nineteenth century witnessed many attempts to reform and improve America. One of the most controversial of these reforms was the women's movement. Women struggled to overcome their social, economic, and political positions of inferiority in American society. The women who led this crusade came mainly from the ranks of the abolitionists. In fact, before the Civil War, the three most significant women leaders—Elizabeth Cady Stanton, Susan B. Anthony, and Lucretia Mott—focused most of their efforts on the battle against slavery.

Women faced many hurdles in their quest for full citizenship. Legal barriers prevented women from voting or serving on juries, and economic laws and traditions, such as coverture, gave husbands complete control over their wives' economic lives. Moreover, women had to combat not only legal obstacles but psychological ones, because most women accepted their inferior place and status in American society. Women were expected to adhere to the values of the Cult of Domesticity and True Womanhood, values that equated true womanhood with submissiveness to men and devotion to family. Stanton, Mott, and others faced great difficulty in raising women's awareness of the injustice of a male-dominated society.

As you study the chart that follows, identify the issues that united women and the ones that divided them. Also, consider why women targeted suffrage as their primary goal.

Directions: Analyze the chart on the nineteenth-century women's movement, and then answer the following questions.

> ### Enhancing Understanding
>
> *MINOR V. HAPPERSETT* (1874) — a court case that found that the 15th Amendment did not include a woman's right to vote. It ruled that the states rather than the federal government determined voting status. It was a victory for the state-by-state strategy of the American Woman's Suffrage Association.

1. The women's movements of the nineteenth century were united around the belief that

   (A) black men's voting rights were more important than women's suffrage

   (B) controlling the use of alcohol was the key to gaining full equality for women

   (C) men were reliable allies in women's crusade for equality

   (D) gaining the right to vote was critical to women's advancement in America

2. A major split developed in the women's movement after the Civil War over

   (A) the use of petition and convention to achieve women's goals of equality

   (B) women working outside the home in jobs traditionally done by men

   (C) the interpretation of the Fifteenth Amendment

   (D) creating a third party only for women

3. The "Cult of Domesticity and True Womanhood" referred to

   (A) women accepting existing societal expectations for themselves

   (B) women forming groups to make homes cheerful for returning soldiers

   (C) women promoting the image of strong individuals capable of maintaining their households without any hired help

   (D) women expanding their sphere of interest and activities outside the home

Major Strands of the Nineteenth Century Women's Movement

	Seneca Falls Movement	National Woman Suffrage Association	American Woman Suffrage Association
Leaders	Elizabeth Cady Stanton Lucretia Mott	Elizabeth Cady Stanton Susan B. Anthony	Lucy Stone Julia Ward Howe
Goals	Right to vote Lessening economic oppression for women Overcoming "Cult of Domesticity and True Womanhood"	Right to vote along with black men Women should be included in 15th Amendment Wide range of reforms	Keep nation aware of women's suffrage, but accept black men as voters for time being 16th Amendment for women's suffrage
Supporters	Middle class women Some male abolitionists such as Frederick Douglass Quakers	Young, educated women Many from Seneca Falls Women in western states Only allowed women officials	More conservative women Strong in Boston area Former abolitionists: Frederick Douglass Welcomed male members
Methods	Published a Declaration of Sentiments Held an annual convention until the beginning of the Civil War	Lobbied to be included in 15th Amendment Later demanded a separate amendment to give women the right to vote	State-by-state approach Worked exclusively for women's suffrage Avoided reforms not directly related to right to vote
Comments	Meetings grew from the snubbing of Mott and Stanton at the World Anti-Slavery Convention in London Women asked James Mott to preside because they felt it inappropriate for a woman to do so	Most radical of women's groups Issued racist rhetoric against the 15th Amendment Hurt by association with Victoria Woodhull Merged with AWSA in 1890, becoming the National American Woman Suffrage Association (NAWSA)—Anthony and Stanton took leadership roles	More accepting of status quo Closer to the ideals of the "Cult of True Womanhood" Merged with NWSA in 1890, becoming the National American Woman Suffrage Association (NAWSA)—Anthony and Stanton took leadership roles

Directions: Using the cartoon below and your knowledge of American history, answer the following questions.

Puck Magazine, June 6, 1894

Multiple-Choice

1. The point of view expressed in the cartoon is that

    (A) women should be arrested when they try to vote

    (B) women could depend on men to help them gain the vote

    (C) women should take care of their children and stop worrying about the vote

    (D) women would face social and legal barriers in gaining the vote

    > The cartoon depicted the social forces working against women (references to women's apparel and the voting booth), and the legal barriers symbolized by the policeman and the issue of public policy (taxes). This combination represented a strong barrier to women achieving equal rights from 1840–1920.
    >
    > *(NAT-1, Analyzing Historical Evidence)*

2. Which of the following mid-nineteenth century reforms most closely resembles the cause presented in the cartoon?

    (A) the movement to establish utopian communities

    (B) the movement to complete America's Manifest Destiny

    (C) the movement to change divorce laws

    (D) the movement to establish equal schools for men and women

> The quest for women's voting rights was similar to women's drive to liberalize the divorce laws in the 1840s and 1850s. Divorce laws greatly limited women's power in society and their change empowered women just as the right to vote would eventually achieve.
>
> *(POL-2, Continuity and Change over Time)*

Short-Answer

Using the cartoon, answer parts a, b, and c.

a) Briefly explain how ONE of the following individuals would respond to the point of view expressed in the cartoon:

- Susan B. Anthony
- Frederick Douglass
- Catherine Beecher

b) Briefly explain how ONE of the other individuals in <u>part a</u> that you did not select would respond to the individual that you did select.

c) Briefly explain ONE important social or political response in the twentieth century to the conditions depicted in the cartoon.

---

a) Answers will vary. Susan B. Anthony would challenge the point of view. She was a strong advocate for women's suffrage regardless of the societal barriers. Frederick Douglass would have mixed feelings about women voting. He had strongly supported the 15th Amendment and wanted women to postpone their drive for suffrage until black men were secure in the voting booth. Catherine Beecher did not support suffrage for women. She was a proponent of the "cult of true womanhood" in the 19th century.

(POL-2, Analyzing Historical Evidence)

b) Answers will vary. *(NAT-1, Analyzing Historical Evidence)*

c) Answers will vary. Students might explain that passage of the 19th Amendment, the League of Women Voters, Title X of the Civil Rights Act of 1964, *Roe v. Wade*, *The Feminine Mystique*, and the formation of the National Organization of Women all helped to expand women's social and political rights in the twentieth century.

(NAT-1, Contextualization, Continuity and Change over Time)

Major Treaties in United States History

As the United States expanded, completed its continental consolidation, and involved itself in world affairs, conflicts with other nations arose. These diplomatic and military disputes grew more numerous and serious as America grew in size, power, and influence, and became more active in international affairs. The nation sought to resolve these clashes and disagreements through treaties and international agreements. The chart on the next two pages summarizes the major diplomatic pacts negotiated and signed by the United States from 1794 to 1954.

You should study the chart in conjunction with Lesson 13, "Freedom of the Seas and Wars with Europe;" Lesson 16, "Cornerstones of United States Foreign Policy;" Lesson 17, "Expansion of the United States, 1783–1853;" and Lesson 18, "Wars in United States History." Collectively these materials provide a picture of America's diplomatic and military relations with the rest of the world. As you review these materials, evaluate the proposition that, in the long run, America accomplished more at the negotiating table than on the battlefield.

Directions: Analyze the chart on major diplomatic pacts, and then answer the following questions.

1. A common outcome in the Adams-Onís Treaty, the Treaty of Guadalupe Hidalgo and the Treaty of Paris 1898 was that all three

   (A) ended wars with major European powers

   (B) were settled without cash payments by the United States

   (C) resulted in territorial acquisition for the United States

   (D) were rejected by the U.S. Senate

2. Both the North Atlantic Treaty Organization and the Southeast Asia Treaty Organization were designed to

   (A) stop the spread of Communism

   (B) involve the United Nations in preserving peace around the world

   (C) acquire spheres of influence in Asia for the United States

   (D) keep Communism out of South America

3. The Treaty of Versailles was a unique agreement in U.S. history because it was the only major treaty

   (A) that resulted in the acquisition of land for the United States

   (B) that respectfully recognized Germany's rights in central Europe

   (C) that was promoted and accepted by both political parties

   (D) that was rejected by the U.S. Senate

Enhancing Understanding

COLLECTIVE SECURITY — the concept embedded in the League of Nations covenant that called on nations to join together to defend the victims of aggression and to solve international problems. It was rejected by the American people in the early 1920s, but found support after World War II with the Containment policy.

Diplomatic Pacts, 1794–1954

Treaty	Nations	Provisions
Jay Treaty, 1794	United States/ England	Britain withdrew from forts in Great Lakes Arbitration of Revolutionary debts Payment for American shipping losses U.S. gained improved trading status with Britain
Treaty of Ghent, 1814	United States/ England	Ended War of 1812 No land concessions by either side No apology by British for impressment Established commission to set boundary between U.S./Canada
Adams-Onís Treaty, 1819	United States/ Spain	U.S. got Florida U.S. paid Spain $5 million Spain recognized U.S. claims to Oregon country Established boundary between New Spain and Louisiana Territory U.S. surrendered its claims to Texas
Treaty of Guadalupe Hidalgo, 1848	United States/ Mexico	Ended Mexican War Mexico recognized Texas annexation Mexico surrendered Mexican Cession U.S. paid Mexico $15 million
Treaty of Paris, 1898	United States/ Spain	Ended Spanish-American War Cuba freed from Spanish rule U.S. got Puerto Rico and Guam from Spain U.S. paid $20 million for Philippines
Treaty of Versailles, 1919	Allies/ Germany	Ended the Great War (World War I) Established the League of Nations Germany punished for starting war U.S. Senate rejected the treaty because of League of Nations and isolationist sentiment in U.S.
North Atlantic Treaty Organization, 1949	United States/ Twelve European Countries	Military alliance to contain Communism in Europe An attack on one country treated as an attack on all A mutual defense pact organized around concept of collective security First entangling alliance for the U.S.
Southeast Asia Treaty Organization, 1954	United States Great Britain France Australia New Zealand Thailand Pakistan Philippines	Mutual defense pact intended to repel common dangers in southeast Asia Committed to protecting countries under pressure from internal subversion and external attack by Communists Helped South Vietnam, Laos, and Cambodia Intended to contain Communism in Asia

Directions: Using the cartoon below and your knowledge of American history, answer the following questions.

OPERATING ROOM
SENATE COMMITTEE ON FOREIGN RELATIONS

PEACE TREATY

THE LAMB FROM THE SLAUGHTER.

The Evening Star, **Washington, D.C., September 5, 1919**

Multiple-Choice

1. Which of the following individuals would most likely support the perspective of the cartoon?

   (A) a person who completely rejected membership in the League of Nations

   (B) a person who rejected the Treaty of Versailles, but accepted membership in the League

   (C) a person who accepted membership in the League, but with some changes to its structure

   (D) a person who accepted membership in the League without question or change

> The cartoon depicted Henry Cabot Lodge, a leading reservationist, shepherding the Treaty of Versailles from the operating room where his amendments had preserved, but also altered, membership in the League of Nations.
>
> *(WOR-2, Analyzing Historical Evidence)*

2. Which of the following consequences most directly resulted from the actions shown in the cartoon?

- **(A)** The United States supported the ideas of collective security.
- **(B)** The United States retreated into traditional isolationism toward Europe.
- **(C)** The United States strengthened its aid to downtrodden people in the world.
- **(D)** The United States proclaimed its policy of containment of Communism.

> After the rejection of the treaty, the United States embarked on a period of retreat from political and military connections with Europe. While maintaining commercial relationships and joining in disarmament agreements, the United States did not join either the League of Nations or the World Court. These isolationist tendencies reached their apex in the mid 1930s with enactment of the Neutrality Acts.
>
> *(WOR-2, Causation)*

Short-Answer

Using the cartoon, answer parts a, b, and c.

a) Briefly explain how ONE of the following individuals would react to the sentiments expressed in the cartoon:

- Henry Cabot Lodge
- William Borah
- Woodrow Wilson

b) Briefly explain how ONE of the other individuals you did not select in <u>part a</u> would challenge the position of your choice.

c) Briefly explain ONE development in the period 1933–1945 that challenged the point of view of the cartoon.

> **a)** Answers will vary. Henry Cabot Lodge approved of the point of view in the cartoon. While supporting much of the Treaty of Versailles and the League of Nations, he led the group that demanded changes (reservations) to the document and the organization. As the leader of the irreconcilables, William Borah wanted the treaty slaughtered (rejected) rather than modified. Woodrow Wilson opposed the point of view of the cartoon. He wanted the treaty and League approved in the same form with which he negotiated it in Paris. He opposed all changes (reservations) proposed by Lodge.
>
> *(WOR-2, Argument Development)*
>
> **b)** Answers will vary. *(WOR-2, Argument Development)*
>
> **c)** Answers will vary. The rise of Fascism in Germany, Italy and Japan in the 1930s all called into question America's refusal to take an active role in the League of Nations and international political affairs. The Lodge reservations, which doomed the Treaty of Versailles, curtailed America's role in Europe and Asia, and set a tone that lingered into the late 1930s.
>
> *(WOR-2, Contextualization, Continuity and Change over Time)*

Lesson 24

Reconstruction of the South

When the Civil War ended in 1865, many questions arose about the political and physical rebuilding of the eleven southern states that had attempted to leave the Union in 1861. During the next three years, the country was convulsed in conflict about Reconstruction. The most contentious issue of the era was the future of the former slaves. The overriding theme of this struggle was whether President Andrew Johnson or the Radical Republicans would decide the fate of the defeated South and freed people.

The political battle became so heated that, in 1868, President Johnson was impeached. Although the radical Republicans in Congress could not convict him, they gained control of Reconstruction and attempted to revolutionize many of the social and political relationships in the United States.

Enhancing Understanding

CIVIL RIGHTS ACT OF 1875 — passed as a tribute to the late Charles Sumner who had drafted the bill, it provided for equal access to public accommodations and public transportation, and prohibited racial exclusions from jury service. Congress removed the desegregation of public schools portion of the bill, and the public accommodation section was overturned by the Supreme Court in 1883.

The chart on the following page offers a concise summary of the major issues and elements of the competing Reconstruction plans. As you study the chart, think about how the plans would appeal to the following groups: freedmen, southern planters, northern Democrats, poor southern whites, moderate northern Republicans, abolitionists, western farmers, and northern factory workers.

Directions: Analyze the chart on reconstruction plans for the American South, and then answer the following questions.

1. The congressional Reconstruction plan proposed at the end of the Civil War found little support among

    (A) former abolitionists

    (B) teachers in the Freedmen's Bureau

    (C) former slaves

    (D) states rights' supporters

2. A major difference between presidential and congressional Reconstruction was that

    (A) the presidential plan did not punish the South at all and the congressional plan did

    (B) the congressional plan expanded the powers of the central government to protect the rights of the former slaves and the presidential plan did not

    (C) the presidential plan allowed the South to rejoin the Union with slavery unchanged and the congressional plan required emancipation

    (D) the presidential plan provided for a Freedmen's Bureau and the congressional plan did not propose a similar organization

3. A major shortcoming of the congressional plan for Reconstruction was that it failed to

    (A) grant black men the right to vote

    (B) put troops in the South after the war

    (C) end slavery

    (D) give land to the former slaves

Reconstruction Plans for the American South

	Presidential	Congressional
Who was in charge?	President Abraham Lincoln President Andrew Johnson	Thaddeus Stevens Charles Sumner Other radical Republicans
Dates	April–December 1865	1866–1877
Had the South left the Union?	No; executive branch believed it needed to restore the states to their proper relationship with the Union	Yes; the southern states had left the Union, were conquered territories, and should be treated accordingly
Acts/Actions	Proclamation of Amnesty and Reconstruction 1863, 1865 Vetoed Wade Davis Bill 1864 Pardoned most ex-Confederates Thirteenth Amendment 1865	Civil Rights Act 1866 Renewed, expanded Freedmen's Bureau Fourteenth Amendment 1868 Reconstruction Acts 1867–1868 Tenure of Office Act 1867 Fifteenth Amendment 1870 Force Acts 1870–1871 Civil Rights Act 1875
Elements of Plans	South must: • renounce secession • ratify Thirteenth Amendment • 10% of voters from 1860 must swear allegiance to Union • Confederate officers, officials, wealthy must make special request for pardon	South must: • ratify Thirteenth, Fourteenth, and Fifteenth Amendments • accept black citizenship • accept black men voting Confederate officials, officers, soldiers could not vote Put 20,000 troops in the South Civil Rights Act of 1875 provided for social integration
Aid for Freedmen	None provided; up to the individual states to decide how and to what extent newly freed slaves would be helped	Created Freedmen's Bureau, providing welfare and education to former slaves Provided troops to protect black voting rights No permanent land distribution, which gave rise to sharecropping and tenant farming

Directions: Using the excerpt below and your knowledge of American history, answer the following questions.

> "...A majority of Congress desires that treason shall be made hateful, not by bloody executions, but by other adequate punishments. ...I am speaking of granting the vote to Negroes in the rebel states. Have not loyal blacks as good a right to choose rulers and make laws as rebel whites? In the second place, it is a necessity in order to protect the white people who are loyal to the Union in the seceded states...
>
> But it will be said, as it has been said, "This is Negro equality!" What is Negro equality about? It means, as understood by honest Republicans, just this much and no more: Every person, no matter what his or her race or color, every human being who has an immortal soul, has an equal right to justice, honesty and fair play. ...The same law which condemns or acquits Africans should condemn or acquit white people..."

— Thaddeus Stevens to the U.S. House
of Representatives, January 3, 1867

Multiple-Choice

1. Which of the following actions would most directly support Stevens' argument in the excerpt above?

   (A) the passage of the 14th and 15th Amendments

   (B) the creation of the Freedmen's Bureau

   (C) the change in property requirements in voting

   (D) the abolition of slavery in the United States

2. The ideas expressed in the passage most clearly reflect the influence of which of the following?

   (A) economic principles expressed in the Constitution

   (B) natural rights principles expressed in the Declaration of Independence

   (C) political principles expressed in the Articles of Confederation

   (D) moral principles expressed in the many colonial constitutions

---

The Radical Republicans, led by Thaddeus Stevens, called upon Congress to guarantee citizenship rights to African Americans and, for Black men, the right to vote. These rights were established and protected by the 14th and 15th Amendments.

(NAT-2, Causation)

The foundation of the Radical Republican program was the promises of unalienable rights to life, liberty and the pursuit of happiness made in the Declaration of Independence to all men. The passage noted that all men had a soul, and were entitled to "justice, honesty and fair play."

(NAT-1, Causation, Continuity and Change over Time)

Short-Answer

Using the excerpt, answer parts a, b, and c.

a) Briefly explain how ONE of the following attempted to punish the South by modifying group identity from 1865–1877:

- The Freedmen's Bureau
- The Fourteenth Amendment
- The Fifteenth Amendment

b) Briefly explain ONE reason why some Americans objected to this modification and punishment.

c) Briefly explain ONE political or social response from 1877–1900 that attempted to negate the sentiment expressed in the passage.

---

a) Answers will vary. The Freedmen's Bureau extended assistance to former slaves. It provided education, welfare, and briefly land to Freedmen. The Bureau performed tasks that the South opposed. The Fourteenth Amendment gave citizenship to African-Americans and made it clear that if states did not protect their citizens, the federal government had the right to step in and offer protection to blacks. The Fifteenth Amendment gave black men the right to vote. In the short run, this allowed the election of African-Americans to political offices throughout the South.

(POL-3, Contextualization)

b) Answers will vary. Students might explain states' rights, racism, lingering resentments from the Civil War, and strict constructionist views of the Constitution.

(Pol-3, Causation)

c) Answers will vary. Students might explain the rise of the Ku Klux Klan, the use of poll taxes and grandfather clauses to restrict voting, the creation of Jim Crow laws, and the court's reduction of the reach of the Fourteenth Amendment.

(Pol-3, Causation)

Judicial Betrayal—The Road to *Plessy v. Ferguson*

When the Supreme Court ruled in 1896 that "separate but equal" facilities for blacks and whites were constitutional in public transportation, the ruling was the culmination of the Court's role in gradually narrowing the interpretation of the Fourteenth Amendment. (See Lesson 19 for a summary of this amendment.) It also gave judicial approval to the Jim Crow system that separated the races in social and cultural settings during the decades following the Civil War. The trend of the Court's decisions from 1870 to 1900 was to restrict the scope of the Fourteenth Amendment, especially its "equal protection" clause for African Americans. By the time of *Plessy*, the nation was in full retreat from the Reconstruction era pledge of full equality for all citizens regardless of race.

The chart on the following page summarizes the four major cases that defined the Court's attitude toward civil rights after the Civil War. In *Plessy*, the majority ruled that "legislation is powerless to eradicate racial instincts or to abolish distinctions based upon physical differences." Can you describe the events from 1877 to 1896 that gave rise to this line of thinking?

ADDITIONAL COMPONENTS

- **Core Chart Worksheet**: "Lesson 25 – Judicial Betrayal"
- **Primary Source Handout**: "Harlan's Dissenting Opinion" (copy p. 130 or print from website)
- **Document Source Worksheets**: "Worksheet for Document Source Analysis" (p. 246)

OBJECTIVES

Review the introductory materials and the chart "Major Civil Rights Cases" on the judicial rulings that led to the *Plessy v. Ferguson* case in 1896 (pages 102–103 in the Student Edition). Have your students discuss the basic assumptions these court cases made about American society and the role of the federal government in race relations from 1873–1896.

After the class discussion on the role of the courts in race relations after the Civil War and reading John Marshall Harlan's dissent which follows, students will be able to:

1. state the basic judicial principles on which the Jim Crow system was based;

2. explain how separate but equal became the law of the land in the first half of the twentieth century;

3. compare John Marshall Harlan's thinking on civil rights to the majority views on the Supreme Court;

4. evaluate the impact of *Plessy v. Ferguson* in creating the Jim Crow system in the United States;

5. assess John Marshall Harlan's role in American judicial history.

Directions: Analyze the chart on the four major civil rights cases, and then answer the following questions.

1. From 1873 to 1896, the general trend of the Supreme Court decisions regarding civil rights was to

    (A) support the idea that all men were created equal

    (B) make no distinction between public and private discrimination

    (C) uphold black rights in all cases of discrimination

    (D) narrow the interpretation of the Fourteenth Amendment

2. Which of the following groups would likely agree with and support the Supreme Court decisions on civil rights from 1873 to 1896?

    (A) Southern blacks

    (B) radical Republicans

    (C) loose constructionists of the Constitution

    (D) strict constructionists of the Constitution

3. When the Supreme Court issued its "separate but equal" decision in *Plessy v. Ferguson*, it provided support for the

    (A) spoils system

    (B) Jim Crow system

    (C) American System

    (D) Lowell labor system

Enhancing Understanding

JOHN MARSHALL HARLAN — an associate Justice on the Supreme Court who, although from a slave holding family, dissented in the *Civil Rights Cases* (1883) and *Plessy vs. Ferguson* (1896). In *Plessy*, he intoned that the Constitution should be color blind and not promote separation of the races.

DISCUSSION QUESTIONS

Hand out or display the document, "Justice John Marshall Harlan's Dissenting Opinion in *Plessy v. Ferguson*," (shown on page 130) and ask the following:

1. What was Harlan's view of the Constitution and race relations?

2. Why does Harlan think the Constitution should be "color-blind"?

3. To what earlier court case does Harlan compare *Plessy*? Why do you think he makes this comparison?

4. What result does he think the *Plessy* decision will have on race relations in the United States?

5. Does the fact that Harlan was once a slaveholder change your opinion of his dissent? Why or why not?

Answers available on the companion website.

Major Civil Rights Cases

Case	Date	Background	Question to be Answered	Ruling
Slaughterhouse cases	1873	Louisiana created state-sanctioned monopolies in slaughterhouse business—butchers believed their 14th Amendment rights were being violated	Did 14th Amendment expand the federal government's authority to protect black citizens?	No, defense of most rights still a job for individual states 13th and 14th Amendments did not greatly expand power of U.S. government 14th Amendment did not create new set of national citizenship rights
U.S. v. Cruikshank	1876	Colfax Massacre resulted in 100 black deaths/ 3 whites killed—no one convicted	Did the 14th Amendment protect blacks from private acts of violence?	No, 14th Amendment did not give U.S. government power to suppress ordinary crimes by individuals U.S. involved only when state actions denied citizen rights
U.S. v. Singleton	1883	Black man denied entry into an opera house in New York City	Did Civil Rights Act of 1875 prohibit private acts of discrimination?	No, Civil Rights Act of 1875 was unconstitutional 14th Amendment only dealt with state discrimination; did not cover private acts of discrimination
Plessy v. Ferguson	1896	Black man tried to sit in "white" railcar to test Louisiana's Jim Crow laws	Did Jim Crow system violate 14th Amendment?	No, legislation was powerless to stop private acts of racial bias Separate facilities were not inherently unconstitutional Facilities could be separate if they were equal

Justice John Marshall Harlan's
Dissenting Opinion in *Plessy v. Ferguson*

In respect of civil rights, common to all citizens, the Constitution of the United States does not, I think, permit any public authority to know the race of those entitled to be protected in the enjoyment of such rights. … But I deny that any legislative body or judicial tribunal may have regard to the race of citizens when the civil rights of those citizens are not involved. Indeed, such legislation, as that here in question, is inconsistent not only with the equality of rights which pertains to citizenship, National and State, but with the personal liberty enjoyed by everyone within the United States.

The white race deems itself to be the dominant race in this country. And so it is, in prestige, in achievements, in education, in wealth and in power. So I doubt not, it will continue to be for all time, if it remains true to its great heritage and holds fast to the principles of constitutional liberty. But in view of the Constitution, in the eye of the law, there is in this country no superior, dominant ruling class of citizens. There is no caste here. Our Constitution is color-blind, and neither knows nor tolerates classes among citizens. In respect of civil rights, all citizens are equal before the law… .

In my opinion, the judgment this day rendered will, in time, prove to be quite as pernicious as the decision made by this tribunal in the Dred Scott case … The present decision, it may well be apprehended, will not only stimulate aggressions, more or less brutal and irritating, upon the admitted rights of colored citizens, but will encourage the belief that it is possible by means of state enactments, to defeat the beneficent purposes which the people of the United States had in view when they adopted the recent amendments to the Constitution, by one of which the blacks of this country were made citizens of the United States and of the States in which they respectively reside, and whose privileges and immunities, as citizens the States are forbidden to abridge. … The destinies of the two races, in this country, are indissolubly linked together, and the interests of both require that the common government of all shall not permit the seeds of race hate to be planted under the sanction of law… .

I am of opinion that the statute of Louisiana is inconsistent with the personal liberty of citizens, white and black, in that State, and hostile to both the spirit and letter of the Constitution… .

Source: John Marshall Harlan, Associate Justice of the Supreme Court

Directions: Using the excerpt below and your knowledge of American history, answer the following questions.

> "…The Court holds that the 14th Amendment applies only to state action. … Individual invasion of individual rights is not the subject matter of the [14th] Amendment…
>
> The wrongful act of an individual, unsupported by any such [state] authority, is simply a private wrong, or a crime of that individual; an invasion of rights of the injured party, it is true…; but if not sanctioned in some way by the state, or not done under state authority, his rights remain in full force, and may presumably be vindicated by resort to the laws of the state for redress."

—Civil Rights Cases, 1883

Multiple-Choice

1. Which of the following developments resulted most directly from the principles established by the ruling?

(A) the rise of racial self-help groups such as the National Urban League

(B) the rise of a strong Republican Party in the southern states

(C) the rise of racial violence in the southern states

(D) the rise of committees to reduce racial prejudice in southern states

2. The Court decision excerpted above was likely written in response to the claim that

(A) separate but equal schools were unconstitutional

(B) the federal government should expand its defense of citizen's rights

(C) every American should have the right to vote

(D) states were powerless to defend the rights of their citizens

---

The Civil Rights cases reinforced the idea that the states were responsible for day-to-day protections of their citizens. The cases reduced the reach of the 14th Amendment and left African Americans at the mercy of their home state. This contributed to attacks such as lynching against blacks.

(NAT-2, Causation)

The abolitionists advocated the ending of slavery and wanted an active federal effort to protect basic rights and safety for all people in the United States. The ruling narrowed the range of action the federal government could undertake under the 14th Amendment and left the protection of African American rights in the hands of indifferent and often hostile state governments in the South.

(NAT-2, Contextualization, Analyzing Historical Evidence)

Short-Answer

Using the excerpt, answer parts a, b, and c.

a)   Briefly explain how ONE of the following individuals would react to the decision presented in the passage:

- J. Strom Thurmond
- Thurgood Marshall
- W.E.B. DuBois

b)   Briefly explain how ONE of the remaining people would challenge the position taken by your choice in <u>part a</u>.

c)   In the mid-twentieth century, the Supreme Court led the way to greater civil rights for African-Americans. Briefly explain ONE court case that best represents the court's leadership role in this endeavor.

---

a)   Answers will vary. J. Strom Thurmond, the leader of the States' Right Party (Dixiecrats) in the late 1940s, would favor the decision because it gave states the power to block federal interference in disputes between whites and blacks. Thurgood Marshall, a lawyer for the National Association for the Advancement of Colored People (NAACP), would oppose the ruling because he looked to the federal government to override the states, and to end the Jim Crow system in America. W.E.B. DuBois, a leading spokesman for civil rights, would oppose the ruling because it tightened the Jim Crow system that he and others spent their lives trying to dismantle.

(NAT-2, Analyzing Historical Evidence)

b)   Answers will vary. *(NAT-2, Analyzing Historical Evidence)*

c)   Answers will vary. Students mostly likely would cite *Brown v. Board of Education*, but they might offer *McLaurin v. Oklahoma State Regents* (1950), which said a student could not be segregated within a classroom and/or *Sweatt v. Painter* (1950), which ruled that a law school created hastily for blacks did not meet the equality requirement of "separate but equal."

(NAT-2, Analyzing Historical Evidence)

Monetary Policy—Gold vs. Silver, 1862–1900

The economic history of the United States from 1862-1900 focuses primarily on the debate over which type of currency should be in circulation: gold or silver. The question turned on whether gold would be the only medium of exchange, and if it provided for widespread economic growth and prosperity. Among eastern bankers and creditors, the answer was a resounding "yes" to "sound money," which gold represented. For farmers and other debtors however, gold was inadequate for the needs of the country and represented class oppression and exploitation.

At first the debate centered on adding paper money to gold as the basis for the currency. Later, after the Depressions of 1873 and 1893 rocked the nation, the cry for "free silver" arose. With farm prices in decline, farmers and debtors demanded that the money supply be expanded, and that silver be coined with gold at a ratio of 16 to 1. Farmers created the Populist Party in the 1890s to promote the coinage of silver, because they believed the resulting inflation would benefit them and improve their lives.

The chart on the next page analyzes many of the acts that informed this currency debate. As you review the chart, think about why the debtors/farmers were unable to convince a majority of the electorate to support their cause. Also evaluate whether "free silver" would have actually solved the agrarian problems in the last quarter of the nineteenth century.

Enhancing Understanding

CROSS OF GOLD SPEECH — William Jennings Bryan's declaration for "free silver" at the Democratic convention in 1896. He pledged that the political establishment "shall not crucify mankind upon a cross of gold." With his dramatic advocacy for silver, he electrified the convention and secured his party's presidential nomination.

Directions: Analyze the chart on monetary policy, and then answer the following questions.

1. Indebted farmers in the years 1862–1900 believed their greatest financial benefit would come from the

    (A) Coinage Act of 1873

    (B) Resumption Act of 1875

    (C) Gold Standard Act of 1900

    (D) Sherman Silver Purchase Act of 1890

2. "Sound money is the only basis for true economic prosperity and gold is the only real money for the United States."

    Which of the following groups would most likely agree with this statement?

    (A) supporters of the Resumption Act of 1875

    (B) supporters of the Populist Party

    (C) supporters of the Greenback-Labor Party

    (D) supporters of the Legal Tender Act of 1862

3. The "Crime of '73" occurred when

    (A) paper money was printed to supplement gold

    (B) bad money drove good money out of circulation

    (C) the use of gold caused the Depression of 1873

    (D) Congress legislated an end to minting silver coins

Monetary Policy

Act	Background	Terms	Political Impact
Legal Tender Act, 1862	As Civil War dragged on, the North was running out of money Passed to help fund the Civil War	Government authorized to print greenback dollars without species backing ($450 million)	Democrats in minority; Republicans pushed the bill through
Coinage Act, 1873	1830-1850, price of silver increased; silver became less and less available for minting 1850s, Congress discontinued silver coins; no real outcry	Demonetization Act Congress decreed silver coins should no longer be minted	Depression of 1873 hits; farmers decried the "Crime of '73" Saw conspiracy by "gold bugs" Demand for "free silver" began
Resumption Act, 1875	Union had printed $450 millions in paper money Fear "soft money" would drive "sound money" out of use	Greenbacks would be redeemed for species Gradually reduced the greenbacks in circulation	Formation of the Greenback party; later called Greenback Labor Demanded repeal of Resumption Act
Bland-Allison Act, 1878	Meant to placate 3rd party demands to expand currency Attempt to stimulate economy from Depression of 1873. Respond to pressure from farmers/miners	Treasury would buy $2–$4 million of silver each month Treasury would coin silver dollars	President Hayes' veto overridden Government purchased/minted minimum amounts of silver Neither party strongly favored act
Sherman Silver Purchase Act, 1890	Response to pressure from 3rd parties Doubled silver purchases under Bland-Allison Act Panic of 1893 caused its repeal	Government purchased 4.5 million ounces of silver monthly Issued certificates redeemable in gold or silver	Republicans supported bill; in turn, Democrats supported McKinley Tariff Populist Party and free silver were on the horizon
Gold Standard Act, 1900	Election of 1896 killed "free silver" Strikes around world increased gold supply Economic recovery lessened cry for silver	All paper money backed by gold Put U.S. on gold standard	Pinnacle of monetary conservatism Bimetallism dead as a political issue

Directions: Using the excerpt below and your knowledge of American history, answer the following questions.

> "Men having a design to injure business by making money scarce, could not easily get hold of all the silver, and hide it away; as they could gold...it [silver] was called the people's money. ...Gold was considered the money of the rich. It was owned principally by that class of people, and the poor people seldom handled it, and the very poor people seldom saw any of it...
>
> You increase the value of all property by adding to the number of monetary units in the land. You make it possible for the debtor to pay his debts; business to start anew and revivify all the industries of the country...The money lenders in the United States, who own substantially all our money, have a selfish interest in maintaining the gold standard..."
>
> —William J. "Coins" Harvey, *Coin's Financial School*, 1894

Multiple-Choice

1. The passage above was likely written in response to a government decision to

    (A) replace species with paper currency

    (B) promote a bimetallist policy for the economy

    (C) expand the money supply by coining silver dollars

    (D) contract the money supply

    The government's decisions after the Civil War to take greenbacks out of circulation and to stop coining silver dollars reduced the amount of currency in circulation. Farmers and debtors were certain that these actions were the root cause of their economic distress.

    (WXT-2, Analyzing Historical Evidence, Causation)

2. Which of the following nineteenth-century debates most closely paralleled the controversy raised in the passage?

    (A) differences over protective tariffs in the 1820s

    (B) differences over banking and finance in the 1830s

    (C) differences over the creation of banking trusts in the 1880s

    (D) differences over the economic value of slavery in the 1850s

    ---

    The debate over currency in the late nineteenth century paralleled the earlier struggle over banking during Jackson's presidency. In both cases, the conflict was framed as a struggle between rich and poor. Also in both eras, agrarian interest struggled with mercantile groups for economic control and advantage.

    (POL-3, Continuity and Change over Time)

Short-Answer

Using the excerpt, answer parts a and b.

a)   Briefly explain how TWO of the following individuals would react to the sentiments expressed in the passage:

- William Jennings Bryan
- James B. Weaver
- Grover Cleveland

b)   Briefly explain how the remaining choice would react to the ideas expressed by the two individuals selected in <u>part a</u>.

---

a)   Answers will vary. William Jennings Bryan, an advocate for free sliver, would agree with the ideas of expanding the money supply by coining silver at a rate of 16 to 1. James B. Weaver, a support of both greenback dollars and later silver would also support the ideas expressed by Harvey. Grover Cleveland, a Gold Democrat, would oppose the ideas in the passage. He supported gold as the only standard currency.

(WXT-2, Analyzing Historical Evidence)

b)   **Answers will vary.** *(WXT-2, Analyzing Historical Evidence)*

Lesson 27

Social Darwinism vs. the Social Gospel Movement

The last quarter of the nineteenth century featured an intellectual struggle over the economic and moral responsibilities of the government to its citizens. On the one side were the Social Darwinists, who transformed the theory of natural selection into a survival of the fittest doctrine that explained human relationships. Citing evolutionary principles, the Social Darwinists defended the growing wealth of the upper classes, warned against government economic interference, and called for little or no direct help for the poor and disadvantaged.

On the other hand, supporters of the Social Gospel movement believed that Christianity could be an engine of social and economic reform. They saw society evolving positively, with salvation, personal growth, and social justice as possible outcomes. Centered primarily in the Protestant churches, they called for government action to alleviate poverty, combat child labor, and promote economic competition. Many of their ideas would provide the foundation for the progressive reforms from 1900–1917.

The chart on the following page compares and contrasts the two schools of thought. As you review it, think about how one group tended to look back, while the other group looked forward in terms of economic and social development in the United States. Also, consider how the ideas of the Social Darwinists influenced American overseas relations at the turn of the century.

Directions: Analyze the chart on Social Darwinists and the Social Gospel movement, and then answer the following questions.

1. Which of the following would a Social Darwinist most strongly support?

   (A) settlement houses for immigrants

   (B) taxes on luxury items

   (C) creation of industrial trusts

   (D) child labor laws

2. Which of the following statements would a supporter of the Social Gospel movement make?

   (A) "What would Jesus do about poverty?"

   (B) "The rich deserve their worldly rewards."

Enhancing Understanding

SETTLEMENT HOUSES — a social movement in the late 19th century that attempted to enrich the lives of slum dwellers. Often focused on immigrants, these houses provided day care, health clinics, educational programs, and art initiatives to relieve the stresses of urban living. One of the most famous was Jane Addams/Ellen Starrs' Hull House in Chicago.

   (C) "No man should eat the bread he has not earned."

   (D) "Darwin's ideas have no place in human society."

3. Supporters of Social Darwinism and the Social Gospel both embraced the ideas of

   (A) William Graham Sumner

   (B) Washington Gladden

   (C) Herbert Spencer

   (D) Charles Darwin

	Social Darwinism	Social Gospel Movement
Precursors of Movement	Charles Darwin Herbert Spencer Thomas Malthus	Charles Darwin Richard Ely Lester Ward
Leading Spokesmen	William Graham Sumner Josiah Strong (Imperialism)	Walter Rauschenbusch Washington Gladden Lyman Abbott Josiah Strong (domestic issues)
Influential Literature	Darwin's *On the Origin of Species* Sumner's *Folkways* Spencer's *Principles of Biology*	Darwin's *On the Origin of Species* Rauschenbush's *Christianity and the Social Crisis* Ward's *Dynamic Sociology*
Impact of Darwin	Both ideologies used Darwin's ideas Natural selection becomes survival of the fittest (Herbert Spencer) Humans, like other life forms, struggle for survival Economic life controlled by natural law	Both ideologies used Darwin's ideas Survival of fittest is not the highest law of civilized society Organic evolution leads to better society Evolution: God's way of doing things
Ideas of Movement	Accumulation of wealth is an index of society's improvement and health Classes do not owe each other anything Competition is the law of nature Government should protect property not upset the social arrangement of nature Poverty is result of struggle for existence "Stateways cannot make folkways" (Sumner) "The world owes no man a living" (Rockefeller)	Humans can direct evolution Humans should create a "Kingdom of God" on earth Religion must play a role in public life Churches speak for those without a voice Government action is necessary in society Christian ethics can be applied to social problems Individuals must improve society Cooperation not competition to promote progress
Supporters	Industrialists: John D. Rockefeller, Andrew Carnegie Upper classes "The Forgotten Man;" tax paying, middle class Some imperialists	Protestant ministers and their congregations The poor Social activist and reformers Some advocates of Socialism
Significance	Promoted *status quo/laissez-faire* Defended the industrialists of 1880s/1890s Basis for Imperialism and unchecked Capitalism Promoted a "negative" definition of freedom Basis for the eugenics and scientific racism of the twentieth century	Justified a more active government in economic matters Addressed moral roots of social injustice Basis for "Christian Socialism" later on Influenced progressive reforms (child labor laws, settlement house movement) Supported labor union movement

Directions: Using the excerpt below and your knowledge of American history, answer the following questions.

"There is a beautiful notion afloat in our literature and in the minds of our people that men are born to certain "natural rights"…In its widest extension it comes to mean that if any man finds himself uncomfortable in this world, it must be somebody else's fault, and that somebody is bound to come and make him comfortable.

…Consequently the doctrine…turns out to be in practice only a scheme for making injustice prevail in human society by reversing the distribution of rewards and punishment between those who have done their duty and those who have not. …The real victim is the Forgotten Man again—the man who has watched his own investments, made his own machinery safe, … it is all wrong to preach to the Forgotten Man that it is his duty to go and remedy other people's neglect. It is not his duty…any reconstruction of society on the plan of some enthusiastic social architect…is only repeating the old error over again, …"

—William Graham Sumner, "What Social Classes
Owe to Each Other," 1883

Multiple-Choice

1. The ideas expressed in the passage above most clearly reflect the influence of which of the following?

(A) beliefs in Biblical calls for protection of the weak

(B) government programs to regulate working conditions

(C) justifications for industrial and financial consolidations

(D) proposals for state ownership of public utilities

2. The sentiments expressed in the passage led most directly to the twentieth-century debate over

(A) the proper role of government in society

(B) the proper role of tariffs in protecting businesses

(C) the proper role of the family in protecting children

(D) the proper role of the Constitution in regulating religious matters

---

The industrialists such as John D. Rockefeller/Andrew Carnegie embraced the ideas of William G. Sumner. He offered justification for their great financial empires and warned against government regulations that might reduce their profits and power.

(WXT-2, Causation)

The twentieth-century economic debate was dominated by the question of how much government involvement the American economic system should tolerate. With the reforms the Progressive Era, the New Deal, and the Great Society, this question was at the forefront of all attempts to expand the government's economic power and to broaden social justice in the nation.

(POL-3, Causation, Continuity and Change over Time)

Short-Answer

Using the excerpt, answer parts a and b.

a) Explain briefly how TWO of the following actions challenged American identity as it was expressed in the passage:

- The Keating Owen Act
- The Hepburn Act
- The Pure Food and Drug Act

b) Briefly explain ONE important social or political response to the needs of the "Forgotten Man" in the period from 1920 to 1970.

---

a) Answers will vary. With each of these acts the government expanded its reach and authority. They all extended help to different groups in society. They tended to challenge the American view of Social Darwinism and self-help that dominated much of the thinking of the Gilded Age. The Keating Owen Act was a federal law regulating child labor. The Hepburn Act regulated and restricted railroad activities and enlarged the Interstate Commerce Commission. Finally, the Pure Food and Drug Act regulated food and drug as it targeted prepared food and patent medicines.

(POL-3, Analyzing Historical Evidence)

b) Answers will vary. The most likely examples of efforts to help the Forgotten Man would be the New Deal of the 1930s and the Great Society of the 1960s. Both followed in the traditions of the Social Gospel movement and the Progressive movement in attempting to change American society through government actions and programs.

(POL-3, Analyzing Historical Evidence)

Lesson 28

Black Leaders, 1880–1968

As the idealism of the Reconstruction era faded during the mid-1870s, black Americans confronted a betrayal of the promise of equal rights. Increasingly the federal government's support retreated, and whites in both the South and North became more hostile toward former slaves and free blacks. As the twentieth century dawned, the shadow of Jim Crow extended across the national landscape.

By the mid-1890s, black leaders stepped forward to offer guidance in dealing with the questions of the "color line" that divided America. Some leaders suggested accommodation and integration, while others demanded a more confrontational approach in dealing with racial inequalities in America.

The chart on the following page outlines the contribution of five black leaders. As you study the chart, which leaders do you think were most constructive in their approach to the racial problems of their times, and which leaders do you think acted out of frustration and anger?

ADDITIONAL COMPONENTS

- **Core Chart Worksheet**: "Lesson 28 – Black Leaders" (website)

- **Primary Source Handout:** "Malcolm X, Press Conference" (copy p. 144 or print from website)

- **Document Source Worksheets:** "Worksheet for Document Source Analysis" (p. 246)

OBJECTIVES

Review the introductory materials and the chart "Influential Black Leaders" (pages 114–115 in the Student Edition). Have your students compare the debate between Booker T. Washington and W.E.B. Du Bois in the early twentieth century with the clashes between Martin Luther King Jr. and Malcolm X in the 1960s. Ask them to identify the man in each of these eras who was the most effective leader of black Americans at the time. Have students defend their answers.

After the class discussion on black leadership and reading Malcolm X's news conference, which follows, students should be able to:

1. compare and contrast the issue faced by African-Americans at midcentury with those they faced in the early 1900s;

2. summarize the philosophy of Malcolm X before his trip to Mecca;

3. evaluate Malcolm X as a civil rights leader;

4. explain the major differences between Martin Luther King Jr. and Malcolm X in 1964;

5. analyze how Malcolm X could appeal to groups of African Americans that other leaders failed to reach.

Directions: Analyze the chart on five black leaders, and then answer the following questions.

1. Booker T. Washington and Marcus Garvey shared a common belief that

   (A) alliances with liberal whites would improve civil rights for blacks

   (B) blacks should concentrate on economic progress to move toward equality

   (C) the only path to full equality is agitation and confrontation

   (D) violence was a likely outcome in the struggle for equality

2. Martin Luther King Jr. could not accept Malcolm X's policy of

   (A) striving to improve the lives of black Americans

   (B) agitation and challenge to the racial status quo

   (C) emphasizing black pride and achievements

   (D) rejecting integration and white help

3. W.E.B. Du Bois expected most of his supporters to be

   (A) black middle-class professionals

   (B) southern black sharecroppers

   (C) black urban youth

   (D) African businessmen

Enhancing Understanding

BLACK POWER — an expression of black militancy in the 1960s. Associated with Stokely Carmichael (aka Kwame Ture), it supported black assertiveness and racial segregation. It included calls for black self-sufficiency, armed protection, racial solidarity, and cultural/educational programs focused on the black experience.

DISCUSSION QUESTIONS

Hand out or display the document, "Malcolm X, Press Conference, March 12, 1964," (shown on page 144) and ask the following:

1. How does Malcolm X define Black Nationalism? Why would this appeal to many African Americans?

2. Why does Malcolm X reject integration?

3. What is his position on the use of violence in the cause of civil rights?

4. How does he believe the government failed blacks?

5. What groups of people would support his message? What groups might feel threatened by his words?

6. Why would Malcolm X have trouble supporting Martin Luther King Jr. and vice versa?

7. Why do you think the memory of Malcolm X has been so powerful in the African-American community since his death in 1965?

Answers available on the companion website.

Influential Black Leaders

	Message	Supporters	Methods	Significance
Booker T. Washington, 1856–1915	Atlanta Compromise Accept social/ political inequality Work for economic equality in farming/ trades Blacks should learn vocational skills	Southern, rural blacks Southern whites Wealthy, white industrialists	Accommodation with whites Created Tuskegee Institute Blacks/whites remain separate socially Emphasized black economic development	Got money for black schools Advised presidents on racial issues Secretly tried to overturn segregation Battled NAACP/ W.E.B. Du Bois
W.E.B. Du Bois, 1868–1963	Talented tenth of the black community must lead for equality Strive for full and immediate equality, including full suffrage	Intellectuals Black professionals Urban, northern blacks White progressives	Founded Niagara Movement in 1905 Helped form NAACP in 1909 Wrote books to energize blacks	Challenged B.T. Washington Agitated for equality Challenged conservative racial policies
Marcus Garvey, 1887–1940	Black self-sufficiency Opposed integration Black pride in African heritage/seek roots in Africa Proposed a "Back-to-Africa" movement Expand black economic power	Urban blacks Some whites who supported segregation of the races	Created Universal Negro Improvement Association Formed Black Star Line, a black-owned shipping company Tried to establish African economic ties	First leader to base much of his program on ties to Africa Reached many urban, northern blacks Arrested for mail fraud, deported
Malcolm X (Little), 1925–1965	Black power Enemy is white man Supported Black Nationalism May have been less separatist, more moderate at end of his life	Northern urban black youth Nation of Islam Northern white student radicals	Militant speeches, confrontations with white establishment Challenged King's nonviolence Urged self-defense against white violence	Black Muslims identified with violence in 1960s Opposed gradualism, accommodation Created an intimidating persona that whites found frightening Assassinated 1965
Martin Luther King Jr., 1929–1968	Justice by religious, moral, peaceful means Whites must see injustices in Jim Crow Later targeted economic inequality	Rural, southern church-going people White northern liberals	Nonviolent protest Marches, demonstrations Speeches, articles, books	Opened eyes of country to immorality of segregation Great moral leader Assassinated 1968

Malcolm X, Press Conference, March 12, 1964

The political philosophy of black nationalism means: we must control the politics and the politicians of our community. They must no longer take orders from outside forces. We will organize, and sweep out of office all Negro politicians who are puppets for the outside forces... .

...Whites can help us, but they can't join us. There can be no black-white unity until there is first black unity. There can be no workers' solidarity until there is first some racial solidarity. We cannot think of uniting with others, until after we have first united among ourselves... .

Concerning nonviolence: it is criminal to teach a man not to defend himself when he is the constant victim of brutal attacks. It is legal and lawful to own a shotgun or a rifle. We believe in obeying the law.

In areas where our people are the constant victims of brutality, and the government seems unable or unwilling to protect them, we should form rifle clubs that can be used to defend our lives and our property in times of emergency... . When our people are being bitten by dogs, they are within their rights to kill those dogs.

We should be peaceful, law-abiding—but the time has come for the American Negro to fight back in self-defense whenever and wherever he is being unjustly and unlawfully attacked.

If the government thinks I am wrong for saying this, then let the government start doing its job.

SOURCE: Malcolm X, Black Activist

Directions: Using the excerpt below and your knowledge of American history, answer the following questions.

> "The political philosophy of Black Nationalism means: we must control the politics and the politicians of our community. They must no longer take orders from outside forces. We will organize, and sweep out of office all Negro politicians who are puppets for the outside forces...Whites can help us, but they can't join us. There can be no black-white unity until there is first black unity...We cannot think of uniting with others, until after we have first united among ourselves...
>
> Concerning nonviolence: it is criminal to teach a man not to defend himself when he is the constant victim of brutal attacks. It is legal and lawful to own a shotgun or a rifle. We believe in obeying the law...We should be peaceful, law-abiding—but the time has come for the American Negro to fight back in self-defense whenever and wherever he is being unjustly and unlawfully attacked."

—Malcolm X, press conference,
March 12, 1964

Multiple-Choice

1. Which of the following individuals from the nineteenth century most closely advocated the ideas expressed in the passage?

(A) William Lloyd Garrison in *The Liberator* newspaper

(B) David Walker in *An Appeal to the Coloured* [sic] *Citizens of the World*

(C) Frederick Douglass in *The North Star* newspaper

(D) Harriet Beecher Stowe in *Uncle Tom's Cabin*

David Walker, a free black man in Boston, called for direct resistance to slavery and racism in the late 1820s. His manifesto was extremely radical for the times and its call for physical confrontations with the white power structure anticipated Malcolm X's message of attacking racism by any means necessary in the 1950s and the 1960s.

(CUL-4, Analyzing Historical Evidence)

2. The sentiment expressed in the passage most directly contributed in developing which of the following?

(A) the judicial rulings of the Supreme Court in the 1960s

(B) President Lyndon Johnson's Civil Rights program in the 1960s

(C) Martin Luther King Jr.'s racial beliefs in the 1960s

(D) the Black Power movement in the 1960s

Malcolm X's call for segregation from whites, arming oneself for defense, and fighting back against discrimination was embraced by the Student Nonviolent Coordinating Committee as they developed their Black Power philosophy in the late 1960s.

(CUL-4, Causation)

Short-Answer

Using the excerpt, answer parts a, b, and c.

a) Briefly summarize the main points of the passage.

b) Briefly explain ONE development in the United States from 1945-1965 that led to the point of view expressed by Malcolm X.

c) Briefly explain ONE action, not mentioned in the passage, that Malcolm X hoped would transform African Americans' views of themselves and their place in American society in the mid-1960s.

---

a) Answers will vary. Malcolm X preached an active, aggressive form of protest against racial discrimination. He wanted blacks to demand their rights and not tolerate discrimination or violence against themselves or their property. He agreed that racial equality was the ultimate goal of the civil rights movement, but he sought to achieve it by direct and possibly violent confrontation with the white establishment.

(CUL-4, Analyzing Historical Evidence)

b) Answers will vary. Several developments helped shape Malcolm X's view of the civil rights movement such as:

(1) his membership in the Nation of Islam;

(2) their militant views on segregation;

(3) the nation's growing interest in racial equality after World War II;

(4) Martin Luther King's non-violent approach to civil rights seemed too slow;

(5) there was a strong white backlash against expanding civil rights in the 1950s and 1960s;

(6) urban riots manifested a more militant approach to civil rights.

(CUL-4, Analyzing Historical Evidence)

c) Answers will vary. Malcolm X called on blacks to:

(1) support anti-colonialism in Africa;

(2) adopt Pan-African ideas;

(3) embrace the Muslim religion;

(4) be wary of mainstream civil rights ideas expressed by Martin Luther King;

(5) be willing to work with like minded whites (at the end of his life).

(NAT-4, Causation)

The Supreme Court and Government Regulation, 1890-1937

After the Civil War, business trusts and holding companies formed. These combinations dominated the economy and abused competitors and consumers alike. In response to a public outcry for action, Congress passed the Sherman Antitrust Act in 1890. Although designed to reign in the power of monopolies, the act was used sparingly (18 times) from 1890–1901. Moreover, the Supreme Court, with its early twentieth-century rulings, contributed to the Act's ineffectiveness with a vague interpretation of what was meant by "combination...in restraint of trade or commerce."

From 1890–1937, the Court confronted the continuing question of whether government regulations of business under the Sherman Act went too far and infringed on the commerce clause, the general welfare clause, and the 5th/14th Amendments. Conservatives argued that the Constitution protected liberty of contracts and clearly differentiated between interstate and intrastate commerce. While reformers asked the Court to uphold laws that expanded interstate commerce, established minimum wages, and restrained child labor. Although the Court tended to support the conservative position in most cases, it also recognized some regulation of businesses, especially when government action protected women.

The following chart outlines eight of the landmark Supreme Court cases concerning the role of government in the economy from 1895–1937. As you study the cases, think about the political climate in which each case was decided, and why the intent of Congress was not always translated into Supreme Court rulings.

Directions: Analyze the chart on impactful Supreme Court cases on the role of government, and then answer the following questions.

Enhancing Understanding

TRUST BUSTER — a nickname given to Theodore Roosevelt for invoking the Sherman Antitrust Act 44 times in the early 1900s. Attempting to institute a "Square Deal," he tried to reign in business trusts. His first major case was the breakup of the Northern Securities Company, which unnerved J.P. Morgan and other prominent business leaders.

---

1. Owners of trusts would be most supportive of which of the following court decisions?

    (A) *Lochner v. New York*

    (B) *Northern Securities v. U.S.*

    (C) *Muller v. Oregon*

    (D) *West Coast Hotel Co. v. Parrish*

2. The court case that provided the greatest encouragement to supporters of government regulation of the economy was:

    (A) *U.S. v. E.C. Knight*

    (B) *Lochner v. New York*

    (C) *Northern Securities v. U.S.*

    (D) *Adkins v. Children's Hospital*

3. When deciding the constitutionality of various state and federal regulations the Court often considered whether a law

    (A) expanded opportunities for minorities

    (B) expanded the economy and jobs

    (C) violated the 2nd Amendment

    (D) violated liberty of contract protection

Case	Issue Raised	Ruling	Significance
***U.S. v. E.C. Knight Co.,* 1895**	Was Sherman Act constitutional? Was manufacturing a part of commerce?	Act was constitutional Manufacturing precedes commerce—E.C. Knight Co. did not violate Sherman Act	Limited definition of commerce and the reach of Sherman Act States should regulate manufacturing
***Northern Securities Co. v. U.S.,* 1904**	Did Sherman Act apply to holding companies like J.P. Morgan had assembled?	Holding companies were covered by Act Morgan's Company did restrain trade	Gave energy to trust busting Temporarily curtailed merging of companies
***Lochner v. New York,* 1905**	Did New York's restriction of baker's hours violate liberty of contracts in Constitution?	NY law exceeded state's police power State unreasonably interfered with right of contract	Established "Lochner Era" of judicial veto of much regulation Ruling used to restrict government actions for next 32 years
***Muller v. Oregon,* 1908**	Did restriction of women's hours violate 14th Amendment? Were women in a "special physical" class?	Restriction constitutional State's police power protected women's physical and maternal function	Established "Brandeis brief" using sociological and medical evidence Did not overturn *Lochner*, but women deemed a special exception
***Standard Oil v. U.S.,* 1911**	Did Rockefeller's Standard Oil Company violate the Sherman Act?	Company represented an "unreasonable" restraint of trade Company must be broken up	Established "rule of reason," a precedent that lasted for many years Added to uncertainty over Sherman Act
***Adkins v. Children's Hospital,* 1923**	Did federal minimum wage for women violate the due process clause in 5th Amendment?	Act did violate liberty of contracts Women could not be restricted anymore than men in marketplace	Overturned *Muller* Nineteenth Amendment had eliminated women's special status Ruling overturned in 1937
***Schechter Poultry Corp. v. U.S.,* 1935**	Did National Industrial Recovery Act (NIRA) violate commerce/general welfare clauses of Constitution?	NIRA unconstitutional Delegated legislative power to executive Violated commerce clause	Message to FDR: economic crisis did allow excessive government actions Played a role in FDR's court packing decision in 1937
***West Coast Hotel Co. v. Parrish,* 1937**	Did Washington state's minimum wage law for women violate liberty of contracts protected by 5th and 14th Amendments?	Law constitutional State could regulate for public interest Law protected community/safety of vulnerable group	Overturned *Adkins* Ended "Lochner Era" Some said reaction to court packing—"switch in time that saved nine"

Directions: Using the excerpts below and your knowledge of American history, answer the following questions.

"The statute necessarily interferes with the right of contract between the employer and employees, concerning the number of hours in which the latter may labor in the bakery of the employer. The general right to make a contract in relation to his business is part of the liberty of the individual protected by the 14th Amendment of the Federal Constitution…

The act…is an illegal interference with the rights of individuals, both employers and employees, to make contracts regarding labor upon such terms as they may think best, or they may agree upon with other parties to such contracts…"

—*Lochner v. New York*, 1905

"The single question is the constitutionality of the statue under which the defendant was convicted so far as affects the work of a female in a laundry. … That woman's physical structure and the performance of maternal functions place her at a disadvantage in the struggle for subsistence is obvious. This is especially true when the burdens of motherhood are upon her…

Differentiated by these matters from the other sex, she is properly placed in a class by herself, and legislations designed for her protection may be sustained even when the legislation is not necessary for men…The limitations which this statute places upon her contractual powers, upon her right to agree with her employer as to the time she shall labor, are not solely for her benefit, but also largely for the benefit of all…we are of the opinion that it cannot be adjudged that the act in question is in conflict with the federal Constitution…"

—*Muller v. Oregon*, 1908

Multiple-Choice

1. The two excerpts best serve as evidence that the Supreme Court of the early twentieth century believed

   (A) that the federal government should not intervene in the workplace

   (B) that all workers must be treated equally in the workplace

   (C) that women were better workers than men in the workplace

   (D) that men and women had different rights in the workplace

> The Court drew a distinction between men and women regarding limitation on their working hours. In Lochner, a law that restricted men to working only ten hours was struck down. In Muller, however, the Court upheld a ten hour working limitation law for women because of their unique physical characteristics and their status as potential mothers.
>
> *(NAT-2, Analyzing Historical Evidence)*

2. Which of the following twentieth-century continuities most resembles the struggle over individual versus corporate property rights?

- **(A)** attempts to expand government power in the 1930s
- **(B)** attempts to expand economic rights for African Americans in the 1910s
- **(C)** attempts to expand gender economic rights in the 1960s
- **(D)** attempts to deregulate industries in the 1980s

> In the mid-1930s the Supreme Court declared nine acts of the New Deal unconstitutional because it viewed various actions of government intervention in the private sector as excessive. The two most notable examples of these decisions were those that invalidated the Agricultural Adjustment Act and the National Industrial Recovery Act.
>
> *(POL-3, Continuity and Change over Time)*

Short-Answer

Using the excerpts, answer parts a and b.

a) Briefly explain how TWO of the following groups would react to the excerpted court decisions:

- Members of the National Woman's Party
- Members of the Bull Moose Party
- Members of the Industrial Workers of the World

b) The two Court decisions excerpted made a statement about American identity in the early twentieth century. Briefly explain how ONE of the following Supreme Court decisions helps define American identity later in the century:

- *Korematsu v. U.S.*
- *Brown v. Board of Education*
- *Roe v. Wade*

a) Answers will vary. The National Women's Party would support Muller because it extended working protection to women. This could be a step in the direction of voting rights for women. The Bull Moose Party would not support Lochner because it restricted government power to regulate working hours and conditions. The Industrial Workers of the World would be opposed to both rulings because they did not go far enough to change the capitalist system.

(NAT-1, Analyzing Historical Evidence)

b) Answers will vary. The Korematsu case upheld the right of the government to imprison Japanese Americans during World War II. It demonstrated that racial prejudice was very strong in the war years among many Americans. The Brown decision declared separate but equal schools unconstitutional. This demonstrated a slow recognition that the Jim Crow system must be disbanded. The Roe decision legalized abolition. The ruling gave women more control over their reproductive rights and helped fuel the feminist movement in the 1970s and 1980s.

(NAT-2, Analyzing Historical Evidence)

Reform Movements of the Twentieth Century

The great domestic political struggle of twentieth-century American history occurred between the impulses of reform and the forces of the status quo. A major issue in this debate was the degree to which the national government should involve itself in the social and economic lives of its citizens—the issue of *laissez-faire*. This conflict over government intervention into the private sector defined the major domestic political and economic debate during most of the twentieth century.

Reformers made three major attempts to alter American social and economic relations during the twentieth century: the progressive reforms early in the century; the New Deal/Fair Deal reforms of the 1930s and 1940s; and the New Frontier/Great Society reforms of the 1960s. The chart on the following page summarizes each of the movements. Historians have noted that these reforms occurred in roughly thirty-year cycles during the twentieth century. That is, a wave of public purpose (reform) was usually followed by a private interlude (i.e., 1920s, 1950s, and 1980s). What factors might explain this cycle of reform?

Directions: Analyze the chart on the three twentieth-century reform movements, and then answer the following questions.

1. A common thread that ran through the Fair Deal, New Frontier, and Great Society was

    (A) each was led by a Republican president

    (B) each occurred after the United States completed a successful war

    (C) each tried to continue and expand New Deal reforms

    (D) each relied on state governments to make societal changes

2. Which pair of twentieth-century reform movements was most effective in changing America?

    (A) The New Deal and the Great Society

    (B) The Great Society and the New Frontier

    (C) The New Deal and the Fair Deal

    (D) The Square Deal/New Freedom and the Great Society

3. In terms of actual accomplishments, which of these reform programs had the least impact on American society?

    (A) New Deal

    (B) New Frontier

    (C) Fair Deal

    (D) Great Society

Enhancing Understanding

COMMITTEE ON CIVIL RIGHTS — created by President Truman, its 1947 report recommended the creation of a civil rights section of the Justice Department, a permanent Fair Employment Practices Commission, the abolition of poll taxes, and anti-lynching legislation. All of these suggestions were enacted in the 1950s and 60s.

Twentieth-Century Reform Movements

	Square Deal/ New Freedom	New Deal	Fair Deal	New Frontier	Great Society
Dates	1901–1916	1933–1939	1945–1953	1961–1963	1963–1969
Leader(s)	T. Roosevelt W. Wilson	F. Roosevelt	H. Truman	J. Kennedy	L. Johnson
Goals	Control corporations, trusts Citizen protection Clean up government Conserve environment	Relief for unemployed Recovery from the Depression Reform of financial institutions, economic system	Continue/expand New Deal with special attention to economic security	Continue/expand New Deal with some attention to civil rights, education	Complete New Deal with special attention to poverty, cities, civil rights, healthcare, education
Actions	Hepburn Act Pure Food and Drug Act Clayton Act Northern Securities Case Federal Reserve Act Federal Trade Commission Newlands Act Keating-Owen Act Progressive Amendments (16th, 17th)	National Industrial Recovery Act Agricultural Adjustment Act Civilian Conservation Corp Public Works Administration Social Security Act Federal Deposit Insurance Corporation Tennessee Valley Authority Securities and Exchange Commission Wagner Act	Desegregated military Employment Act 1946 Raised minimum wage Expanded Social Security Proposed civil rights program	Proposed: • Medicare • Civil Rights Act • Aid to education • Public housing • Mass transit	Medicare/ Medicaid Act Civil Rights Act Voting Rights Act 60 education acts Economic Opportunity Act Housing Act Immigration Act Highway Safety Act Head Start program Model Cities Act

Directions: Using the excerpt below and your knowledge of American history, answer the following questions.

> "I have called for a national war on poverty. Our objective: total victory.
>
> There are millions of Americans—one fifth of our people—who have not shared in the abundance which has been granted to most of us, and on whom the gates of opportunity have been closed. ...The war on poverty is not a struggle simply to support people, to make them dependent on the generosity of others...
>
> It is an effort to allow them to develop and use their capacities, as we have been allowed to develop and use ours, so that they can share, as others share, in the promise of the nation.
>
> Our history has proved that each time we broaden the base of abundance, giving more people the chance to produce and consume, we create new industry, higher production, increased earnings and better income for all. ... Because it is right, because it is wise, and because for the first time in our history, it is possible to conquer poverty, I submit for the consideration of the Congress and the country, the Economic Opportunity Act of 1964."
>
> —President Lyndon B. Johnson, 1964

Multiple-Choice

1. Which of the following activities from the early years of the twentieth century most closely resembled President Johnson's call for action in the passage?

   (A) governmental promotion of high tariffs on imported goods

   (B) governmental expansion of suffrage in the United States

   (C) governmental regulation of working hours for women

   (D) governmental calls for private donations to help the poor

   ---

   In an approach similar to President Johnson's call to "broaden the base of abundance," the progressive reformers of the early 20th century hoped to improve the quality of life for women by regulating their working hours and conditions in American factories and businesses.

   (POL-3, Continuity and Change over Time)

2. Which of the following controversies in the 1980s arose most directly from the sentiment expressed in the passage above?

   (A) a debate over the amount of government spending on social programs

   (B) a debate over whether whites and blacks should receive government help

   (C) a debate over federal versus state regulation of corporations

   (D) a debate over government aid to parochial schools

   Much of the conservative agenda of the 1980s was directed at scaling back the programs of the Great Society of the 1960s. The consensus among many people was that the federal government's size and spending policies had gotten out of hand.

   (POL-3, Causation, Continuity and Change over Time)

Short-Answer

Using the excerpt, answer parts a, b, and c.

a)   Briefly explain how ONE of the following movements sought to change the federal government's role in the social and economic life of the nation:

- The New Deal
- The Fair Deal
- The Great Society

b)   In both the early twentieth century and the 1960s, the federal government attempted to address the question of poverty and social justice. Briefly explain ONE important similarity in the reasons why this spirit of reform emerged in both time periods.

c)   Provide ONE piece of evidence from the 1960s, that is not included in the passage, and explain how it supported President Johnson's message.

> **a)**   Answers will vary. Each of these reform movements sought to extend the reach of the federal government into the lives of the poor, minorities, and, in the 1960s, women. Students should reference the 3 Rs of the New Deal, and the Great Society mission to complete Roosevelt's and Truman's reform agendas.
>
> *(POL-3, Analyzing Historical Evidence)*
>
> **b)**   In both eras there was intellectual support for action (the muckrakers in the Progressive Era and Michael Harrington's The Other America in the 1960s). There were strong Presidents in both eras (Theodore Roosevelt, Woodrow Wilson, and Lyndon Johnson). There was a belief that the gap between rich and poor was deleterious to the nation both philosophically and practically. The federal government had the financial and political resources to address some of the problems.
>
> *(POL-3, Comparison)*
>
> **c)**   Under the leadership of Lyndon Johnson, Congress enacted the Civil Rights Acts of 1964 and 1965, Head Start, the Job Corp, Food Stamps, Medicare, Medicaid, the Immigration Act of 1965, and over 70 bills for federal support for education.
>
> *(POL-3, Analyzing Historical Evidence)*

Lesson 31

Isolationism vs. Internationalism, 1919-1941

Between the two World Wars, isolationists and internationalists struggled over what role America should play in the military and political affairs of Europe. Both sides realized the United States could not withdraw from world affairs completely, yet the isolationists consistently opposed membership in the League of Nations and the World Court. They did, however, support multilateral disarmament treaties that saved taxes, reduced the power of the federal government, and, theoretically, the chances of war.

The onset of the Great Depression strengthened the isolationists' (non-interventionists') hand. The nation, preoccupied with economic problems during this time, accepted a series of Neutrality Acts that reinforced its nonentangling, foreign policy stance. When Germany invaded Poland in September 1939, however, public opinion shifted toward the internationalist position. Between 1939 and America's entry into the war in 1941, President Roosevelt gradually sought more aid for, and involvement with, potential European allies, such as Great Britain.

The chart on the following page compares the two contrasting viewpoints from 1919 to 1941. Do you think Roosevelt was too timid in his approach to foreign relations during the 1930s? Why is the label "isolationism" somewhat inaccurate during these years?

OBJECTIVES

Review the introductory material and the chart "Comparing Internationalists and Isolationists" (pages 126–127 in the Student Edition). Have your students discuss the reasons why America rejected "collective security" as envisioned by Woodrow Wilson in the League of Nations.

After the class discussion on the isolationist-internationalist struggle and reading Gerald P. Nye's "Is Neutrality Possible for America?" which follows, students will be able to:

1. outline the basic beliefs of the noninterventionists (isolationists) in the 1920s and 1930s;

2. evaluate the "isolationist impulse" as the most realistic policy for America in the world in the 1930s;

3. explain why alternatives to the isolationists' position were not effectively presented in the 1930s;

4. analyze how America's World War I experiences formed the foundation for the isolationists' rationale of the 1920s and 1930s.

ADDITIONAL COMPONENTS

- **Core Chart Worksheet**: "Lesson 31 – Isolationism vs. Internationalism" (website)

- **Primary Source Handout**: "Is Neutrality Possible for America" (copy p. 158 or print from website)

Directions: Analyze the chart on internationalism and isolationism, and then answer the following questions.

1. The issue that divided the isolationists and internationalists most deeply immediately after the Great War (World War I) was whether the United States should

   (A) make a permanent alliance with Great Britain

   (B) reduce spending on the military

   (C) raise taxes to support foreign aid

   (D) accept membership in the League of Nations

2. Between 1919–1941, William Borah, Charles Lindbergh, and Gerald Nye all shared the belief that

   (A) the U.S. should cease trading with most nations in the world

   (B) European alliances would make America safer

   (C) England's security was vital to America's security

   (D) America should avoid involving itself in European politics

3. Internationalists between 1919 and 1941 strongly believed in

   (A) nonentangling foreign alliances

   (B) collective security

   (C) reducing military spending

   (D) disarmament and immigration restriction

Enhancing Understanding

ARTICLE 10 — part of the covenant of the League of Nations that committed members to respect and defend the territorial integrity of nations. In the case of aggression against a member, the League would advise upon the means to assist the targeted country. This article was the central point in the debate and rejection of the Treaty of Versailles by the U.S.

DISCUSSION QUESTIONS

Hand out or display the document, "Is Neutrality Possible for America?," (shown on page 158) and ask the following:

1. What were the major ideas in the noninterventionists' (isolationists') arguments in the 1930s?

2. How did the events of 1914–1917 affect American isolationists' thinking in the 1930s?

3. Why did the isolationists reject collective security between the wars?

4. What anticolonial arguments did the isolationists make?

5. Why was it difficult to counter the isolationists' position in the 1930s?

6. Did President Roosevelt handle American foreign policy effectively in the 1930s? Defend your answer.

Answers available on the companion website.

Comparing Internationalists and Isolationists

	Internationalists	Isolationists
Principles	Collective security U.S. had interest in European security Confront overseas aggression Axis powers a threat to U.S. Quarantine aggressors British and American security linked Atlantic Charter	Avoid entangling foreign alliances Great War a mistake Arms makers had manipulated U.S. into Great War Avoid defending England's interests Reduce military Keep taxes low Domestic issues more important than foreign affairs Defend continental U.S.
Actions	Should accept Article 10 Should join League of Nations Should join World Court Stimson Doctrine Reciprocal trade agreements Offer aid short of war Provide lend-lease	Alter/reject Article 10 Reject League of Nations Reject membership in World Court Washington Naval agreement Kellogg-Briand Pact Immigration restrictions Hawley-Smoot tariff Nye munitions investigation Neutrality Acts 1935, 1936, 1937
Personnel	Woodrow Wilson Franklin Roosevelt Cordell Hull Henry Stimson Frank Knox Tom Connally Committee to Defend America	Henry Cabot Lodge William Borah Gerald Nye Charles Lindbergh Hiram Johnson Robert Taft America First Committee
Comments	Reeling during 1920s from League of Nations' defeat In 1930s, first priority was economic recovery No European support against Axis Roosevelt unwilling to challenge isolationists in Congress When France fell in June of 1940, the internationalists gained political strength	Sought economic internationalism Avoid political/military overseas connections Keep America's freedom of action abroad Reached height with Neutrality Acts

Is Neutrality Possible for America?

No one is more jealously interested in my country's maintaining adequate national defense than I am. But I am sick of things that are being done in the name of national defense. …

…But there is still another side of this outlay for war preparedness and conduct of war. Dr. Nicholas Murray Butler has made an inventory of what we could do for mankind if we had the money today. Every city of approximately 20,000 people in those countries [in western Europe] could have a two million dollar hospital, a three million dollar library, and a ten million dollar university. With part of the balance invested at five per cent, we could pay salaries of a thousand dollars apiece to 125,000 teachers and 125,000 nurses.

The serious danger to our peace, to say nothing about our standards of common honor and decency, is so obvious that a way out of the bog in which we find ourselves must be found. A policy of strict neutrality, to become mandatory as soon as the war infection manifests itself, appears to be such a way of escape. The advantages of such mandatory legislation are easily apparent. It is simply the law of the land, a law familiar to every foreign power. Nations intent upon war are given notice and may weigh for themselves the effect of such a policy upon their ability to buy arms and other war supplies in our markets. These are very definite advantages which cannot be lightly dismissed. To such a mandatory embargo against the shipment of munitions was added, specifically for our own protection against involvement in war, the so-called cash and carry provision.

The truth is that unless a halt is called upon war preparations that are not for defense and upon the enactment of laws for the complete mobilization of our civil organization in wartime, America will succumb to war psychology and will be drawn inevitably into actual conflict. Neutrality, aided by the natural advantages of our physical so-called isolation, or neutrality, happily in co-operation with other nations, if that can be safely accomplished, appears to be the solution.

When we are asked to underwrite a campaign for collective security, it is plain that we are not being invited to assist in the defense of powers, or to co-operate with powers that can properly be called democratic. The defense of the British and French empires, were we to lend ourselves to a policy of collective security with those countries, would involve the continued subjugation of hundreds of millions of black and brown peoples among whom the spirit of revolt is already manifest.

For better or worse, we are part of a world order, and it is always possible that challenges may come which we cannot ignore and which will take us as a co-operator into another world war. But let us refrain from writing the ticket of procedure even before we know who our allies are to be, what the cause is to be, what the jeopardy is going to be, what the cost is going to be, and, above all, what the chances [are] of winning the cause for which we may be willing to fight.

SOURCE: Gerald P. Nye, U.S. Senator

Directions: Using the excerpt below and your knowledge of American history, answer the following questions.

> "No one is more jealously interested in my country's maintaining adequate national defense than I am. But I am sick of things being done in the name of national defense. ...The serious danger to our peace, to say nothing about our standards of common honor and decency, is so obvious that a way out of the bog in which we find ourselves must be found. A policy of strict neutrality...appears to be such a way of escape...
>
> The truth is that unless a halt is called upon war preparations that are not for defense and upon the enactment of laws for the complete mobilization of our civil organization in wartime, America will succumb to war psychology and will be drawn inevitably into actual conflict...
>
> For better or worse, we are part of the world order...But let us refrain from writing the ticket of procedure even before we know who our allies are to be, what cause is to be, what the jeopardy is going to be..."

—Senator Gerald P. Nye, "Is Neutrality Possible for America?" in *Tomorrow in the Making*, 1939

Multiple-Choice

1. Which of the following nineteenth-century issues raised concerns that were similar to those expressed in the passage?

   (A) tariff wars between the United States and Europe

   (B) conflicts over fishing rights in the Atlantic Ocean

   (C) armed conflicts between European countries

   (D) troubles with Spain over ownership of Florida

> George Washington's warning about entangling alliances dominated much of the foreign policy debate over America's role in European affairs in the nineteenth century. The issue of political/diplomatic isolationism carried over into the 1930s debate over America's role in Europe as war clouds began to gather there.
>
> *(WOR-2, Continuity and Change over Time, Contextualization)*

2. The sentiments expressed in the passage above led most directly to the 1940s controversy over

   (A) membership in the World Court

   (B) involvement in European trade agreements

   (C) sending anti-communist aid to China

   (D) membership in the North Atlantic Treaty Organization

> When the North Atlantic Treaty Organization was proposed, many isolationists saw the alliance as a repudiation of the warning that George Washington gave in the late 1790s. The debate over joining the organization renewed the cry of avoiding "entangling foreign alliances." In fact, N.A.T.O. was the first time that the United States actually joined a formal European alliance.
>
> *(WOR-2, Causation)*

Short-Answer

Using the excerpt, answer parts a, b, and c.

a) Briefly explain how ONE of the following foreign policy actions affected the debate over American isolationism from 1919–1941:

- The rejection of the Treaty of Versailles
- The Neutrality Acts of the mid-1930s
- The Atlantic Charter

b) United States non-involvement in Europe had a long history before the 1930s. Briefly explain ONE example of America's reluctance to entangle itself in European affairs from 1790–1825.

c) Briefly explain ONE development that challenged the sentiment expressed in the passage from 1945–1955.

---

a) Answers will vary. The rejection of the Treaty of Versailles strengthened America's commitment to avoid European affairs. The nation rejected Article X's and collective security and curtailed American involvement in Europe for almost two decades. The Neutrality Acts prevented the United States from loaning money, providing weapons to belligerent nations, and prohibited American citizens from traveling into the war zone. These laws were the apex of isolationist sentiment in the 1930s. The Atlantic Charter pulled the United States closer to breaking its isolationism as America and Great Britain laid out a series of internationalist goals to be achieved when the fascists were defeated in Europe.

(WOR-2, Causation)

b) Answers will vary. Students might explain one of the following:

(1) Washington's Neutrality Proclamation of 1793;

(2) the Farewell Address of 1796;

(3) overall neutrality in the Anglo-French conflict 1793-1812;

(4) Monroe's restatement of Washington's policies in the Monroe Doctrine 1823.

(WOR-2, Analyzing Historical Evidence)

c) Answers will vary. Students might explain the onset of the Cold War in the mid- and late 1940s, the Korean War, the Fall of China, and/or Soviet aggression in Greece, Iran and Eastern Europe.

(WOR-2, Causation, Contextualization)

Transformation of Capitalism in the 1930s

The New Deal was Franklin Roosevelt's plan to restore economic prosperity to the United States during the 1930s. Though Roosevelt expanded the powers of the federal government enormously from 1933 to 1939 and alleviated the suffering of millions of Americans, his economic programs failed to end the Depression. It would take the Second World War to accomplish that.

Roosevelt's program to alleviate the Depression had two distinct phases. A First New Deal from 1933 to 1935 concentrated on economic relief and recovery and attempted to establish a government partnership with American corporations and businesses. A Second New Deal from 1935–1939 focused on long-term reforms in the American economy and took a confrontational stance toward the business community and the wealthy by imposing higher taxes and new, stricter regulations.

The chart on the next page outlines the basic differences between the First and Second New Deals. As you study it, consider the factors that undermined cooperation between big business and the government. Further, in what ways did the First and Second New Deals attempt to alter the capitalist system?

Directions: Analyze the chart on the First and Second New Deals, and then answer the following questions.

1. During the First New Deal, Franklin Roosevelt believed

    (A) the National Recovery Administration should nationalize the major industries

    (B) corporations that provided public services must accept government regulations and limitations on their profits

    (C) businessmen should be left alone to make as much money as possible

    (D) the government must cooperate with the business community to lift the country out of the Depression

2. In the Second New Deal, the government's attitude toward wealthy Americans was that

    (A) the gap between the wealthy and other classes should be narrowed through taxing policy

    (B) rich people should be protected because their spending could stimulate prosperity

    (C) the incomes of all Americans should be roughly equal

    (D) inherited wealth hurt the country and prolonged the depression

3. The primary goal of the First New Deal was

    (A) to control all aspects of the American economic system

    (B) to provide relief and recovery from the Depression

    (C) to break up the trusts that had formed since the Progressive era

    (D) to establish cooperative ownership of America's farms and businesses

    Enhancing Understanding moved to the following page.

Comparing the First and Second New Deals

	First New Deal	Second New Deal
Dates	1933–1935	1935–1939
Goals	Direct relief to unemployed; recovery from the Depression Cooperated with business community to restore pre-1929 prosperity Helped organized labor to improve position in society Provided assistance to agriculture	Revived progressive tradition of trust regulation Strengthened organized labor Sought to meet needs of workers, elderly, disabled, farmers, unemployed Narrowed class differences by taxing the wealthy Supported industrial workers and small farmers
Position on Business	Partnership Cooperation Suspended antitrust actions	Confrontational toward corporate interests Strong regulation of public utilities
Actions	National Industrial Recovery Act Agricultural Adjustment Act Federal Emergency Relief Act Emergency Banking Act Civilian Conservation Corp Tennessee Valley Authority Act	Public Utility Holding Company Act Wealth Tax Act (Revenue Act) National Labor Relations Act (Wagner Act) Works Progress Administration Social Security Act Fair Labor Standards Act
Comments	Brief honeymoon between business community and the Roosevelt administration First New Deal told business what it must do Business found New Deal regulations increasingly confining and intrusive Supreme Court sided with business interests as it struck down several major New Deal acts	Stronger controls and higher taxes on the wealthy and large businesses Responded to attacks by Liberty League and Supreme Court's judicial review Second New Deal told business what it must *not* do

Enhancing Understanding

AMERICAN LIBERTY LEAGUE — an organization of conservative politicians and businessmen opposed to the New Deal. Heavily financed by the DuPont Company and supported by Democrats such as Alfred Smith and John W. Davis, the group viewed Roosevelt's intervention in the economy as tilting toward fascism. It disbanded in 1940.

Directions: Using the cartoon below and your knowledge of American history, answer the following questions.

The Washington Star, **June 2, 1935**

Multiple-Choice

1. The ideas expressed in the cartoon most directly reflect which of the following continuities in United States history?

   (A) debates over the role of the federal government in economic matters

   (B) debates over the transportation system that best suited the nation

   (C) debates over presidential power to amend the Constitution

   (D) debates over the role of the federal government in religious matters

   In the cartoon, the United States system of democracy and capitalism is symbolized by an old-fashioned horse and buggy. Franklin Roosevelt is seen as offering a modern, state-of-the-art program of federal control. This debate over the degree of federal involvement in the lives of Americans continued throughout the nation's history.

   (POL-3, Causation, Continuity and Change over Time)

2. The question highlighted in the cartoon was raised earlier in the twentieth century when the federal government began to

- **(A)** desegregate the schools in the South
- **(B)** provide healthcare for immigrant groups
- **(C)** establish a uniform currency in the United States
- **(D)** regulate corporate business practices

> The question of federal control over the economy was raised when progressive reformers tried to curtail business and trust abuses in the early 20th century. Their use of the Sherman Act and Clayton Act raised controversy as did the New Deal programs of the 1930s.
>
> *(POL-3, Continuity and Change over Time, Contextualization)*

Short-Answer

Using the cartoon, answer parts a, b, and c.

a) Briefly explain how ONE of the following individuals would react to the ideas expressed in the cartoon:

- Harry Hopkins
- Norman Thomas
- Herbert Hoover

b) Briefly explain how ONE of the remaining individuals would challenge the response of the individual selected in <u>part a</u>.

c) Briefly explain ONE example of how President Roosevelt sought to implement the point of view expressed in the cartoon from 1933–1941.

---

a) Answers will vary. Harry Hopkins, a principal strategist for the New Deal, would support the idea of federal government control in the economy. Norman Thomas, a socialist, would want much more federal control of the economy and social system than the New Deal offered. Herbert Hoover, a Republican, would caution against too much federal control. He would fear that such actions would lead to totalitarianism.

(POL-3, Analyzing Historical Evidence)

b) Answers will vary. *(POL-3, Causation)*

c) Answers will vary. Students might explain various elements of the 3 Rs such as the National Industrial Recovery Act, Agricultural Adjustment Act, Glass-Steagall Act, Social Security Act, Wagner Act, Federal Emergency Relief Act, Tennessee Valley Authority Act, Civil Works Administration, Works Progress Administration.

(POL-3, Analyzing Historical Evidence)

Presidential Civil Rights Records, 1945-1974

The Second World War helped launch the civil rights movement of the 1950s and 1960s. After defeating the racist philosophy of the Axis powers, President Truman began to evaluate race relations in the United States. Influenced by African-Americans' wartime sacrifices and their mistreatment in America, the president proposed a civil rights program. Although Truman's program met opposition from his own party and Republicans in Congress, he marked the path toward greater racial justice in America.

Building on Truman's momentum, the Supreme Court issued a series of rulings that culminated in *Brown v. Board of Education* (1954), which outlawed Jim Crow in America. During the next fifteen years, leaders such as Martin Luther King Jr. and Lyndon Johnson promoted racial equality and changed the face of America.

From 1945 to 1974, presidential motives and actions on civil rights varied greatly. Most chief executives weighed the political costs before taking action on behalf of African-Americans. The chart on the next page compares the proposals and actions of the presidents from Truman to Nixon. As you study the information, which one of these five presidents would you nominate as African-Americans' greatest ally in the quest for equality?

Directions: Analyze the chart on civil rights proposals and actions, and then answer the following questions.

1. In terms of civil rights, Dwight Eisenhower and Richard Nixon shared

 (A) a desire to achieve racial equality regardless of the political costs

 (B) a desire to make civil rights a weapon in fighting the Cold War

 (C) a weak commitment toward civil rights

 (D) a belief that federal laws could change people's racial attitudes

2. For John F. Kennedy, civil rights was an issue

 (A) of the highest moral priority from the very beginning of his presidency

 (B) to be managed without political conflict within his party

 (C) to be completely ignored until it required action

 (D) to be postponed until he was re-elected

3. Lyndon Johnson's civil rights program was undermined by

 (A) opposition from liberal Democrats and the Supreme Court

 (B) budget deficits and economic recession

 (C) affirmative action and the Republican controlled Congress

 (D) domestic unrest and the war in Vietnam

Enhancing Understanding

AFFIRMATIVE ACTION — preferential government programs in employment and educations for women and minorities. Arguing these groups had experienced past injustices, institutions provided special consideration to them for jobs and college enrollment. Since the 1990s, the programs have been attacked as unnecessary and promoting reverse discrimination against white men.

Civil Rights Proposals and Actions, 1945–1974

President	Proposals	Actions	Comments
Harry Truman	Anti-lynching law Voter protection End discrimination in military, interstate travel, government hiring End poll tax	Created Civil Rights Committee First president to address the NAACP Desegregated the armed forces Reduced government job discrimination	Civil rights program blocked by Congress Won African Americans to Democratic Party Alienated South (Strom Thurmond's Dixiecrat revolt)
Dwight Eisenhower	Work for mildest forms of civil rights Racial justice part of Cold War struggle	Appointed Earl Warren to Supreme Court Civil Rights Acts of 1957/1960 Ended segregation in D.C. and on military bases Sent federal troops to Little Rock	Lacked conviction on civil rights Avoided compulsory action on civil rights Sought change through reason and prayer Believed government could not legislate morality
John Kennedy	Enforce existing laws End discrimination in public housing Made civil rights a moral issue in June 1963	Defended freedom riders Enforced desegregation of universities Ended public housing discrimination Proposed Civil Rights Act	Hoped to contain civil rights pressures/actions Feared southern Democrats in Congress Came late to supporting civil rights Clashed with King, wiretapped him
Lyndon Johnson	Include African-Americans in Great Society Wage war on poverty Overcome racism Improve cities and urban schools	Civil Rights Act of 1964 Voting Rights Act of 1965 Economic Opportunity Act Appointed Thurgood Marshall to Supreme Court 60 education laws, including Head Start	Greatest presidential supporter of civil rights Great Society very strong on civil rights Urban riots 1964–1968 undermined program Great Society damaged by Vietnam War
Richard Nixon	Bring nation together Restore law and order Called for extra help for urban blacks	Supported affirmative action briefly Desegregated many schools Extended Voting Rights Act Condemned busing Appointed conservative federal judges	In the past, he had a moderate record on civil rights Lacked commitment to true racial equality Used race to divide Democrats Gradually followed a southern racial strategy

Directions: Using the excerpt below and your knowledge of American history, answer the following questions.

> "For a few minutes this evening I want to talk to you about the serious situation that has arisen in Little Rock. ...In that city, under the leadership of demagogic extremists, disorderly mobs have deliberately prevented the carrying out of proper orders from a Federal Court. Local authorities have not eliminated that violent opposition, and, under the law, I yesterday issued a Proclamation calling upon the mob to disperse.
>
> This morning the mob again gathered in front of the Central High School of Little Rock, obviously for the purpose of again preventing the carrying out of the Court's order relating to the admission of Negro children to that school. ...I have today issued an Executive Order directing the use of troops under Federal authority to aid in the execution of Federal law at Little Rock, Arkansas. ...Our personal opinions about the decision have no bearing on the matter of enforcement; the responsibility and authority of the Supreme Court to interpret the Constitution are very clear. ...Mob rule cannot be allowed to override the decision of our courts."

—President Dwight D. Eisenhower, 1957

Multiple-Choice

1. The sentiments expressed in the passage above most clearly show the influence of which of the following?

(A) late nineteenth-century states' rights claims to manage racial conflicts

(B) mid twentieth-century judicial rulings on racial conflicts

(C) early twentieth-century military interventions in racial conflicts

(D) late nineteenth-century judicial rulings on racial conflicts

2. Which of the following events in the nineteenth century most closely parallels the controversy described in the passage?

(A) the use of troops to end racial violence during labor strikes

(B) the use of troops to put down urban rioting among African Americans

(C) the use of troops to implement Reconstruction in the South

(D) the use of troops to maintain racially segregated schools in the North

---

The Little Rock crisis flowed from the Brown v. Board of Education decision of 1954. This ruling overturned the separate but equal doctrine that had been in place since 1896. Attempts to integrate the schools of Little Rock resulted in mob violence and intimidation. This resistance prompted President Eisenhower to send troops to quell the disorders.

(NAT-2, Causation)

During the Reconstruction era, federal troops were dispatched to force the South to abide by the Radical Reconstruction program, and to put down the violence of the Ku Klux Klan. By 1876 most of the 20,000 troops that had occupied the South had been withdrawn and Reconstruction was over.

(POL-3, Comparison, Contextualization)

Short-Answer

Using the excerpt, answer parts a, b, and c.

a) Briefly explain how ONE of the following documents influenced President Eisenhower's message in the passage:

- *Brown v. Board of Education*, 1954
- The Southern Manifesto, 1956
- "To Secure These Rights," 1947

b) The "Second Reconstruction" is a term often used by historians to mark the launching of the modern civil rights movement. Briefly explain how ONE of the documents listed in <u>part a</u> best represented the beginning of that era.

c) Briefly explain why ONE of the other options is not as useful in marking the beginning of the period as your choice in <u>part b</u>.

---

a) Answers will vary. The Brown decision was the catalyst for the desegregation of the schools when the court struck down the separate but equal doctrine. This was the cause of the violence in Little Rock. The Southern Manifesto was a statement signed by 101 southern Congressmen denouncing the Brown decision as "a clear abuse of judicial power." To Secure These Rights was a report to President Truman that placed the executive branch behind an expansion of civil rights. It helped awaken the country to the plight of African Americans and set a precedent for future President to be more involved in the equal rights movement.

(POL-1, Causation)

b) Answers will vary. Students might explain To Secure These Rights as the best example since it was the first real attempt by a modern President (Truman) to put civil rights on the national political agenda in a meaningful way. Others might cite the Brown decision since it overturned Plessy v. Ferguson, which was the bedrock of Jim Crow system.

(POL-1, Causation)

c) Students should recognize and explain that the "Southern Manifesto" was not in tune with the onset of the modern civil rights era. In fact, it was a pledge by southern members of Congress to block any changes in the Jim Crow system.

(POL-1, Causation, Analyzing Historical Evidence)

Lesson 34

Containment, 1945-1975

At the end of the Second World War, the tenuous wartime alliance between the United States and Soviet Union broke apart. Unable to agree over the future of Eastern Europe, the two superpowers began a non-shooting competition that columnist Walter Lippmann labeled a "Cold War."

The United States' strategy in this struggle was to contain communist expansion around the world. Largely influenced by George Kennan's article "The Sources of Soviet Conduct" and his "Long Telegram," the Truman administration viewed the Soviet Union as an ideologically driven power, bent on world conquest. Faced with this enemy, Truman decided to follow the "patient, but firm and vigilant containment" of Soviet expansion. Although labeled in different ways, and focused on varying geographical regions, this policy became the foundation of United States Cold War strategy for the next thirty years.

The chart on the next page outlines how five presidents approached containment from 1945 to 1975. As you study this information, consider the following: Were there alternatives to containment? What domestic political factors influenced containment? Was the containment policy too reactive and costly?

Directions: Analyze the chart on containment, and then answer the following questions.

1. During the late 1940s, the Truman administration implemented containment by

   (A) sending combat soldiers to repel communist attacks

   (B) using air power and atomic bombs to stop Communism

   (C) using China as a diplomatic tool to contain Communism

   (D) sending economic aid to countries threatened by Communism

OBJECTIVES

Review the introductory materials and the chart "Containment Approaches, 1945-1975" (pages 138–139 in the Student Edition). Have your students discuss the pros and cons of the policy of containment in protecting the security of the United States and preserving world peace during the Cold War.

After the class discussion on containment and reading the excerpts from "National Security Council Paper 68 (NSC–68)," which follows, students will be able to:

1. outline the basic assumption of America's containment policy;

2. trace the evolution of containment from 1945–1951;

3. evaluate the efficacy of containment in preserving world peace;

4. assess America's understanding of Soviet intentions and capabilities during the Cold War.

ADDITIONAL COMPONENTS

- **Core Chart Worksheet:** "Lesson 34 – Containment, 1945-1975" (website)

- **Primary Source Handout:** "National Security Council Paper 68 (NSC-68)" (copy p. 172 or print from website)

- **Document Source Worksheets:** "Worksheet for Document Source Analysis" (p. 246); "Worksheet for Visual Source Analysis" (p. 247)

2. President Kennedy believed that America's containment policy should

   (A) rely on many types of military force to block Communism

   (B) abandon Vietnam since it was not critical to American security

   (C) negotiate with Fidel Castro to weaken his alliance with the Soviet Union

   (D) not be concerned about Communism in the Third World

3. President Nixon differed from his predecessors with a containment policy that

   (A) used the CIA to spy on the Soviet Union

   (B) sent military and economic aid to allies in Europe

   (C) used diplomacy with China as a means of containing the Soviet Union

   (D) relied on nuclear weapons to maintain world peace

> **Enhancing Understanding**
>
> **LONG TELEGRAM** — written by George Kennan in 1946, it was a response to Soviet aggressions. He stated the USSR was expansionistic because of its history and neurotically suspicious of capitalism. He further asserted that the U.S. should block the U.S.S.R. with economic/political pressure. The idea was expanded in "The Sources of Soviet Conduct" and became the containment strategy of the Cold War.

DISCUSSION QUESTIONS

Hand out or display the document, "National Security Council Paper 68 (NSC–68)," (shown on page 172) and ask the following:

1. According to NSC–68, what was at stake in the Cold War?

2. In the view of NSC–68, what were the Soviet Union's motivations and goals in the Cold War?

3. In retrospect, do you think this view of the Soviet Union was accurate?

4. How do the authors of NSC–68 frame the conflict in the Cold War? (That is, what forces does it suggest were in combat?) Does this seem overblown?

5. Compare the ideas and the outlook expressed in NSC–68 with the Truman Doctrine. How are they similar and different? What does this tell you about the evolution of containment?

6. What actions do the authors of NSC–68 want the United States to take?

7. What impact on American society do you think the recommendations of NSC–68 had?

Answers available on the companion website.

Containment Approaches, 1945-1975

President	Strategy	Means/Implementation	Comments
Harry Truman	Containment	Used economic and military aid Sent troops where necessary Programs: • Truman Doctrine • Marshall Plan • North Atlantic Treaty Organization (NATO) Sent troops to Korea	Communist threat in Greece and Turkey required U.S. aid Sent aid to Europe 1948–1953 NATO first entangling alliance for U.S. Korean conflict—first limited war
Dwight Eisenhower	"New Look" to contain Communism	Massive retaliation Rollback of Communism Brinkmanship Used CIA to spy on, and topple communist regimes Eisenhower Doctrine in Middle East	Relied on air power, nuclear weapons Made empty pleas for freeing communist-controlled areas in Europe Take USSR to brink of nuclear war if necessary Used CIA to keep Iran, Guatemala friendly to U.S.; U-2 spy planes
John Kennedy	"Flexible response" to contain communist aggression Stand firm in Europe	Combated wars of national liberation in the Third World Used counterinsurgency forces Strong stand in Berlin Blocked Communism in Cuba, Vietnam	Berlin wall erected Used guerrilla as well as conventional forces Tried to topple Castro, but resulted in Bay of Pigs Cuban Missile Crisis brought world to brink of nuclear war Sent 16,000 troops to Vietnam
Lyndon Johnson	Containment in Asia Stand firm in Europe by maintaining NATO	Sent 500,000+ troops to Vietnam; tried for political settlement with military forces Bombed North Vietnam	Widened Vietnam War Tried to negotiate with Soviets in Europe
Richard Nixon	Vietnamization Détente Nixon Doctrine Opened China	Reduced U.S. troops in Vietnam Maintained NATO Negotiated with USSR Diplomatic agreements with China	Withdrew U.S. troops from Vietnam Kept commitments in other parts of world Used China to contain the Soviet Union Peace settlement in Vietnam

National Security Council Paper 68 (NSC–68)

The issues that face us are momentous, involving the fulfillment or destruction not [only] of this Republic but of civilization itself. They are issues which will not await our deliberations. With conscience and resolution this Government and the people it represents must now take new and fateful decisions … The fundamental design of those who control the Soviet Union and the international communist movement is to retain and solidify their absolute power, first in the Soviet Union and second in the areas now under their control. In the minds of the Soviet leaders, however, achievement of this design requires the dynamic of their authority and the ultimate elimination of any effective opposition to their authority.

The design, therefore, calls for the complete subversion or forcible destruction of the machinery of government and structure of society in the countries of the non-Soviet world and their replacement by an apparatus and structure subservient to and controlled from the Kremlin. To that end Soviet efforts are now directed toward domination of the Eurasian land mass …

The Kremlin regards the United States as the only major threat to the achievement of its fundamental design. There is a basic conflict between the idea of freedom under a government of laws, and the idea of slavery under the grim oligarchy of the Kremlin … The implacable purpose of the slave state to eliminate the challenge of freedom has placed the two great powers at opposite poles …

This broad intention embraces two subsidiary policies. One is a policy which we would probably pursue even if there were no Soviet threat. It is a policy of attempting to develop a healthy international community. The other is the policy of "containing" the Soviet system …

… The frustration of the Kremlin design requires the free world to develop a successfully functioning political and economic system and a vigorous political offensive against the Soviet Union. These, in turn, require an adequate military shield under which they can develop. It is necessary to have the military power to deter, if possible, Soviet expansion, and to defeat, if necessary, aggressive Soviet or Soviet-directed actions of a limited or total character. The potential strength of the free world is great; its ability to develop these military capabilities and its will to resist Soviet expansion will be determined by the wisdom and will with which it undertakes to meet its political and economic problems.… .

In summary, we must, by means of rapid and sustained build-up of the political, economic and military strength of the free world, and by means of an affirmative program intended to wrest the initiative from the Soviet Union, confront it with convincing evidence of the determination and ability of the free world to frustrate the Kremlin design of a world dominated by its will.… . The whole success of the proposed program hangs ultimately on recognition by this Government, the American people, and all free people, that the cold war is in fact a war in which the survival of the free world is at stake.

SOURCE: Paul Nitze, et al., National Security Adviser

Directions: Using the cartoon below and your knowledge of American history, answer the following questions.

The Minneapolis Star, 1947

Multiple-Choice

1. The idea expressed in the cartoon above most directly reflected the Cold War belief that the United States should

    (A) provide medical assistance to deal with the chaos in Western Europe

    (B) accept communist domination of Western Europe

    (C) work with communist nations to preserve the peace in Western Europe

    (D) become more active in stopping Communism in Western Europe

As a result of the economic collapse in most of Western Europe after the war, the United States believed it must reject its pre-war isolationism and become more engaged in European affairs.

(WOR-2, Causation, Contextualization)

2. The sentiments expressed in the cartoon most directly led to which of the following Cold War actions by the United States?

    (A) the extension of economic and financial aid to Europe

    (B) the creation of the World Health Organization in Europe

    (C) the use of tactical nuclear weapons in Europe

    (D) the recreation of the Grand Alliance in Europe

The United States began a series of economic and financial programs after the war to stabilize European economies and to keep the countries from turning to alternative political and economic systems such as communism.

(WOR-2, Causation)

Short-Answer

Using the cartoon, answer parts a, b, and c.

a) Briefly explain how the beliefs expressed in the cartoon impacted ONE of the following Cold War developments:

- The creation of the Truman Doctrine, 1947
- The development of the Marshall Plan, 1947
- The establishment of the North Atlantic Treaty Organization, 1949

b) Briefly explain how the point of view expressed in the cartoon caused a major departure in American foreign policy after World War II.

c) Briefly explain ONE development in foreign affairs after 1975 that challenged the point of view of the cartoon.

---

a) Answers will vary. The Truman Doctrine was the first aid program established in 1947. It provided $400 million in economic assistance to Greece and Turkey. The Marshall Plan was grander is scope as it involved $22 billion of aid to most of Western Europe from 1947-1952. The North Atlantic Treaty Organization was the first time the United States joined a military alliance. It was designed to safeguard Western Europe from a military attack by the Soviet Union.

(WOR-2, Causation)

b) Answers will vary. The United States rejected its isolationist policies of the past and became deeply involved in collective security arrangements in Europe and elsewhere in the world. The nation came to see the communist threat as worldwide.

(WOR-2, Analyzing Historical Evidence)

c) After the fall of Vietnam in 1975 to the communists, the United States became less interested in assisting other nations either militarily or economically. We turned inward to address domestic problems that affected the nation.

(WOR-2, Analyzing Historical Evidence, Contextualization)

Lesson 35

Failure of Containment—The Vietnam War

For the United States, the Vietnam War was the most divisive and controversial conflict of the post-World War II era. It divided America internally and ended with a communist victory in South Vietnam in 1975. Initiated as a minor part of United States's postwar containment policy, aid to South Vietnam eventually grew into a full-scale American military commitment that, by the late 1960s, had become the centerpiece of American foreign policy. The Vietnam struggle was a thread that wove itself through post-World War II history from Truman to Nixon. Each administration contributed in some way to the tragedy that the war became for the United States.

The chart on the next page will help place the war in perspective and provide a review of critical information. It presents an overview of the war from the Truman years through the end of the conflict in 1975. As you study the information, identify three or four critical turning points in America's descent into the tragic quagmire of the war.

Directions: Analyze the chart on the Vietnam War, and then answer the following questions.

1. Presidents Eisenhower, Kennedy, and Johnson sent aid and troops to Vietnam because they believed

    (A) that Vietnam had been a long-term ally of the United States and deserved support

    (B) that the United States Congress supported Diem's reform policies

    (C) that Ho Chi Minh would abandon Communism if confronted by American force

    (D) that the domino theory was correct and Vietnam was critical to containing Communism

OBJECTIVES
Review the introductory material and the chart "Overview of the Vietnam War" (pages 142-143 in the Student Edition). Have your students identify two or three turning points in the war where the United States might have avoided being pulled into the quagmire that the war became. Students should defend their choices.

After the class discussion on the Vietnam War and America's failure at containment, and reading "Letter from President Eisenhower to Ngo Dinh Diem," which follows, students will be able to:

1. identify the motivation that propelled American involvement in Vietnam;

2. analyze the assumptions about Communism that America held in the 1950s;

3. list the mistakes the United States made as it became involved in the Vietnam War;

4. assess the role of the Eisenhower administration on U. S. involvement in Vietnam.

ADDITIONAL COMPONENTS
*   **Core Chart Worksheet**: "Lesson 35 – Failure of Containment" (website)
*   **Primary Source Handout**: "Letter from President Eisenhower ... Diem" (copy p. 178 or print from website)

2. Lyndon Johnson escalated the war in Vietnam because he

   (A) hoped to block French colonialism in the region

   (B) feared the war's loss would hurt his domestic agenda and America's credibility in the world

   (C) believed the Soviet Union was sending thousands of troops to North Vietnam

   (D) believed U.S. assistance was the only way to maintain Ngo Dinh Diem in power

3. A critical decision made by Dwight Eisenhower in Vietnam was to

   (A) select and support Ngo Dinh Diem as an American ally

   (B) abandon the domino theory in South East Asia

   (C) send 540,000 combat soldiers to fight in Vietnam

   (D) begin bombing North Vietnam

> **Enhancing Understanding**
>
> **DOMINO THEORY** — proposed by President Eisenhower in April 1954, it theorized that a communist takeover in one country would pressure neighboring nations to yield to communism as well. The fall of one nation would set off a political/economic chain reaction. The idea was a central justification for U.S. involvement in Vietnam as a means to protect all of Southeast Asia. The theory has been largely discredited by historians.

DISCUSSION QUESTIONS

Hand out or display the document, "Letter from President Eisenhower to Ngo Dinh Diem," (shown on page 178) and ask the following:

1. What evidence is there in Eisenhower's letter that the United States might encourage Diem not to follow the Geneva agreement?

2. Why did Eisenhower offer to assist Diem's government?

3. What was Eisenhower's goal in Vietnam? Why did this goal prove unattainable for the United States?

4. What did Eisenhower require of Diem's government in return for aid?

5. Why was this requirement never met, and how was it the heart of the problem for the United States in Vietnam?

6. What assumption does Eisenhower make about the threat that Diem's government faced?

7. To what extent did the ideas outlined in Eisenhower's letter lead to America's ultimate failure in Vietnam?

Answers available on the companion website.

Overview of the Vietnam War

President	Background	Actions/Events	Significance of Action
Harry Truman	1945–1949 France tried to recolonize Indochina Ho Chi Minh and communists resisted U.S. opposed French recolonization, but feared Communism	1949–1953 U.S. began massive aid to France; by 1953 was paying 80% of French bills in Indochina Sent O.S.S./C.I.A. to work with French to combat communists	Fall of China, Korean War put pressure on Truman to hold line on Communism in Asia Supported French colonialism in order to stop Communism
Dwight Eisenhower	1954, Dien Bien Phu fell; French defeated Geneva Conference divided Indochina Proposed unification elections be held in 1956	Selected Ngo Dinh Diem as U.S. ally Supported Diem's decision not to hold elections in 1956 Gave economic aid Sent 1,000 advisers to Vietnam	Domino theory made Vietnam critical to Asian containment Support of Diem laid foundation for future commitments
John Kennedy	Worried by Diem's repression of Buddhists and Diem's refusal to reform political corruption in South Viet Cong grew in strength	JFK resisted call to send combat troops Increased advisers to 16,000 Supported domino theory Tacitly supported Diem's ouster in 1963	Postponed either escalation or withdrawal No clear future direction on war Diem's death left South in political and military chaos
Lyndon Johnson	Faced political chaos in Vietnam Believed in domino theory Feared conservative political attacks on Great Society Realized fighting war could destroy his presidency	Gulf of Tonkin Resolution 1964 gave LBJ authority to fight war Began bombing North Vietnam Sent combat troops to Vietnam; by 1968, 540,000 troops in South Vietnam Opposition to war grew	Saw war as test of U.S. will as superpower Escalated the war and gradually divided nation Tet Offensive set stage for U.S. desire to withdraw from Vietnam War destroyed Johnson's presidency and tarnished his legacy
Richard Nixon (Ford)	Pledged to "Vietnamize" war Claimed he had a secret plan to end the war	Reduced U.S. role in war Invaded Cambodia Bombed North Vietnam Peace accords in 1973 left communists in South Vietnam	Ended draft; withdrew U.S. troops Watergate removed Nixon and reduced public support for South Vietnam Communists took over South Vietnam in 1975

Letter from President Eisenhower
to Ngo Dinh Diem

DEAR MR. PRESIDENT: I have been following with great interest the course of developments in Viet-Nam, particularly since the conclusion of the conference at Geneva. The implications of the agreement concerning Viet-Nam have caused grave concern regarding the future of a country temporarily divided by an artificial military grouping, weakened by a long and exhausting war and faced with enemies without and by their subversive collaborators within.

Your recent requests for aid to assist in the formidable project of the movement of several hundred thousand loyal Vietnamese citizens away from areas which are passing under a de facto rule and political ideology which they abhor are being fulfilled. I am glad that the United States is able to assist in this humanitarian effort.

We have been exploring ways and means to permit our aid to Viet-Nam to be more effective and to make a greater contribution to the welfare and stability of the Government of Viet-Nam. I am, accordingly, instructing the American Ambassador to Viet-Nam to examine with you in your capacity, as Chief of Government, how an intelligent program of American aid given directly to your Government can serve to assist Viet-Nam in its present hour of trial, provided that your Government is prepared to give assurances as [to] the standards of performance it would be able to maintain in the event such aid were supplied.

The purpose of this offer is to assist the Government of Viet-Nam in developing and maintaining a strong, viable state, capable of resisting attempted subversion or aggression through military means. The Government of the United States expects that this aid will be met by performance on the part of the Government of Viet-Nam in undertaking needed reforms. It hopes that such aid, combined with your own continuing efforts will contribute effectively toward an independent Viet-Nam endowed with a strong government. Such a government would, I hope, be so responsive to the nationalist aspirations of its people, so enlightened in purpose and effective in performance, that it will be respected both at home and abroad and discourage any who might wish to impose a foreign ideology on your free people.

Sincerely,

Dwight Eisenhower

SOURCE: President Dwight D. Eisenhower, October 23, 1954

Directions: Using the photograph below and your knowledge of American history, answer the following questions.

Veterans for Peace rally, San Francisco, 1969

Multiple-Choice

1. The action in the photograph reflects most directly on which of the following continuities in United States history?

    (A) the debate over using public property for private protests in wartime

    (B) the debate over who should be allowed to protest in wartime

    (C) the debate over military service in wartime

    (D) the debate over the Constitutional limits of protest in wartime

> While there was a significant anti-war movement in the United States by 1967, many Americans questioned whether it was patriotic to protest an overseas war while American soldiers were in danger on the battlefield. This question was debated throughout American history from the Hartford Convention during the War of 1812 to the anti-war marches on Washington in the 1960s and 1970s.
>
> *(POL-2, NAT-3, Continuity and Change over Time)*

2. The controversy expressed in the photograph most directly contributed to which of the following developments in the 1960s and 1970s?

    (A) frustration and anger over unemployment among minorities

    (B) boycotts of goods produced by defense contractors

    (C) conflict and turmoil within the political parties

    (D) conflict over the ending of student draft deferments

> The protest movement raised debate about the justification for the war in Vietnam in both the Republican and Democratic parties. The greatest turmoil, however, was among Democrats. The conflict was so great that President Johnson decided not to seek another term as president in 1968.
>
> *(POL-2, NAT-3, Causation)*

Short-Answer

Using the photograph, answer parts a, b, and c.

a) Briefly explain how ONE of the following individuals would react to the point of view expressed in the photograph:

- A member of the Student Non-Violent Coordinating Committee
- A member of Students for a Democratic Society
- A member of a World War II veterans organization

b) Briefly explain how ONE of the remaining individuals would react to the point of view expressed in your answer to <u>part a</u>.

c) There is a long tradition of Americans protesting United States involvement in armed conflicts. Briefly explain ONE instance, besides the one depicted in the photograph, of domestic opposition to America's warfare against another nation.

---

a) Answers will vary. The Student Nonviolent Coordinating Committee, while ostensibly concerned with civil rights, supported the protest over the war. Its members believed young black men bore a disproportional burden of the fighting. The Students for a Democratic Society supported the idea of stopping the war. They were likely participants in the protest depicted in the photograph. A World War II veteran would likely believe the protest were wrongheaded and unpatriotic. He would believe that all Americans should rally round the flag.

(POL-2, Analyzing Historical Evidence)

b) Answers will vary. *(POL-2, Analyzing Historical Evidence)*

c) Answers will vary. Students might explain one of the following protests during war time:

(1) Loyalists during the American Revolution;

(2) the Hartford Convention during the War of 1812;

(3) the Abolitionists and Transcendentalists during the Mexican War;

(4) Copperheads during the Civil War;

(5) the Anti-Imperialist League members during the Spanish American War;

(6) Socialist who protested during World War I (Eugene Debs).

(POL-2, Analyzing Historical Evidence)

Lesson 36

Famous Doctrines—from Monroe to Nixon

On several occasions in American history, presidents have unilaterally asserted American intentions in various parts of the world. These presidential doctrines have been issued without the force of either treaty or international agreement. Yet, because they have coincided with American interests in the region, they have been accepted by the American people, supported by Congress, and heeded by the international community. In all cases, the doctrines were only assertions by presidents and their foreign policy advisers of America's goals and desires in specific regions of the world. Other nations have usually acquiesced to the doctrines because of America's power and position in the regions affected by the pronouncements.

The chart on the next page outlines the four major doctrines in U.S. history. As you study the information, consider under what authority America made its decrees about other parts of the world. Did the United States possess the moral right to tell the rest of the world what to do? Also, were the doctrines merely reflections of American self-interest or did they serve international peace and order?

Directions: Analyze the chart on four famous doctrines in American history, and then answer the following questions.

1. One of the objectives of the Truman and Eisenhower Doctrines was to

   (A) save China from Communism

   (B) oust Fidel Castro from Cuba

   (C) conserve American foreign aid and money

   (D) contain communist expansion

2. The principal goal of the Monroe Doctrine was to

   (A) warn Europe against colonizing in the Western Hemisphere

   (B) prevent the seizure of American shipping during European wars

   (C) stop Britain from impressing U.S. sailors

   (D) block the spread of democracy in South America

3. The Nixon Doctrine was a modification of the policy of

   (A) isolationism

   (B) watchful waiting

   (C) containment

   (D) massive retaliation

Enhancing Understanding

UNILATERALISM — a concept in international affairs that defines many presidential doctrines, it often calls for one-sided action by the U.S. with a disregard for other nations' input. This "go it alone" approach avoids alliances and has been criticized in the 20 century. It has, however, been a foundation of various doctrines in U.S. history.

Famous Doctrines in U.S. History, Monroe to Nixon

	Monroe	Truman	Eisenhower	Nixon
Year	1823	1947	1957	1969
Area of World	Western Hemisphere	Greece and Turkey	Middle East	Asia
Reason(s) for Issuance	Feared Spain would try to recolonize Latin America Feared Russian claims on west coast of U.S.	Part of containment strategy Feared Soviet pressure in Greece and Turkey	Designed to block Communism in oil-rich Middle East Feared Soviet moves in the region	Redefined U.S. containment policy, yet reassured allies that U.S. would not retreat to isolationism Responded to U.S. experience in Vietnam
Principles	No new colonies in Western Hemisphere Existing colonies left alone by U.S. U.S. would stay out of European affairs Discouraged the extension of monarchies into Americas	U.S. would provide economic aid to help nations resisting internal or external communist threat	Congress gave president power to provide economic and military aid to nations resisting communist aggression Put Soviets on notice of America's resolve	U.S. would maintain collective security and containment by economic and diplomatic means U.S. would aid allies, but not with American troops
Example of Action	U.S. intervened in Venezuela British boundary dispute in 1895	Sent $400 million to Greece, Turkey	Sent troops to Lebanon in 1958 to restore order and to support America's ally	Gradual removal of U.S. troops from Vietnam (Vietnamization)

Directions: Using the excerpt below and your knowledge of American history, answer the following questions.

> "...the American continents, by the free and independent condition which they have assumed and maintain, are henceforth not to be considered as subjects for future colonization by any European powers...In the wars of the European powers in matters relating to themselves we have never taken any part, nor does it comport with our policy so to do.
>
> ...We owe it, therefore,... to declare that we should consider any attempt on their part [Europe] to extend their system to any portion of this hemisphere as dangerous to our peace and safety. With the existing colonies or dependencies of any European power we have not interfered and shall not interfere...
>
> ...Our policy in regard to Europe...is, not to interfere in the internal concerns of any of its powers; ...It is impossible that the allied powers should extend their political system to any portion of either continent without endangering our peace and happiness..."

—President James Monroe, December, 1823

Multiple-Choice

1. Which of the following efforts most directly resulted from the ideas expressed in the passage?

   (A) United States intervention into the internal affairs of many Caribbean nations

   (B) United States refusal to make collective security agreements in the Caribbean

   (C) United States cooperation with European nations to protect Caribbean nations

   (D) United States promotion of self-determination in many Caribbean nations

2. The ideas expressed in the passage above most clearly reflect the influence of which of the following?

   (A) self-determination ideals expressed in the Declaration of Independence

   (B) isolationist sentiments expressed in the early days of the Republic

   (C) support for European expansion into the Caribbean after the War of 1812

   (D) acceptance of free trade agreements with Caribbean nations in the 1820s

The non-involvement in European affairs of the Monroe Doctrine was a reinforcement of the isolationist policy set forth by George Washington during his administration.

(NAT-3, Causation)

The Monroe Doctrine became the foundation for America's aggressive foreign policy in the late 19th c. and early 20th c. President Theodore Roosevelt, in particular, expanded the original Doctrine to include a broader justification for American intervention in Latin American affairs.

(WOR-2, Causation, Continuity and Change over Time)

Short-Answer

Using the excerpt, answer parts a, b, and c.

a) Briefly outline the main points of President Monroe's 1823 message.

b) Briefly explain how Monroe's ideas influenced ONE of the following twentieth-century policies:

- Big Stick
- Dollar Diplomacy
- Good Neighbor

c) The Monroe Doctrine was both a reflection of continuity as well as change in America's foreign policy toward Latin and South America in the 1820s. Briefly explain ONE important reason EITHER for the change or the continuity expressed in the Doctrine.

---

a) President Monroe set forth the following principles:

(1) no further colonization in Latin America by European powers;

(2) no establishment of new monarchies in Latin America;

(3) non interference with existing Latin American colonies or with European affairs.

(WOR-2, Analyzing Historical Evidence)

b) The Big Stick Policy grew directly from the Monroe Doctrine. Its aggressive approach to managing the events in Latin America was an extension of the 1823 warning. Dollar Diplomacy was a variation on the Big Stick Policy. If a country failed to respond to financial assistance (or pressure) then the United States would resort to the Big Stick. The Good Neighbor Policy of the late 1920s and 1930s attempted to soften the intervention edge of the Monroe Doctrine by trying to cooperate with Latin America through multi-lateral agreements and actions.

(WOR-2, Causation)

c) Answers will vary. The United States changed its stance toward Latin America in the 1820s because:

(1) Many Latin American countries had become independent from 1810-1823;

(2) There were rumors that the Holy Alliance was forming to help Spain recover her colonies;

(3) The United States was in the midst of a nationalistic period that the Monroe Doctrine reflected. The reason for the continuity in the Doctrine was its restatement of America's policy of the long-time tradition of non-involvement in European affairs dating back to the earliest days of the Republic.

(WOR-2, Continuity and Change over Time)

Lesson 37

Dealing with Terrorism, 1993-2015

With the collapse of the Soviet Union, the Cold War ended. A new challenge for America quickly arose abroad, however. It came from nebulous Muslim groups who harbored religious fanaticism, strong anti-American beliefs, and sought to punish non-believers in the West. In the 1990s, these groups gathered strength, but were off the political radar in the United States. All of that changed on September 11, 2001.

The attacks on the World Trade Center in New York and the Pentagon in Virginia, along with the crash of United Flight 93, killed nearly 3,000 Americans and injured over 6,000 others. 9/11 became the Pearl Harbor of the new fight. The struggle against terrorism at home and abroad was the number one foreign policy issue for Presidents Bush and Obama in the new millennium.

The chart on the following page summarizes the fight against terrorism from 1993 to 2015. As you study the chart, compare the origins, policies, and philosophies of this struggle with the one outlined in Lesson 34 on the containment of Communism. How are the two similar yet very different?

Directions: Analyze the chart on terrorism during the Clinton, Bush, and Obama presidencies, and then answer the following questions.

1. A common approach to fighting terrorism shared by Presidents Clinton and Obama was that they both

    (A) ignored the terrorist threat in the United States

    (B) relied on the military to stop terrorism

    (C) used air power as a principal action against terrorism

    (D) mainly focused on terrorism at home

2. The major setback for President Bush in his fight against terrorism was his

    (A) failure to find weapons of mass destruction in Iraq

    (B) invasion of Afghanistan that failed to rout the Taliban

    (C) refusal to use the military to fight terrorism

    (D) refusal to see the terrorist threat as a national priority

3. President Obama would mostly likely support which of the following in the fight against terrorists?

    (A) military trials for suspected terrorists

    (B) economic assistance to Middle Eastern countries

    (C) suppression of basic rights to keep America safe

    (D) a declaration of war against all forms of terrorism

Enhancing Understanding

PATRIOT ACT — passed in the wake of the 9/11 attack in 2001, it gave the F.B.I. enhanced powers to combat terrorism by expanding its ability to search homes, emails, and business records of suspected terrorists. It also expanded government surveillance powers with easier access to search warrants. Critics suggested that the law gave too much power to the government.

Dealing with Terrorism, 1993-2015

	Bill Clinton	George W. Bush	Barack Obama
Major Terrorist Events	Domestic terrorism dominated: Waco, Oklahoma City Failed attack on World Trade Center, 1993 American targets attacked overseas	September 11, 2001 attack in NYC and Washington, D.C. Rise of Osama bin Laden and *al Qaeda*	Series of "lone wolf" attacks in U.S.A. Killing of bin Laden, 2011 Rise of Islamic State (ISIS or ISIL) in Syria and Iraq Continuing conflict in Afghanistan
Philosophy in Dealing with Terrorist Threat	Dealt with both domestic and foreign terrorism as a law enforcement issue	Use of military force to root out and punish terrorists "Bush Doctrine" – either with U.S. or against it Identified the "axis of evil": Iran, Iraq, North Korea	Diplomacy rather than unilateral military force Outreach to Muslim World Not at war with Muslim religion Opposed use of ground troops
Actions Taken	Suppressed militia movements at home Arrested terrorists; tried in court Used airpower overseas to punish terrorists	Passage of Patriot Act Creation of Homeland Security Department Established the prison at Guantanamo Bay Invasion of Afghanistan and Iraq	Tried to close Guantanamo Lead "from behind" in Middle East Withdrew troops from Iraq Air strikes against terrorist leaders
Comments	Used FBI to investigate terrorism As 1990s progressed, American embassies and naval facilities overseas targeted Fighting terrorism not high on President's or nation's agenda	Routed the Taliban in Afghanistan, but bin Laden escaped Seeking weapons of mass destruction in Iraq, U.S. embarked on a disastrous invasion of the country in 2003	Backed away from military solutions to terrorism Believed must address economic and social problems in Middle East Often criticized for lack of response to terrorism

Directions: Using the excerpts below and your knowledge of American history, answer the following questions.

> "…The United States will use this moment to extend the benefits of freedom across the globe. We will actively work to bring the hope of democracy, development, free markets, and free trade to every corner of the world… In building a balance of power that favors freedom, the United States is guided by the conviction that all nations have important responsibilities. Nations that enjoy freedom must actively fight terror. Nations that depend on international stability must help prevent the spread of weapons of mass destruction…. Today, humanity holds in its hands the opportunity to further freedom's triumph over all these foes. The United States welcomes our opportunity to lead in this great mission."

—The National Security Strategy of the United States, September 2002

> "I have come to seek a new beginning between the United States and Muslims around the world; one based on mutual interest and mutual respect…. I also believe that events in Iraq have reminded America of the need to use diplomacy and build international consensus to resolve our problems whenever possible. … The fear and anger that it [9/11 attack] provoked was understandable, but in some cases, it led us to act contrary to our ideals…. I have unequivocally prohibited the use of torture by the United States, and I have ordered the prison at Guantanamo Bay closed by early next year. … So let me be clear: no system of government can or should be imposed upon one nation by any other…."

—Barack Obama, Cairo, June 2009

Multiple-Choice

1. Which earlier action by the United States promoted ideas closest to those expressed in the 2002 National Security Strategy?

   (A) Henry Cabot Lodge's attempt to amend the Treaty of Versailles in 1919

   (B) Franklin Roosevelt's "Day of Infamy" speech in 1941

   (C) James Monroe's warning to Europe in 1823

   (D) Harry Truman's decision to aid Greece and Turkey in 1947

> In both the 2002 Security Strategy excerpt and President Truman's decision to aid Greece and Turkey, the United States committed itself to leadership in meeting an international threat. For Truman it was the battle against Communist challenge after World War II, and for the Bush's administration it was the struggle against global terrorism. Also, in both cases, the United States hoped to promote its economic and political values overseas.
>
> *(WOR-2, Continuity and Change over Time)*

2. Which of the following factors contributed most directly to the sentiments expressed by President Obama in 2009?

    (A) the death of Osama bin Laden

    (B) the chaotic invasion of Iraq

    (C) the lack of international support for America's terrorist campaign

    (D) America's outrage over torture and imprisonment of terror suspects

> The Obama administration sought to reverse the aggressive military policies of the Bush years. The invasion of Iraq developed into a confusing civil conflict that costs American lives, destabilized the country, and failed to find weapons of mass destruction, which was the reason for the invasion in the first place.
>
> *(WOR-2, Causation)*

Short-Answer

Using the excerpts, answer parts a, b, and c.

a) Briefly explain ONE major difference expressed by the Bush and Obama administrations in fighting terrorism.

b) Briefly explain ONE action taken by the Bush administration, and not mentioned in the excerpt, that supported the philosophy expressed in the National Security Strategy.

c) Briefly explain ONE action taken by the Obama administration, and not mentioned in the excerpt, that supported the philosophy expressed in June 2009.

---

a) Answers will vary. Major differences expressed in the two excerpts could include:

(1) The Bush administration believed the United States should spread its values and system of government overseas. The Obama administration sought cooperation and respect from countries overseas.

(2) The Bush administration put the United States in a leadership position in the battle against terrorism, while the Obama administration favored a more collegial, consensus approach with other nations.

(3) The Bush administration viewed American values as steeped in democracy, free markets, and free trade. The Obama administration emphasized American values of leaving other countries alone, and upholding international law against torture.

(WOR-2, Comparison)

b) Answers will vary. The Bush administration led a coalition of countries that invaded Afghanistan (2001) and Iraq (2003). The administration was dedicated to nation building in Afghanistan and Iraq. It sought to change the government and the societies in each country. It also created a "coalition of the willing" to combat terrorism throughout the Middle East.

(WOR-2, Analyzing Historical Evidence)

c) Answers will vary. The Obama administration began the process of withdrawing troops from both Afghanistan and Iraq. It abandoned the use of waterboarding and other types of "enhanced interrogation" of terrorist suspects. It closed "black sites" where terror suspects were held without charges. Overall, it tried to reduce the nation's "perpetual war footing" against terrorism.

(WOR-2, Analyzing Historical Evidence)

Acknowledgments

Sherpa Learning, LLC. has made every effort to obtain permission for the reprinting of all selections contained herein. If any author or publisher is not acknowledged herein, please contact the publisher for proper acknowledgment in all future editions or reprintings of this title.

Document Credits: p. 5, from *Sources in American History*, Orlando: Harcourt Brace Jovanovich, 1986; p. 12, James G. Randall, *The Civil War and Reconstruction*, Boston: D.C. Heath, 1937; p. 12, W.E.B. DuBois, *Black Reconstruction*, New York: S.A. Russell Company, 1935; pp., 18, 19, 24, 25, 34, from *Viewpoints USA*, Bernard Feder, New York: American Book Company, 1967; p. 39, from Charles G. Finney, *Lectures on Revivals of Religion*, New York: Fleming H. Revell, 1868; pp. 45, 46, 54, 63, 72, 83, 93, 107, Feder; p. 112, Lydia Maria Child, "Colonization Society, and Anti-Slavery Society," from *An Appeal in Favor of That Class of Americans Called Africans*, Boston: Allen & Ticknor, 1833; pp. 113, 125, 135, 139, 153, Feder; pp. 158, 159, Senator Gerald P. Nye, "Is Neutrality Possible for America?" in *Tomorrow in the Making*, New York: Whittlesey House, 1939; pp. 167, 178, 183, Feder

Image Credits: p. 6, data from *The Atlantic Slave Trade: A Census*, by Philip D. Curtin, Univ. of Wisconsin Press, 1972; p. 40, "Camp Meeting at Eastham, Mass," Boston Athenæum, Boston, MA; p. 68, "The Grange Awakening the Sleepers," The Granger Collection, New York City; p. 88, "Hands Off!" from Puck Magazine, 1906; p. 117, "A Squelcher for Women's Suffrage," from Puck Magazine, 1894; p. 121, cartoon by CK Berryman from The Evening Star, 1919, Library of Congress; p. 163, cartoon by CK Berryman from The Washington Star, 1935; p. 173, cartoon by Roy Justus from the Minneapolis Star, 1947; p. 179, photograph by Paul Richards, 1969, Harvey Richards Media Archive; p. 226, The introduction of African slavery into the American colonies at Jamestown, Virginia, August, 1619, wood engraving, late 19th century, The Granger Collection, New York City; p. 231, cartoon of the Ninth National Women's Rights Convention, May 12, 1859, *Harper's Weekly*, June 11, 1859; p. 237, "A Giant Straddle," by William Allen Rogers, *Harper's Weekly*, March 28, 1896

Cover Image: Map Quilt (detail); Artist unidentified; Possibly Virginia, 1886; Silk and cotton with silk embroidery; 78 3/4 x 82 1/4"; Collection American Folk Art Museum, New York; Gift of Dr. and Mrs. C. David McLaughlin; 1987.1.1; Photo by Schecter Lee, New York

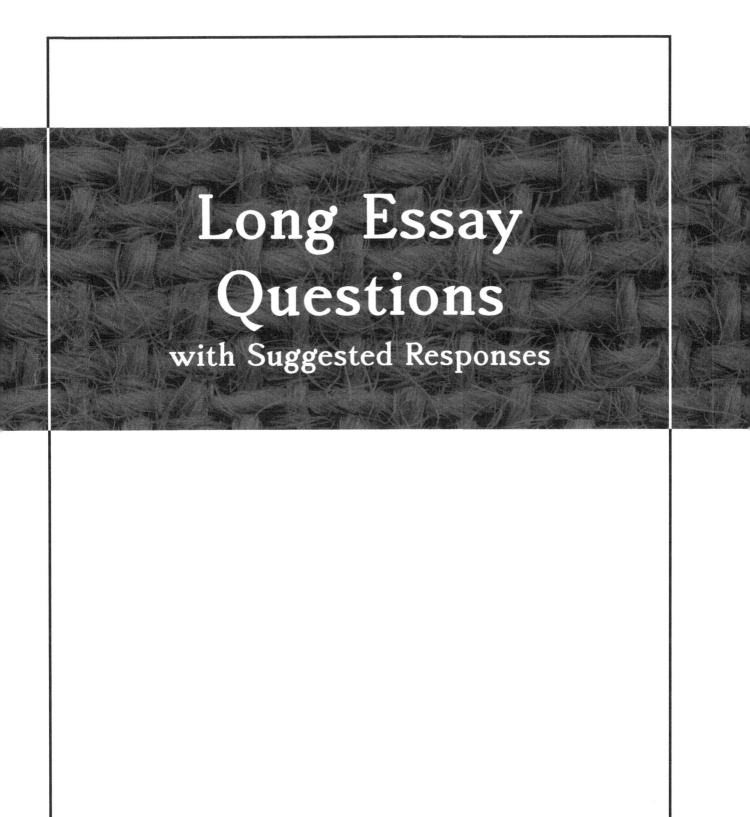

Long Essay Questions

with Suggested Responses

The 19 Long Essay Questions that follow are available on the Teacher Companion Website so that you can easily print and copy for your students, or copy/paste into your own assessment activities. Please note that the suggested responses begin on page 195.

LEQ 1

Evaluate the extent to which political and religious dissent shaped colonial development in New England and the Chesapeake regions from 1619–1750.

(NAT-1, POL-1; Continuity/Change, Causation; Lessons 2, 3)

LEQ 2

"America's greatest presidents transformed and strengthened the relationship between the government and the people."

Evaluate this statement by comparing and contrasting the policies of TWO United States presidents with regards to their views on the role of government in society.

(POL-1, POL-3; Comparison; Lessons 4, 17, 30, 32)

LEQ 3

Historians often consider Thomas Jefferson a liberal and Alexander Hamilton a conservative leader in the 1790s. To what extent is this assessment valid about the two men's political philosophy and actions in the era?

(POL-1; Comparison; Lessons 8, 9, 11)

LEQ 4

Evaluate the extent to which political compromises maintained continuity as well as promoted change in American politics from 1787–1850.

(POL-1; Continuity/Change; Lesson 14)

LEQ 5

Evaluate the extent to which the struggle between liberals and conservatives from 1940 to 1980 was part of the presidential legacy of Franklin Roosevelt.

(POL-3; Continuity/Change, Causation; Lessons 9, 10, 30, 32)

LEQ 6

Evaluate the extent to which the platforms and beliefs of political parties promoted the coming of the Civil War from 1840–1860.

(POL-1; Continuity/Change, Causation; Lessons 11, 12)

LEQ 7

Evaluate the extent to which the Federalist Party contributed to the development of the American economic system from 1790–1825.

(POL-3; Continuity/Change, Causation; Lessons 8, 11, 15)

LEQ 8

Evaluate the extent to which the ideas of the Second Great Awakening and the development of utopian societies in the 1830s and 1840s maintained continuity as well as promoted changes in Americans' views of themselves and their society.

(POL-2; Continuity/Change; Lessons 6, 20)

LEQ 9

To what extent did nineteenth-century armed conflicts promote new directions in American foreign policy from 1812-1898?

(WOR-2; Causation; Lessons 13, 17, 18)

LEQ 10

Compare and contrast the successes and failures of the abolitionist and women's movements in expanding democracy in the 19th century.

(POL-2; Comparison; Lessons 12, 21, 22)

LEQ 11

Evaluate the extent to which Congress and the Supreme Court helped the South win the peace after the Civil War. Consider the years 1868–1900.

(POL-3, NAT-2; Causation; Lessons 24, 25)

LEQ 12

To what extent did the debate over the appropriate role of the federal government in the American economy change the lives of American workers from 1880–1910?

(POL-3; Continuity/Change; Lessons 26, 27, 29)

LEQ 13

Compare and contrast the role of TWO civil rights leaders in combating the Jim Crow system from 1890–1925.

(POL-2; Comparison; Lesson 28)

LEQ 14

Evaluate the extent to which political and economic reform movements promoted social justice in the United States from 1900–1940. Consider at least TWO movements.

(POL-2; Continuity/Change, Causation; Lesson 10, 30, 32)

LEQ 15

Evaluate the extent to which American foreign policy from 1920–1941 maintained continuity as well as promoted change in America's view of itself in world affairs.

(WOR-2; Continuity/Change; Lessons 23, 31)

LEQ 16

To what extent did private individuals rather than political figures promote civil rights after World War II? Cite at least two individuals from 1945–1960 to justify your answer.

(POL-2; Causation; Lesson 28, 33)

LEQ 17

Compare and contrast the successes and failures of containment of TWO Cold War presidents from 1945–1974.

(WOR-2; Comparison; Lessons 34, 35, 36)

LEQ 18

Compare and contrast the foreign policies of President George H.W. Bush with George W. Bush.

(WOR-2; Comparison; Lessons 5, 37)

LEQ 19

Evaluate the extent to which the presidency of Bill Clinton changed the political and economic policies of the Democratic Party in the 1990s. Analyze what changed and what stayed the same in this time period.

(POL-2; Continuity/Change, Causation; Lessons 5, 37)

Long Essay Questions with Suggested Responses

LEQ 1

Evaluate the extent to which political and religious dissent shaped colonial development in New England and the Chesapeake regions from 1619-1750.

(NAT-1, POL-1; Continuity/Change, Causation; Lessons 2, 3)

Students can use a variety facts and ideas to answer this prompt. In addition to the information in Lessons 2 and 3, your students could include some of the following ideas:

OVERALL THEMES

1. In New England the intolerance and inflexible religious attitudes of the Puritans, especially in the early years, caused clashes and encouraged splinter religious groups to form.

2. In the Chesapeake region, Bacon's Rebellion had a direct impact on the labor system. Virginia became increasingly alarmed about the indentured servant system after the revolt, and began to rely more heavily on slavery.

3. The Great Awakening of the 1730s and 1740s reflected an attempt to promote Calvinist religious views, challenge established church authority, and increase religious freedom.

POSSIBLE INFORMATION

Puritan Religious Beliefs

- wanted to create a "city upon a hill"
- believed they had "the true religion and holy ordinance of Almighty God"
- believed "if God be with us, who can be against us"
- only one true way to God
- people better whipped than damned
- strong enforcement of religious procedures

Roger Williams

- called for separation of Church and State
- fairer treatment of Native Americans
- public denunciation of the Church of England
- opposed requiring non-church members to go to church
- banished from Massachusetts Bay in 1635
- founder of Rhode Island with very liberal religious views

Anne Hutchinson

- challenged Puritans in Massachusetts Bay
- spoke out against idea that salvation could be achieved through good works
- wanted to discuss and interpret sermons
- publicly criticized ministers
- claimed God had spoken directly to her
- "troubled the peace of the commonwealth"
- did not know "her place" as a woman
- acted more like "husband than a wife"
- banished in 1638
- traveled from place to place after banishment
- killed by Indians in 1643

Thomas Hooker

- believed Massachusetts Bay was too narrow in its teachings
- said godly people could be admitted to church membership even if they had not had conversion experience

- people should be able to elect officials and then guide their decisions
- left Massachusetts in 1635
- settled in Hartford, Connecticut
- 1639 helped to write Fundamental Orders of Connecticut
- Orders allowed all freemen, whether church members or not, to vote

Mary Dyer and the Quakers

- Puritans made it clear Quakers were not welcome in colony
- Quakers believed in many roads to God
- all people had light of God within them
- Quakers seen as dangerous, seditious by Puritans
- during mid-1650s Puritans punished Quakers who tried to practice religion
- 1658 passed law that prescribed death to Quakers for worshipping in Massachusetts
- 1660 executed Mary Dyer for her religious activities
- this persecution began to undermine the Crown's confidence that Massachusetts should keep its charter; lost it in 1690s

Great Awakening

- a religious revival in 1730s and 1740s
- led by George Whitefield and Jonathan Edwards
- an attempt to combat the growing secularism of the colonies

- Calvinist in its message
- return to Calvinist views of:
  - predestination
  - original sin
  - a harsh and angry God
- message summarized by Edwards' "Sinners in the Hands of an Angry God"
- promoted religious pluralism

Political Dissent: Bacon's Rebellion

- 1676
- caused by frontier clashes with Native Americans
- Bacon and his followers wanted to attack Native Americans to gain their land
- Governor William Berkeley said no
- Bacon and his men marched against Jamestown
- briefly ousted Berkeley
- rebellion collapsed when Bacon died
- Bacon's forces included many black/white former indentured servants
- rebellion had several levels of significance:
  - made Virginia question the indentured servant system
  - colony turned increasingly to permanent African slavery to solve labor problems
  - some historians view it as first attack on insensitive, autocratic British rule, as a prelude to the American Revolution

LEQ 2

"America's greatest presidents transformed and strengthened the relationship between the government and the people."

Evaluate this statement by comparing and contrasting the policies of TWO United States presidents with regards to their views on the role of government in society.

(POL-1, POL-3; Comparison; Lessons 4, 17, 30, 32)

Students could select among several presidents to answer this prompt. In addition to the information in Lessons 4, 17, 30, 32, your students might select the three presidents most likely to be rated as great: Thomas Jefferson, Abraham Lincoln, and Franklin Roosevelt. Your students could also include some of the following:

OVERALL THEMES

1. Each of these men enhanced the powers of the presidency to assist the people. In all cases, they expanded the executive power in government at the expense of the Congress through bold action and superb political skills.

2. All three men were excellent politicians, that is, manipulators of men and controllers of Congress. Also, they were able to communicate their vision of America's future to the people.

3. All reversed the direction of the country when they took power. They altered the policies of their discredited predecessor in the White House.

4. All were strong partisans who transformed their parties into dominant political forces for years to come.

5. Each man viewed the role of government in a different way. Jefferson sought to limit the role of government, while both Abraham Lincoln and Franklin Roosevelt, for different reasons, expanded it.

POSSIBLE INFORMATION

Thomas Jefferson

- reversed the elitist, centralizing political attitudes of the Federalists, especially John Adams' last two years in power (Sedition Act, Alien Acts, and "midnight judges")

- presided over the first transfer of power between the two political factions

- set the nation on a path of decentralization that marked America as unique in the era of monarchies

- his policies:
  - created a government favorable to independent yeoman farmers
  - reduced the concentration of power in the central government
  - abolished excise taxes on such items as whiskey
  - pardoned the victims of the Sedition Act
  - repealed the Judiciary Act of 1801
  - doubled the size of the United States through the Louisiana Purchase 1803
  - cut national debt from $83 million to $45 million

- his election in 1800 placed the government on a frugal, more egalitarian path

- began the "Virginia Dynasty" (1801–1825) of Democratic-Republican presidents, all from Virginia

- followed by James Madison and James Monroe

Abraham Lincoln

- reversed James Buchanan's weak response to secession

- restored the Union—his greatest achievement

- ended slavery—slowly and reluctantly—but he did it

- by saving the Union and ending slavery he reaffirmed and strengthened the ideals of the Declaration of Independence and Constitution

- kept foreign nations out of the Civil War and isolated the South diplomatically

- persuaded Congress to:
  - pass the Homestead Act of 1862, which opened the west to settlement by giving away land
  - begin to build the transcontinental railroad (completed 1869)
  - create a national banking system with the National Banking Acts of 1863–1864

- was the first of four consecutive Republican presidents elected from 1860–1880

Franklin Roosevelt

- energized the country and restored hope after economy reached its nadir during the last year of the Hoover presidency

- expanded the federal government's efforts to combat the Great Depression

- communicated to the people that the government had not forgotten them

- doubled the amount of money spent by Hoover

- administered direct relief to the people who could not work

- expanded the federal government's role in the health, education, and welfare of the American people

- extended government regulation of the banking industry and stock market

- created the Social Security system to help the elderly

- restored the nation's faith in democracy and capitalism and increased its expectation for government action in economic hard times

- alleviated the suffering of millions of Americans

- led the nation through World War II

- established the Democrats as the dominant political party for the next 35 years

LEQ 3

Historians often consider Thomas Jefferson a liberal and Alexander Hamilton a conservative leader in the 1790s. To what extent is this assessment valid about the two men's political philosophy and actions in the era?

(POL-1; Comparison; Lessons 8, 9, 11)

Students can use many facts and ideas to answer this prompt. In addition to the information in Lessons 8, 9, and 11, your students could include some of the following ideas:

OVERALL THEMES

1. Hamilton represented the conservative position of the 1790s. He believed that America would thrive under a strong central government with a concentration of financial and military power at the national level.

2. Since monarchies ruled Europe at this time,

Hamilton's philosophy represented the status quo (conservative) thinking of the 1790s.

3. Throughout Europe during the 1790s, strong central governments ruled with little or no input from the governed.

4. Jefferson's ideas represented a challenge to this thinking, thus he was a liberal.

5. Jefferson sought a political system that promoted decentralization of power, states' rights, and an active, vocal role for the "people" (i.e., yeoman farmers).

POSSIBLE INFORMATION

Hamilton's Conservative Position:

- national government must have power

- national government and mercantile interests must cooperate for economic progress

- Congress and the president should expand their authority through the "necessary and proper clause" (elastic clause)

- nation would benefit from the creation/ existence of a National Bank

- national debt should be funded at par value, but not paid off too quickly

- tariffs and other taxes must remain high to pay down the debt

- the "common people" should allow the elites to govern the nation

- opposition such as the Whiskey Rebellion should be repressed decisively and forcefully

- good commercial and political relations with Great Britain should be the sine qua non of America's foreign policy

Jefferson's Liberal Position:

- states should maintain as much power as possible

- agrarian interests should be promoted and protected by the government

- the Constitution must be strictly interpreted; the elastic clause should not be stretched

- the national debt is harmful and should be eliminated as quickly as possible

- taxes such as the one on whiskey are oppressive and impose too much control by the central government over people's lives

- government should heed the people's protests

- government should encourage average people to participate in its decision-making

- America should align itself with the antimonarchical philosophy sweeping France during the French Revolution

LEQ 4

Evaluate the extent to which political compromises maintained continuity as well as promoted change in American politics from 1787–1850.

(POL-1; Continuity/Change; Lesson 14)

Students can use a variety of facts and ideas to answer this prompt. In addition to the information in Lesson 14, your students could include some of the following ideas:

OVERALL THEMES

1. The question of representation in Congress dominated the Constitutional Convention. The delegates expected Congress to be the most important branch of government. With state sovereignty in the forefront of the delegates' minds, representation in Congress was the number-one issue to be resolved.

2. As slavery became more important economically in the South, its preservation and extension became a growing controversy between the two sections.

3. On two occasions in the 1820s and 1850s, the nation reached an impasse over the extension of slavery into the territories.

4. Both compromises postponed a national crisis over the issue of slavery.

POSSIBLE INFORMATION

The Great Compromise

- sometimes called the Connecticut Compromise
- reached July 12, 1787
- a blend of the Virginia and New Jersey Plans
- both plans called for strengthening the powers of Congress
- Virginia Plan based congressional representation on population:
  - two houses of Congress
  - lower house determined by state population
  - upper house elected by lower house
- New Jersey Plan called for one house of Congress with each state having one vote gave Congress more taxing power and regulatory authority retained unicameral aspect of legislature as it had existed under Articles of Confederation
- Compromise:
  - two houses of Congress
  - lower house based on population
  - upper house with equal representation from each state
  - all money bills start in lower house (House of Representatives)
- Compromise broke deadlock between small and large states and allowed the convention to continue its work in creating the Constitution

The Missouri Compromise

- also called Compromise of 1820
- Missouri applied for statehood in 1819 as slave state
- there was a balance of 11 free and 11 slave states
- since the Articles of Confederation, states had entered union in pairs—one free, one slave
- South believed Missouri, as part of Louisiana Territory, should maintain its status as slave territory

- February 1819, James Tallmadge from New York introduced a resolution that slavery be gradually ended in Missouri after it became a state
- his proposal roiled Congress
- Speaker of the House Henry Clay proposed a compromise:
  - Missouri would become a slave state;
  - Maine would become a free state;
  - a line dividing the Louisiana Territory into a northern free area; and
  - a southern slave area would be established (at 36° and 30′ North latitude)
- while the South opposed dividing the Louisiana Territory, the Compromise narrowly passed
- Clay's Compromise partially restored sectional harmony; the agreement held until 1854 when the Kansas-Nebraska Act opened territory north of the 36° 30′ line to slavery

Compromise of 1850

- December 1849, California sought admission to Union as a free state
- South opposed the move because it would disrupt balance in Senate (15 free and 15 slave)
- an aging Henry Clay tried one last compromise:
  - California enters as a free state
  - formation of territorial government in Mexican Cession with status of slavery to be determined by popular sovereignty
  - abolition of slave trade in District of Columbia, but retention of slavery there
  - stronger Fugitive Slave Law
- Clay failed to get the package passed, and he withdrew
- Stephen Douglas stepped forward and, after the death of John C. Calhoun and President Zachary Taylor (both of whom opposed the measure), shepherded the compromise through Congress
- provided only short-term solutions to a growing problem over slavery in territories

- much less effective than Missouri Compromise
- did suppress movement for secession among southerners at the Nashville Convention in 1850
- delayed Civil War for 11 years, giving North time to expand advantage over South in population and industrialization

LEQ 5

Evaluate the extent to which the struggle between liberals and conservatives from 1940 to 1980 was part of the presidential legacy of Franklin Roosevelt.

(POL-3; Continuity/Change,Causation; Lessons 9, 10, 30, 32)

Students can use many facts and ideas to answer this prompt. In addition to the information in Lessons 9, 10, 30, and 32, your students could include some of the following ideas:

OVERALL THEMES

1. From 1940–1980 the major division between liberal and conservatives was the question of the role of the federal government in domestic affairs. The New Deal was the catalyst for this debate, with its unprecedented expansion of government power in the 1930s.

2. For liberals who supported government activism, the expansion of the New Deal was a measure of America's commitment to the "forgotten man" (average people) of America.

3. For conservatives, who questioned the consequences of government activism on American political and economic institutions, the issue was which parts of the New Deal to accept, which programs to limit, and which programs to eliminate.

4. Although the New Deal had no civil rights program in the 1930s, after 1954 the issue of minority rights also divided conservatives and liberals, with conservatives resisting government intervention on behalf of minorities and liberals promoting government assistance in achieving equality.

POSSIBLE INFORMATION

Harry Truman

- his Fair Deal was clearly an attempt to continue the New Deal agenda
- he increased the minimum wage
- he signed the National Housing Act, providing 800,000 low-cost housing units
- he expanded Social Security benefits
- he signed G.I. Bill of Rights
- he signed Full Employment Act, committing government to managing economy
- he proposed:
  - national health insurance
  - a civil rights program that included a national anti-lynching law
- he signed Executive Order 9981, which desegregated the military

Dwight Eisenhower

- called his program "Modern Republicanism"
- hoped to reverse the direction of New Deal, but accepted much of it

- called for a "pay as you go" approach to social spending—balance the budget
- he removed wage and price controls
- lowered price supports for farm products
- kept Social Security (actually expanded it)
- increased minimum wage
- created Department of Health, Education, and Welfare
- Highway Act (1956) $31 billion for interstate highway system
- National Defense Education Act (1958)
- little support for civil rights

John Kennedy

- proposed expansion of the New Deal, but little actually accomplished
- proposed:
  - national health insurance (Medicare)
  - extension of unemployment benefits
  - Civil Rights Act (1963)
- accomplished:
  - increase of minimum wage
  - broadening of Social Security
  - Area Redevelopment Act—federal aid for poor regions
  - Manpower Development and Training Act—$435 million to train workers
  - establishment of a Women's Bureau in Labor Department and enactment of Equal Pay Act
- more style than substance domestically yet dedicated to an active role for government

Lyndon Johnson

- the president most committed to completing the New Deal
- he had most ambitious and successful domestic program of the twentieth century
- with his "War on Poverty" he changed the face of the welfare state
- he accomplished:
  - a tax cut
  - Food Stamp program

  - Civil Rights Act of 1964 and Voting Rights Act of 1965
  - Medicare and Medicaid
  - Economic Opportunity Act (Head Start, Job Corps)
  - Office of Economic Opportunity
  - more than sixty education bills
- percentage of Americans in poverty fell from 20 percent in 1963 to 13 percent in 1968
- his administration represented the high point of twentieth-century liberalism

Richard Nixon

- a moderate Republican in the mold of Eisenhower
- accomplished:
  - increased federal funding for low-cost housing
  - increased spending on mandated social programs
  - Environmental Protection Act
  - Occupational Safety and Health Administration
  - Consumer Product Safety Act
  - Clean Water Act
  - National Air Quality Standards Act
- proposed:
  - a major overhaul of welfare system— Family Assistance Plan
- accepted that big government was here to stay
- on civil rights:
  - first two years showed moderate support for civil rights by expanding
  - minority hiring and contracting programs
  - by 1971, had turned against civil rights by opposing busing, attempting to put conservatives on Supreme Court

Jimmy Carter

- inflation and economic stagnation undermined Carter's support for the New Deal ideals

- a growing generational split emerged during the Carter years as younger Democrats began to wonder whether massive government programs were impeding economic development
- many Democrats opposed higher taxes and expanded social programs

- Carter: "more [government] is not necessarily better"
- maintained rather than expanded the core of the New Deal/Fair Deal/Great Society
- he tended to admire Fair Deal Democrats more than the New Dealers

LEQ 6

Evaluate the extent to which the platforms and beliefs of political parties promoted the coming of the Civil War from 1840–1860.

(POL-1; Continuity/Change, Causation; Lessons 11, 12)

Students can use a variety of facts and ideas to answer this prompt. In addition to the information in Lessons 11 and 12, your students could include some of the following ideas:

OVERALL THEMES

1. All three parties were caught in the dispute over slavery in the late 1840s and 1850s.

2. Each of the parties addressed the question of where slavery should be allowed to expand and whether it should be tolerated in the southern states.

3. All three parties were buffeted by the issue.

4. None of the parties called for the immediate abolition of slavery, but they all played a role in dividing the nation.

5. The Republican Party eventually became the political home for most members of the other two parties.

POSSIBLE INFORMATION

Liberty/Free Soil Party

- Liberty Party formed in 1840; in 1848 it was "translated" into the Free Soil Party
- 1840, 1844 Liberty Party ran James Birney for president

- 1844 Birney drew votes from Clay, giving victory to Polk
- 1848 Free Soil Party nominated Martin Van Buren and 1852 John P. Hale
- by 1854 Free Soil Party had been absorbed into the Republican Party
- platform:
  - abolish slavery wherever constitutionally possible
  - end slavery in Washington D.C.
  - 1844 opposed annexation of Texas
- endorsed:
  - cheap postage
  - internal improvements
  - limiting government spending
  - free homesteads
  - a tariff for revenue only
- motto: "free soil, free speech, free labor and free men"
- in 1852 Hale denounced the Compromise of 1850, called for the repeal of the Fugitive Slave Law
- impact: weakened the Whig Party, inserted slavery into the political arena, paved way for Republican Party of 1850s

The American Party

- nicknamed "Know Nothings"
- antiforeign and anti-Catholic
- very strong in early 1850s—many thought they could replace the Whigs as a second major party
- tried to link Catholics to slavery; claimed Catholics were trying to spread slavery
- hoped to avoid the divisive issue of slavery by focusing on immigrant threat
- many saw them as the party that might preserve the nation's purity and the Union
- captured control of several state legislatures, dozens of seats in Congress
- by 1855, the party had split over slavery
- platform:
  - extend naturalization period from five to twenty-one years
  - literacy test to vote
  - tax on immigrants
  - supported temperance laws
  - opposed Fugitive Slave Law
  - opposed Kansas-Nebraska Act
  - condemned "Rum, Romanism and Slavery"
  - anti-Catholic, especially opposed to separate parochial schools

- impact: by emphasizing an issue other than slavery, the party hoped to draw support, but it became enmeshed in the controversy just like other political groups

The Republican Party

- formed in response to the passage of the Kansas-Nebraska Act 1854
- clearly a sectional party (North and West)
- not abolitionists—made clear the party favored the interests of the white man
- dedicated to fighting "the slave power conspiracy" of the South
- platform:
  - motto: "free soil, free labor, and free men"
  - opposed the spread of slavery into the territories
  - no interference with slavery in the southern states
  - supported high protective tariff
  - favored government program of internal improvements—especially railroads
  - supported a homestead act
- impact: although not directly attacking slavery, the Republican Party was seen by the South as a threat to the institution and the southern way of life; its founding set stage for a major political confrontation
- 1860 election of Republican Abraham Lincoln led several southern states to secede from the Union

LEQ 7

Evaluate the extent to which the Federalist Party contributed to the development of the American economic system from 1790–1825.

(POL-3; Continuity/Change, Causation; Lessons 8, 11, 15)

Students can use a variety of facts and ideas to answer this prompt. In addition to the information in Lessons 8, 11, and 15, your students could include some of the following ideas:

OVERALL THEMES

1. The Federalist Party's economic policy favored and supported the mercantile, commercial interests in the United States during the nation's formative period.

2. The Federalists established the financial foundation of the country with the creation of the National Bank and the tax system.

3. The Federalists sought to strengthen America's economic self-sufficiency by enhancing manufacturing and commerce.

4. The Federalists hoped to see the nation linked more closely by roads and canals that would expand markets and make raw materials more accessible to businesses.

POSSIBLE INFORMATION

Hamilton's Financial Plan

- creation of a National Bank

- assumption of states' debt

- payment of debt at par value

- excise tax on whiskey, other products

- Report on Manufactures (1791) called for tariff designed to raise revenue and to protect American manufacturing interests

Republicans' Adoption of Federalists' Ideas

- after War of 1812, Henry Clay proposed "American System," an updated version of the Federalist economic blueprint; it included:

  ◦ a second national bank (established 1816)

  ◦ a protective tariff (Tariff of 1816)

  ◦ increased spending on internal improvements (roads and canals); however, Bonus Bill, providing federal funding for these, was vetoed by Madison

Marshall's Court and the Federalist Tradition

- John Marshall served as Chief Justice of Supreme Court, 1801–1835

- Led Court to uphold Federalist economic principles

- *McCulloch v. Maryland* 1819—decided National Bank was constitutional

- Dartmouth College Case 1819—strengthened sanctity of contracts, encouraging commerce

- *Gibbons v. Ogden* 1824—struck down monopolies, affirmed federal power over interstate commerce

LEQ 8

Evaluate the extent to which the ideas of the Second Great Awakening and the development of utopian societies in the 1830s and 1840s maintained continuity as well as promoted changes in Americans' views of themselves and their society.

(POL-2; Continuity/Change; Lessons 6, 20)

Students can use a variety of facts and ideas to answer this prompt. In addition to the information in Lessons 6 and 20, your students could include some of the following ideas:

OVERALL THEMES

The changing nature of identity might include Americans:

1. continued belief in democracy and capitalism

2. continued belief in the righteousness of the people

3. continued belief in progress and improvement for society

4. supporting the expansion of democratic ideals

5. questioning (women and African Americans) their inferiority in the American political and social system

6. worrying about their personal salvation and the direction of society

7. replacing secular materialism with a commitment to helping others

8. taking greater responsibility for their lives and personal salvation

9. considering themselves "free moral agents"

POSSIBLE INFORMATION

The Second Great Awakening contributed to these changes with:

- belief in personal and societal perfection
- belief that salvation could be earned by good works
- belief in personal effort and free will
- rejection of the materialism of the Market Revolution
- accepting equality for all people before God
- praising human abilities and activities

- belief in universal salvation for those who sought it
- trying to establish a "Benevolent Empire" on earth

Utopian societies contributed to a changing identity by:

- replacing competitive individualism with a spiritual unity and group cooperation
- belief in perfectionism and millennialism
- accepting unusual sexual arrangement between members (in some cases)
- promoting great equality and authority for women
- attempting to abolish social divisions and injustices
- countering perceived social degradation that accompanied the Market Revolution
- rejecting capitalism and accepting a socialistic economic order
- trying to create a new moral world

LEQ 9

To what extent did nineteenth-century armed conflicts promote new directions in American foreign policy from 1812-1898?

(WOR-2; Causation; Lessons 13, 17, 18)

Students can use a variety of facts and ideas to answer this prompt. In addition to the information in lessons 13, 17, and 18, your students could include some of the following ideas:

OVERALL THEMES

1. Attempts by the United States to settle disputes through warfare with other countries produced mixed results in the nineteenth century.

2. In all three conflicts the United States sought territory owned by other countries.

3. Only in the Mexican-American War did the United States achieve clear ownership and control over the coveted land (Mexican Cession and disputed parts of Texas).

4. The War of 1812 brought on new economic and political relationships with Great Britain and Europe.

5. The Mexican War, with the addition of the Mexican Cession, divided the nation further and made the Civil War more likely.

6. The Spanish-American War made the United States a world, colonial power.

POSSIBLE INFORMATION

War of 1812

- causes:
  - United States wanted to defend its honor on seas
  - hoped to maintain neutrality in war between England and France
  - United States wanted to stop British maritime interference
  - humiliated by impressments of American sailors
  - United States hoped to acquire land in Canada and Florida
  - United States angry that British were inciting Native Americans to attack in Ohio and Indiana
- results:
  - war ended with the restoration of the status quo ante
  - no territorial changes
  - British stopped seizure of ships and impressment, but not because of American military pressure
  - British agreed to abandon western forts and stop inciting Indians
  - war sparked a feeling of nationalism because we stood up against England
- political/diplomatic impact:
  - mixed diplomatic record for the United States
  - America did not gain land it wanted
  - showed America's willingness to defend honor and protect rights on the seas
  - yet United States went to war prematurely in 1812; problems could have been solved at bargaining table

Mexican-American War

- causes:
  - America annexed Texas in March 1845
  - Mexico claimed it owned Texas; did not recognize the Treaty of Velasco (1836)
  - United States tried to negotiate, buy land, settle boundary at Rio Grande

- President Polk sent John Slidell to settle issues, but reached no diplomatic agreement
- border clash between the United States and Mexico in April 1846; in May, Polk asked for declaration of war
- results:
  - Treaty of Guadalupe Hidalgo signed February 2, 1848
    - » Mexico recognized Texas independence, surrendered the Mexican Cession, and agreed to Rio Grande as Texas border
    - » United States paid Mexico $15 million for land (529,000 square miles, 48 cents per acre)
    - » Mexican Cession included California, New Mexico, Utah, and many other western states
    - » America assumed financial claims its new citizens still had against Mexico
- political/diplomatic impact:
  - Mexican Cession became a "dose of poison" for the United States because it raised divisive slavery issue
  - Wilmot Proviso, calling for ban on slavery in newly acquired territories, led to increasingly bitter arguments
  - set off sectional dispute that helped divide nation and brought on Civil War
  - soured relations with Mexico for decades to come

Spanish-American War

- causes:
  - uprising among Cubans against Spanish rule in 1895 was principal cause
  - United States businesses had $50 million invested in Cuban sugar industry
  - U.S. had $100 million in trade with Cuba
  - part of a general imperialistic mood of the 1890s
- other causes:
  - yellow press—William Randolph Hearst's and Joseph Pulitzer's sensational news stories about Spanish atrocities

- DeLôme letter criticizing McKinley
- destruction of battleship Maine
- United States gave Spain an ultimatum:
  - » immediate armistice with rebels
  - » stop brutal treatment and killing of Cubans
  - » release prisoners
  - » allow United States to mediate a resolution to rebellion
- Spain did not heed ultimatum; United States declared war April 25, 1898
- results:
  - Cuba freed
  - Teller Amendment (1898) pledged the United States would not acquire Cuba

- Platt Amendment (1901) said Cuba must clear all treaties with United States
- United States acquired Puerto Rico, Guam, and the Philippine Islands
- United States paid Spain $20 million
- political/diplomatic impact:
  - war did resolve the Cuban conflict, but Cuba eluded clear American acquisition
  - United States joined the march for empire
  - United States became a colonial, imperialist power
  - United States became very aggressive in Caribbean

LEQ 10

Compare and contrast the successes and failures of the abolitionist and women's movements in expanding democracy in the 19th century.

(POL-2; Comparison; Lessons 12, 21, 22)

Students can use a variety of facts and ideas to answer this prompt. In addition to the information in Lessons 12, 21, and 22, your students could include:

OVERALL THEMES

1. The two movements were closely related, many women reformers receiving their training and experience in the abolitionist movement.

2. The abolitionists achieved their primary goal when the Thirteenth Amendment ended slavery in 1865.

3. Women did not have the same successes. Between 1848 and 1865, women subordinated their efforts to the antislavery cause.

4. After the Civil War, the women's suffrage movement divided over the Fifteenth Amendment and the question of African-American male suffrage.

5. At the end of the century, women were still without their primary goal—suffrage.

POSSIBLE INFORMATION

Abolitionist Movement

- William Lloyd Garrison:
  - led abolitionists 1831–1865
  - began publishing The Liberator 1831
  - helped found the American Anti-Slavery Society 1833
  - very controversial
  - many fellow abolitionists thought him rancorous and abusive

- he called for:
  - » immediate abolition of slavery
  - » no compensation for owners
  - » attacks on the churches for not speaking out against slavery
  - » attacked the Constitution—called it a pact with the devil
  - » active and equal role for women in the movement
- by 1838 American Anti-Slavery Society claimed to have 250,000 members
- Garrison was always opposed to political action—he wanted slavery ended through moral persuasion
- Lewis and Arthur Tappan
  - allies of Garrison in early 1830s, broke with him in 1840
  - formed American and Foreign Anti-Slavery Society
  - called for:
    - » gradual emancipation
    - » compensation to owners
    - » political action—supported Liberty Party, later Free Soil Party
    - » alliance with churches
    - » women must accept a secondary and inferior role in the movement
- by early 1850s, Society was in trouble and faded in mid-1850s
- impact of abolitionists:
  - insisted the North choose between principles of antislavery and the Union
  - South believed abolitionists would bring on a "holocaust of blood"
  - many northerners did not like being forced to think about slavery
  - helped to bring on the Civil War
  - achieved their goal of ending slavery

The Women's Movement

1848–1865

- women were active in temperance and abolition crusade before the Civil War

- diluted their work for suffrage
- William Lloyd Garrison very influential—he suggested:
  - the principle of absolute human equality
  - the theory of social change: must change people's hearts and ideas as well as laws
- The Liberator had a "Ladies Department"—issues for and about women
- in 1830s, women formed several female antislavery societies
- women's role in the abolitionist movement became a flash point of controversy between Garrison and his supporters
- Seneca Falls Convention:
  - organized by Elizabeth Cady Stanton, Lucretia Mott
  - held July 19–20, 1848
  - 300 participants (40 men)
  - issued Declaration of Sentiments
  - first demand was for the right to vote
- women's rights activists held an annual convention from 1848 to the beginning of the Civil War (except in 1857)
- in 1840s and 1850s made progress in getting fairer divorce laws for women, right to own property and keep wages
- during Civil War, women organized the Women's Loyal National League
  - worked for Union and emancipation

1865–1900

- women divided over Fifteenth Amendment
- leaders like Susan B. Anthony and Elizabeth Stanton wanted women included in Fifteenth Amendment
- others like Lucy Stone and Julia Ward Howe said women should wait—it was the Negro's hour
- rival organizations evolved from this dispute
  - American Woman Suffrage Association, 1869
    - » leader Lucy Stone
    - » accepted Fifteenth Amendment as it was

» worked at state level for women's suffrage

» focused on the suffrage exclusively

» more conservative—accepted "cult of true womanhood"

○ National Woman Suffrage Association, 1868

» leaders Anthony and Stanton

» demanded Fifteenth Amendment include women as well as black men

» more aggressive, militant—only women allowed to be officers

• became increasingly antiblack in rhetoric

• 1890 two groups combined into National American Woman Suffrage Association

• Elizabeth Cady Stanton first president

• tended to diminish the role of the American Woman Suffrage group

• some states gave women suffrage— Colorado, Idaho, Wyoming—but no national right to vote achieved

• 1875 Minor v. Happersett ruled that suffrage was not attached to women's citizenship

• summary: although women made speeches, tried to vote, and staged demonstrations, they failed to achieve their overarching nineteenth-century goal of suffrage

LEQ 11

Evaluate the extent to which Congress and the Supreme Court helped the South win the peace after the Civil War. Consider the years 1868–1900.

(NAT-2, POL-3; Causation; Lessons 24, 25)

Students can use a variety of facts and ideas to answer this prompt. In addition to the information in Lessons 24 and 25, your students could include some of the following ideas:

OVERALL THEMES

1. Congress began to lose interest in Reconstruction after 1868.

2. The failure to convict Andrew Johnson and the death of Thaddeus Stevens in 1868 undermined Radical Republican reformers in Congress.

3. The election dispute in 1876 set the stage for an end to Congressional reconstruction of the South.

4. The Supreme Court began to shrink the legal impact of the Fourteenth Amendment in the early 1870s.

5. From 1873–1896, the Court issued a series of rulings that strengthened the rights of the states to enforce laws within their boundaries.

6. The Court restricted the federal government's authority to involve itself in cases of private discrimination.

7. The Court found the Fourteenth Amendment did not require integrated facilities for races, only required they be equal in quality.

POSSIBLE INFORMATION

Congressional Role

• Johnson's impeachment

○ the failure to convict Andrew Johnson for his violation of the Tenure of Office Act in 1868 weakened the Radical Republicans

- Thaddeus Stevens' death further hurt the goal of transforming the South
- Grant's presidency
  - Grant wanted peace, and he did not challenge Congress on the gradual return to power of southern conservative redeemers
  - Panic of 1873 focused nation's attention on economic issues rather than civil rights
  - Grant scandals crowded other issues from national agenda
- Compromise of 1877
  - in order to get Rutherford B. Hayes certified as president, northern Republicans withdrew troops from the last southern states
  - left South to restore its economic and social system
  - showed that the nation was ready to put war behind it and wanted
  - reconciliation
  - "The hour of the Negro had passed"
  - Reconstruction was over
- Hayes's presidency featured reconciliation with the South
  - no attempt to enforce statutes protecting civil rights
  - desire to heal the sectional wounds of the war

The Supreme Court

- Court followed government's overall philosophy of returning power to southern states and reconciling North with South

- In Slaughterhouse cases, *U.S. v. Cruikshank, Reese v. U.S., U.S. v. Singleton*, Court established that:
  - citizenship rights should be protected at state level
  - protection of rights to assemble and bear arms would remain state
  - responsibility
  - federal government could prevent only cases of state-sponsored
  - discrimination; could not intervene in cases of private bias
  - paved way for *Plessy v. Ferguson* (1896)
- Court rejected centralizing tendencies of the Fourteenth Amendment
- Struck down Civil Rights Act of 1875 in Singleton case (1883)
- *Plessy v. Ferguson*
  - upheld Jim Crow system in railroads
  - allowed separate facilities as long as they were equal
  - Court also ruled/implied:
    » Fourteenth Amendment did not abolish all distinction based on race
    » government could not force social integration
    » government cannot put blacks on same social plane as whites
    » separation is badge of inferiority only if blacks interpret it that way
    » "law ways cannot change folkways"
    » laid foundation for entire Jim Crow system

LEQ 12

To what extent did the debate over the appropriate role of the federal government in the American economy change the lives of American workers from 1880–1910?

(POL-3; Continuity/Change; Lessons 26, 27, 29)

Students can use a variety of facts and ideas to answer this prompt. In addition to the information in Lessons 26, 27, and 29, your students could include some of the following:

OVERALL THEMES

1. Main struggle between the forces supporting government intervention and the forces of *laissez-faire*.

2. Social Darwinist and their ideas dominated the late 19th century economic discussion.

3. According to Social Darwinists the proper role of the government was to protect private property and avoid upsetting the natural order of unbridled competition.

4. Reformers called for more government regulation to achieve a balanced social and economic order.

5. Government in the Progressive Era became active in regulating the environment and the consumer market place.

6. The Supreme Court tended to limit government actions in the economy from 1880–1910.

7. The currency issue faded after McKinley election victory in 1896.

8. From 1880–1900 the government tried to address the currency issue by purchasing and coining limited amount of silver.

POSSIBLE INFORMATION

Social Darwinists

- followed the writing of Herbert Spencer and William Graham Sumner

- warned against government intervention and interference with social and economic evolution

- believed helping poor impeded progress in United States

- believed the gold standard was the best for the economy

- applauded Supreme Court rulings such as E.C Knight and Lochner, which limited the government's power to regulate the economic system

- believed the poor were responsible for their fate

Reform Darwinists (Social Gospel Members)

- believed freedom and spiritual self-development required equalization of wealth and power

- believed unbridled competition mocked Christian ideals of brotherhood

- drew inspiration from writers such as Walter Rauschenbusch, Lyman Abbott

- did not take a strong position on the currency question

Progressive Reformers

- drew inspiration from writers such Henry George, Edward Bellamy, Henry Demarest Lloyd

- reformer Presidents included Theodore Roosevelt, William Howard Taft, Woodrow Wilson

- used Sherman Act, Hepburn Act, Mann Elkins Act to control corporations

- supported Supreme Court rulings in Northern Securities Case, *Muller v. Oregon*

- enacted laws to regulate child labor

- called for a "Square Deal" for laboring people and the middle class

- believed freedom was the power of the government to act on behalf of the people

- rooted out corruption with initiative, recall, and referendum

LEQ 13

Compare and contrast the role of TWO civil rights leaders in combating the Jim Crow system from 1890-1925.

(POL-2; Comparison; Lesson 28)

Students can use a variety of facts and ideas to answer this prompt. In addition to the information in Lesson 28, your students could include:

OVERALL THEMES

1. Great struggle between Booker T. Washington and W.E.B. Du Bois to lead African Americans against Jim Crow.

2. Washington called for accommodation and some acceptance of the Jim Crow system. He emphasized economic advancement for African Americans rather than social and political agitation.

3. Washington favored acceptance of the racial status quo from 1895–1915.

4. Du Bois emphasized agitation and immediate changes.

5. Du Bois called for full equality and the dismantling of the entire Jim Crow system.

6. Marcus Garvey was closer to Washington in philosophy in his call for economic progress to lead to a better quality of life. He also accepted segregation in many aspects of black life. Yet, his separatist, back-to-Africa ideas placed him in a more radical position than either Washington or Du Bois.

POSSIBLE INFORMATION

Booker T. Washington

- born a slave, grew up in South
- educated at Hampton Institute
- ceased to have "bitterness against southern whites"
- became president of Tuskegee Institute
- gained national prominence in 1895 with his "Atlanta Compromise" speech which:

- emphasized economic issues
- said blacks SHOULD NOT:
  - » run from work; rather they should embrace it
  - » worry about political rights
  - » agitate on social questions
  - » let grievances overshadow economic opportunities
  - » seek social equality—remain as "separate as fingers on a hand" from white people
- said blacks SHOULD:
  - » cast down economic buckets where they were and work hard for white acceptance
  - » live by the production of their hands
  - » obtain training in agriculture and trades
  - » do right and the world would be all right
  - » accept conditions as they now exist
- Washington received support from white industrialists
  - George Eastman gave $10,000 annually to Tuskegee
  - John D. Rockefeller gave $10,000 as well
  - Andrew Carnegie added $600,000 to Tuskegee endowment, 1903
- Washington became influential leader with political and economic connections throughout the white world
- criticism:
  - no real progress made by blacks—whites still discriminated and held blacks back
  - his don't-rock-the-boat policies made him seem like an "Uncle Tom"
  - did not challenge whites and the Jim Crow system

- deeply hurt by the Atlanta Riot and Brownsville Raid in 1906
- secretly worked behind the scenes to try to tear down Jim Crow

W.E.B. Du Bois

- born after the Civil War in Massachusetts
- never a slave, grew up in Massachusetts
- earned Ph.D. from Harvard in 1895
- at first supported Washington's position on Jim Crow
- broke with Washington in 1903 with publication of his book The Souls of Black Folk
- founding member of the Niagara Movement and the National Association for the Advancement of Colored People (NAACP)
- taught at several southern colleges
- said: "the problem of the twentieth century is the problem of the color line"
- called for:
  - direct assault on the Jim Crow system
  - black agitation for all social, political, and economic benefits that America offered to white people
  - putting responsibility for racial solutions on white people not blacks
  - the "Talented Tenth" of the black community to lead the charge for equal rights (educated people like DuBois and his friends)
  - blacks should study liberal arts and seek professional education opportunities
- critics said he:
  - was out of touch with average black people
  - did not know the South
  - was an elitist
- eventually he broke with the NAACP
- more and more critical of America and capitalism
- in 1950s and 1960s, left country and joined the Communist Party

Marcus Garvey

- came to United States from Jamaica in 1916 to get support from Booker T. Washington
- connected with urban, poor African Americans
- message:
  - black pride
  - blacks should seek African roots
  - economic self-sufficiency
  - seek lands where blacks were in the majority—Africa
  - motto: "One God, One Aim, One Destiny"
  - blacks should follow separate course of economic advancement
- strongly promoted cultural, economic links with Africa
- founded the Universal Negro Improvement Association (UNIA)
- created the Black Star Line—black-owned shipping company
- founded the Negro Factory Corporation
- tried to connect the UNIA with Liberia
- criticized NAACP and Du Bois as outdated and too close to whites
- arrested in 1922 for mail fraud
- deported in 1927
- criticism:
  - his separatist message was actually endorsed by the Ku Klux Klan
  - his elaborate costumes and flamboyant behaviors were ridiculed by many people
  - his fraud represented his betrayal of the thousands of blacks who had invested in his economic schemes

LEQ 14

Evaluate the extent to which political and economic reform movements promoted social justice in the United States from 1900–1940. Consider at least TWO movements.

(POL-2; Continuity/Change, Causation; Lessons 10, 30, 32)

Students can use a variety of facts and ideas to answer this prompt. In addition to the information in Lessons 10, 30, and 32, your students could include:

OVERALL THEMES

1. Social justice refers to equal access to due process and equal opportunity to society's bounty and riches regardless of gender, class, religion, ethnicity, or race.

2. The economic reforms of the Progressives (1901–1917) and the New Dealers (1933–1939) placed the government on the side of the middle class and against special and powerful interests.

3. In both cases, government actions involved business regulation, taxing the rich, and reducing barriers to economic advancement.

4. Both movements had limited success in changing the economic and political structure and improving conditions for the middle class and working poor.

5. However, both movements began the march to a fairer, more equal America.

POSSIBLE INFORMATION

Square Deal and New Freedom Actions

- regulation of corporations
  - Theodore Roosevelt, William Howard Taft, and Woodrow Wilson brought 214 suits against corporations from 1902–1917 under the Sherman Antitrust Act
  - Congress passed:
    - » Hepburn Act (1906)—expanded Interstate Commerce Commission
    - » Elkins Act (1904)—outlawed railroad rebates

- » Mann-Elkins Act (1910)—further regulated railroads
- » Clayton Antitrust Act (1914)—regulated trusts, unfair competition
- » Federal Trade Commission (1914)—outlawed unfair trade practices
- » Federal Reserve Act (1913)—regulated banking industry

- citizen protection
  - Pure Food and Drug Act (1906)
  - Meat Inspection Act (1906)
  - Keating-Owen Act (1916)—prohibited the interstate shipment of goods
  - manufactured by firms employing children under fourteen years old
  - created Children's Bureau within Department of Labor

- Sixteenth Amendment enacted (1913)—an income tax that required the rich to pay at least partially for maintaining government services

- Progressives made business more cautious, and offered some protection and services to the middle class

- progressives supported the movement that eventually resulted in the Nineteenth Amendment granting women's suffrage

- failed to alter the unequal distribution of power and wealth in the country

- did not address the inequality of the Jim Crow system

- did not provide welfare payments to the poor and those unable to work

New Deal Actions

- FDR used the Three Rs—relief, recovery, and reform—to promote limited social justice in the 1930s

- the New Deal built on the progressive tradition of Theodore Roosevelt and Woodrow Wilson

- through a series of programs, the New Deal assisted the forgotten people of the middle class
    - Agricultural Adjustment Act—helped farmers
    - Emergency Relief Act—provided money for direct relief
    - many work programs (WPA, CWA, PWA, CCC)—created temporary jobs for the unemployed
    - Glass-Steagall Act—regulated banks and set up the Federal Deposit Insurance Corporation
    - Security and Exchange Commission—regulated Wall Street and stock market

- Roosevelt's Second New Deal confronted businesses and the rich, and tried to assist workers, the middle class, and the poor

    - Holding Company Act—designed to break up the utility holding companies
    - Revenue Act—higher taxes on rich
    - Wagner Act—made unionizing easier for workers
    - Social Security Act—government-mandated retirement system

- Roosevelt made permanent changes in the country's attitude toward government intervention on behalf of farmers, unionized workers, and small businessmen

- New Deal indirectly helped African Americans and won their votes, but Roosevelt did not propose a civil rights program

- nor did the New Deal directly help women, although Eleanor Roosevelt was an active and vocal proponent for women's rights; Molly Dewson headed the Women's Division of the Democratic National Committee, which helped women obtain federal appointments in the government

- summary: New Deal did promote social justice by empowering new interest groups and allowing them to compete more effectively in the market

LEQ 15

Evaluate the extent to which American foreign policy from 1920–1941 maintained continuity as well as promoted change in America's view of itself in world affairs.

(WOR-2; Continuity/Change; Lessons 23, 31)

Students can use a variety of facts and ideas to answer this prompt. In addition to the information found in Lessons 23 and 31, your students could include:

OVERALL THEMES

1. After rejecting membership in the League of Nations, the United States returned to its classic policy of avoiding entangling political and military alliances with Europe.

2. During these years, the United States practiced economic isolationism by maintaining high tariffs, immigration restrictions, and inflexible war debt policies.

3. During the 1920s, however, the nation did initiate and sign a series of international disarmament treaties.

4. The onset of the Great Depression reinforced the nation's determination to avoid Europe's military and political turmoil.

5. When World War II began in Europe, the United States realized its security was threatened, so it abandoned its policy of neutrality and isolation.

POSSIBLE INFORMATION

1920–1933

- U.S. refused to join the League of Nations and World Court
- U.S. practiced economic isolationism
  - restricted immigration—number of immigrants declined from 800,000 in 1920 to 150,000 in 1929
  - refused to offer forgiveness or flexibility on payments of $20 billion in war debts owed by Europe
  - maintained high tariffs
    - » Fordney-McCumber 1922
    - » Hawley-Smoot 1930
      - U.S. did, however, involve itself in a series of multinational disarmament treaties with Europe and Japan
    - » Washington Conference (1921)—naval reduction, ten-year moratorium on battleship construction
    - » Five-Power Pact (1922)—established ratios for naval building
    - » Kellogg-Briand Pact (1928)—outlawed war as a means of settling international disputes

1933–1939

- Roosevelt, although an internationalist, was more concerned about the domestic Depression than world developments
- FDR did lower tariffs through Reciprocal Trade Agreement Act of 1934

- Isolationists controlled legislative agenda
  - 1935–1937 passed a series of Neutrality Acts that called for:
    - » mandatory arms embargo
    - » restriction of Americans' travel on belligerent ships
    - » prohibition on loans to belligerents
    - » cash-and-carry for all exports in time of war
    - » as historian Thomas Bailey said about the Neutrality Acts: "In retrospect, the United States was one war too late in its attempt to legislate itself into neutrality"
- Roosevelt was unable to use the Panay incident or his quarantine speech (both in 1937) to move the nation toward a strong international stance

1939–1941

- When war broke out in September 1939 in Europe, the United States began to dismantle its neutrality policy
  - November 1939 repealed the arms embargo
  - September 1940 established conscription
  - September 1940 made destroyer-for-bases deal with England
  - January 1941 enacted Lend-Lease
- undeclared shooting war on the seas between the U.S. and Germany brought America to the brink of war by autumn 1941
- U.S. economic pressure on Japan and the continued stalemate over the Japanese invasion of China led to Japanese attack on Pearl Harbor in December 7, 1941
- December 10, 1941, Germany declared war on U.S.

LEQ 16

To what extent did private individuals rather than political figures promote civil rights after World War II? Cite at least two individuals from 1945–1960 to justify your answer.

(POL-2; Causation; Lessons 28, 33)

Students can use a variety of facts and ideas to answer this prompt. In addition to the information found in Lessons 28 and 33, your students could include:

OVERALL THEMES

1. Truman was the first president to put a true civil rights program on the legislative agenda.

2. Lyndon Johnson's War on Poverty included a strong civil rights component.

3. Johnson was the greatest presidential leader for civil rights in the twentieth century.

4. Martin Luther King Jr. was the most influential civil rights leader in America from 1956–1968.

5. During the early and mid-1960s, Malcolm X and other militant leaders began to challenge and question King's effectiveness and strategies.

POSSIBLE INFORMATION

Harry Truman

- became concerned about civil rights because of the treatment of black soldiers returning to America after World War II

- saw the glaring hypocrisy of fighting to stamp out Fascist racism around the world and perpetuating racism at home

- December 1946 appointed Civil Rights Committee; their report To Secure These Rights became core of Truman's program

- June 1947 became first president to address the NAACP

- July 1948 issued Exec. Orders 9980 and 9981
  - 9980: integrated the federal workforce
  - 9981: integrated U.S. armed forces

- during election campaign of 1948 called for:
  - creating civil rights division in Department of Justice
  - permanent commission on civil rights
  - Fair Employment Practices Commission
  - end to the poll tax
  - end to discrimination in interstate transportation
  - home rule/suffrage for the District of Columbia
  - statehood for Alaska and Hawaii
  - settlement of Japanese-American evacuation claims from WWII
  - split his party in election of 1948
  - Truman could not get Congress to act on most of his proposals, but he led the way in awakening nation's conscience on civil rights

Martin Luther King Jr.

- came to prominence in December 1955 with the Montgomery Bus Boycott
  - spokesman for the cause
  - when Supreme Court required Montgomery bus system to abandon Jim Crow in November 1956, King came into the national spotlight

- organized 30,000 people to come to Lincoln Memorial May 17, 1957

- founded the Southern Christian Leadership Conference (SCLC)
  - called for nonviolent coercion to achieve goals
  - used public protests to pressure whites to dismantle Jim Crow system

- supported but did not start the sit-ins and the freedom rides of the early 1960s

- came to true national prominence in spring of 1963
  - organized the protest against segregation in Birmingham, Alabama
  - arrested and wrote his famous "Letter from Birmingham Jail"
    - » emphasized direct action
    - » said cup of endurance and forbearance was overflowing for blacks
    - » blamed white moderates for slow pace of racial change
    - » also criticized the churches for inaction
- violence in Birmingham pressured President Kennedy to propose a civil rights act in June of 1963
- King organized march to lobby the president and Congress to approve the act
  - initially, march was to feature civil disobedience
  - Kennedy administration opposed this
  - 250,000 who joined King at Lincoln Memorial heard his "I Have a Dream" speech
  - high point of King's influence
  - 1963 fully 88 percent of blacks supported King's effort
- Civil Rights Act passed July 1964
- King won Nobel Peace Prize in 1964
- urban rioting began in 1964 and started to erode King's support
- Selma protest led to Voting Rights Act of 1965
- urban riots increased violence, gave rise to militancy of Student Nonviolent Coordinating Committee and individuals such as Malcolm X
- 1967 King criticized war in Vietnam
  - King said U.S. is greatest purveyor of violence in world
  - Johnson felt betrayed
- 1968 under increasing pressure from radicals
- April 1968 assassinated in Memphis, Tennessee

Lyndon Johnson

- although a southerner, he had a moderate record on civil rights as a legislator
  - one of three southern Senators who refused to sign the southern manifesto of resistance to the *Brown v. Board of Education* decision in 1957
  - helped pass Civil Rights Acts of 1957 and 1960
- as president, declared a War on Poverty, which included civil rights programs
- achievements:
  - Civil Rights Act of 1964—most far-reaching civil rights law since Reconstruction
  - Voting Rights Act of 1965—voting rights, changed the political face of the South
  - 1964 created Equal Employment Opportunity Commission—investigated and prevented job discrimination
  - 1965 Immigration Act—revised 1924 quota system
  - Congress enacted food stamp program and public housing assistance
  - Congress passed sixty bills providing aid to education, 1964–1969
  - riots and Vietnam War undermined his program
    - » in 1964, rioting starts in cities
    - » in 1966, 128 cities had some type of disorder
    - » in 1967, 164 cities had riots
- summary: greatest civil rights record in history of the country

Malcolm X

- member of the (Black) Muslims of America
- criticized the nonviolent, integration approach of Martin Luther King Jr.
- opposed:
  - integration—he asked: Why integrate with a burning house?
  - March on Washington in 1963
    - » called it the "Farce on Washington"

» said it was controlled by white power structure

» said blacks could not end racism by holding hands and singing songs

- called for:
  ◦ black self-defense
  ◦ realization that whites were the devil
  ◦ racial pride and unity
  ◦ projection of black manhood

- had some influence with undereducated, unemployed urban black males

- broke with Elijah Muhammad over Muhammad's personal behavior

- claimed his trip to Mecca in 1964 softened his anti-white beliefs

- assassinated in 1965 by another faction of Muslims

- on fringes of the civil rights movement; in 1965 only 5 percent of blacks said he was doing the best job on their behalf

LEQ 17

Compare and contrast the successes and failures of containment of TWO Cold War presidents from 1945-1974.

(WOR-2; Comparison; Lessons 34, 35, 36)

Students can use a variety of facts and ideas to answer this prompt. In addition to the information in Lessons 34, 35, and 36, your students could include:

OVERALL THEMES

1. The concept of containment became America's overriding strategy throughout the Cold War.

2. Each president fine-tuned the implementation of the policy and labeled it differently, but all remained committed to its assumptions and overall strategy.

3. The concept of containment grew from the pre-World War II experiences of trying to appease totalitarianism in Europe and Asia.

4. American leaders came to see the Communists as "the new Nazis" who could not be allowed to seize territory incrementally.

5. The Vietnam War proved to be both the apex and the turning point in the implementation of containment.

POSSIBLE INFORMATION

Harry Truman

- based containment on ideas of George F. Kennan's "Long Telegram" and "Sources of Soviet Conduct"

- saw Soviets as expansionistic and threatening to American interests

- implementation of containment
  ◦ Truman Doctrine (1947)—$400 million to help Greece and Turkey resist Communist guerrillas
  ◦ Marshall Plan (1948–1951)—$12.5 billion to aid Europe
  ◦ Berlin Airlift (1948–1949)—supplied West Berlin for 324 days when it was threatened by Soviets

- North Atlantic Treaty Organization (1949)—military alliance with Western Europe to stop potential Soviet aggression

- NSC 68 (1950)—called for tripling the defense budget; putting country on a state-of-war readiness to prevent world domination by the Soviet Union

- Korean War (1950–1953)

- Truman outlined parameters of containment that all future presidents would largely follow
- U.S. committed to being "the world's policeman"

Dwight Eisenhower

- came to power calling for a "New Look" in foreign policy
- spokesman was Secretary of State John Foster Dulles
- viewed Communism as monolithic
- implementation of containment
  - massive retaliation—nuclear response to Communist aggression
  - no more limited wars like Korean conflict
  - take Soviets to brink of war if necessary to stop their aggression
  - rollback and liberate areas under Communist control
  - increased spending on atomic weapons, missiles, and bombers
  - gave Central Intelligence Agency broad power
  - called for "peaceful coexistence" with Soviets
  - proposed "domino theory" as justification to help Vietnam resist Communist aggression
  - used force in Middle East to keep out Communists (Eisenhower Doctrine)
- summary: while using different rhetoric, Eisenhower "traveled the well-rutted road" of containment

John Kennedy

- accepted basic outline of containment
- altered Eisenhower's massive retaliation with his "flexible response"—expanded options for fighting Communist threat
- focused on Berlin as great trouble spot and "wars of liberation" in Asia, Africa, and Latin America
- implementation of containment
  - April 1961 tried to overthrow Fidel Castro in Cuba—failed invasion at Bay of Pigs
  - October 1962 confronted the Soviet Union and forced the removal of nuclear weapons from Cuba (Cuban Missile Crisis)
- accepted domino theory and deepened American commitment in Vietnam
  - sent 16,000 advisors to South Vietnam
  - November 1963 supported a coup that eliminated Ngo Dinh Diem—set off chaos in country and set stage for America's quagmire in Vietnam
- summary: Kennedy was a traditional cold warrior in mold of Truman and Eisenhower

Lyndon Johnson

- accepted basic ideas of Cold War and containment—believed communism:
  - was monolithic—controlled from Moscow
  - must be contained
  - threatened America's prestige as world power
- believed in domino theory and that Vietnam was critical to all of Southeast Asia's future
- remembered how Truman's presidency had been damaged by the fall of China to the Communists in 1949
- wanted to protect support for his domestic programs by being tough with Communists
- wanted to honor John Kennedy's memory
- reduced tension with Cuba and sought status quo in Europe with Communists
- faced crisis in Vietnam
  - death of Diem resulted in chaos throughout country
  - by 1964 estimated that 40 percent of land and 50 percent of people in South Vietnam were controlled by Communists
  - Gulf of Tonkin Resolution gave him a blank check to wage war in Vietnam
- eventually sent 540,000 troops to South Vietnam and heavily bombed North Vietnam
- war divided the nation and destroyed Johnson's presidency
- Vietnam showed the limits of containment and of America's ability to shape the world

- summary: country began to question the assumptions and reality of being the world's police force

Richard Nixon

- although committed to broad outline of containment, Nixon began to redefine the concept
- realized United States must disengage in Vietnam
- saw great opportunity for United States with the rivalry between the Soviet Union and China for control of the international Communist movement
- Nixon dropped idea that Communism was monolithic
- Nixon realized the United States must remain a world power, but must rethink its international approach
- Nixon and Henry Kissinger tried to construct a new global strategy with less emphasis on traditional containment:
  - Vietnamization in Vietnam—withdraw combat troops but pressure Communists to negotiate a settlement
  - use tension between the USSR and China to America's strategic advantage

- » Nixon visited China in February 1972
- » United States offered China American technology
- » signed a Strategic Arms Limitations Treaty (SALT) with Soviet Union
- ○ looked for peaceful coexistence and cooperation (détente) with Soviet Union
- ○ wound down war in Vietnam
  - » June 1969 withdrew 25,000 troops from Vietnam
  - » 1970–1972 continued to pull American troops out and tried to force Communists to negotiate for peace
- ○ 1973 ended draft
- ○ 1973 withdrew last American troops and signed peace accord
- supported containment of Communist power, but hoped the carrot-and-stick approach would transform both countries into more traditional powers
- summary: the Watergate scandal short-circuited Nixon/Kissinger's vision of a new phase of containment

LEQ 18

Compare and contrast the foreign policies of President George H.W. Bush with George W. Bush.

(WOR-2; Comparison; Lessons 5, 37)

Students can use a variety of facts and ideas to answer this prompt. In addition to the information in Lessons 5 and 37, your students could include:

OVERALL THEMES

1. H.W. dealt with a post-Cold War world while W. dealt with a post- 9/11 world

2. H.W. focused on issues in Central America, Europe, and Iraq while W. mainly involved in the Middle East

3. Both faced trouble in Iraq with Saddam Hussein

4. Both presidencies were criticized over their Iraq policy: H.W. for not completing the task of toppling Hussein; W. for his failed attempt to nation-build in Iraq

POSSIBLE INFORMATION

Policies of George H.W. Bush:

- Berlin Wall fell November 1989

- October 1990 Germany reunified

- December 1991 the Soviet Union ceased to exist

- Invaded Panama and arrested Manuel Noriega as a drug trafficker

- January to February 1991 First Gulf War (Kuwait Invasion)

- Popularity quickly vanished after war with the onset of a severe recession

Policies of George W. Bush:

- Saw the rise of well-financed, well-armed terrorists

- United States attacked by al Qaeda September 11, 2001 (3000 Americans killed)

- Attacked Osama bin Laden in Afghanistan in October 2001

- Launched Operation Enduring Freedom in October to get bin Laden and the Taliban

- Established the "Bush Doctrine" of preemptive military action against suspected terrorists

- March 2003 United States attacked Iraq— removed Saddam Hussein with "Operation Iraqi Freedom"

- Violence and chaos followed in Iraq with the removal of Hussein

- No weapons of mass destruction found

- Presidency was in shambles by 2008

Possible Outside Information

- Michael Dukakis

- Election of 1988

- Dan Quayle

- Mikhail Gorbachev

- "New World Order"

- Tiananmen Square

- Boris Yeltsin

- Manuel Noriega

- Operation Desert Shield

- Bill Clinton

- World Trade Center

- Al Gore

- Osama bin Laden

- Taliban

- al Qaeda

- Jihad

- Operation Enduring Freedom

- USA Patriot Act

- Operation Iraqi Freedom

- Weapons of mass destruction

LEQ 19

Evaluate the extent to which the presidency of Bill Clinton changed the political and economic policies of the Democratic Party in the 1990s. Analyze what changed and what stayed the same in this time period.

(POL-2; Causation; Lessons 5, 37)

Students can use a variety of facts and ideas to answer this prompt. In addition to the information in Lessons 5 and 37, your students could include:

OVERALL THEMES

1. Should be careful not to overstate Clinton's deviation from past Democratic policies

2. While Clinton rhetorically represented a turning point in the Democratic Party, his actions/policies were more in line with the party's past

3. His major change was in the area of welfare reform and deregulation

4. He also tried to position himself to the right of the liberal wing of the Democratic Party

5. He acknowledged the power of conservatives in Congress and bowed to many of their demands

POSSIBLE INFORMATION

Pre-Clinton Democratic Policies:

- A party of high taxes and government spending
- Supporters found in organized labor, minorities, and blue collar workers
- Promoted social justice through government actions
- Expanded government bureaucracy
- Government should regulate the economy to protect the middle class
- Should maintain the programs of the New Deal and Great Society
- Maintain a strong safety net of protection for minorities
- Supported Civil Rights programs
- Deficit spending a necessity for maintaining government services

Clinton's attempt at change:

- He promised to cut taxes
- Promised to reign in government spending
- He supported North American Free Trade Agreement (NAFTA) which was opposed by traditional Democratic constituencies of organized labor and environmentalists.

- He retreated from government regulations of broadcast companies, banks, and telephone companies.
- He tempered his support for affirmative action.
- He signed Welfare Reform Act which limited the amounts and time allowed on welfare rolls.
- He claimed to have "ended welfare as we knew it."
- He proclaimed the "era of big government is over."
- His triangulation strategy included embracing the anti-government outlook of Republicans, but rejected their more extreme measures of their program.

Possible Outside Information

- George H.W. Bush
- Ross Perot
- Al Gore
- North American Free Trade Agreement (NAFTA)
- Hillary Clinton
- Oklahoma City bombing
- Contract with America
- Newton Gingrich
- Personal Responsibility and Work Opportunity Act
- Bob Dole
- Monica Lewinsky
- Impeachment
- Ken Starr
- Telecommunication Act of 1996
- Triangulation

Document–Based Questions

with Suggested Responses

DBQ 1: EMERGING COLONIAL IDENTITY

Analyze the changes in the political structure and social fabric in British North America from 1620–1680 that promoted an emerging colonial identity.

(NAT-1; Continuity/Change and Historical Causation)

Document 1

Source: The introduction of African slavery into the American colonies at Jamestown, Virginia, August, 1619

INTRODUCTION OF SLAVERY.

Document 2

Source: The Mayflower Compact, 1620

…We whose names are underwritten … do by these presents solemnly and mutually in the presence of God, and one of another, covenant and combine ourselves together into a civil body politics for our better ordering and preservation and furtherance of the ends aforesaid; and by virtue hereof, to enact, constitute, and frame such just and equal laws, ordinances, acts, constitutions, and offices from time to time, as shall be thought most meet and convenient for the general good of the colony unto which we promise all due submission and obedience…

Document 3

Source: Roger Williams, 1644

Sixth. It is the will and command of God that since the coming of his Son, the Lord Jesus a permission of the most pagan, Jewish, Turkish, or anti-Christian consciences and worships be granted to all men in all nations and countries…

Eighth. God requires not a uniformity of religion to be enacted and enforced in any civil state…enforced uniformity…is the greatest occasion of civil war, ravishing of conscience, persecution of Christ Jesus in his servants, and of the hypocrisy and destruction of millions of souls.

Twelfth. …the Church of Christ does not used the arm of secular power to compel men to the true profession of the truth, for this is to be done with spiritual weapons, whereby Christians are to be exhorted, not compelled.

Document 4

Source: Navigation Acts, 1660

I. For the increase of shipping and encouragement of the navigation of this nation wherein, under the good providence and protection of God, the wealth, safety, and strength of this kingdom is so much concerned; be it enacted by the king's most excellent Majesty,…no goods or commodities whatsoever shall be imported into or exported out of any lands, islands, plantations, or territories to his Majesty…in any other ship or ships, vessel or vessels whatsoever, but in such ships as do truly and without fraud belong only to the people of England or Ireland….

II. And be it enacted, that no alien or person not born within the allegiance of our sovereign lord the king…[shall] exercise the trade or occupation of a merchant or factor in any the said place;

Document 5

Source: Increase Mather, 1675

August 12. This is the memorable day wherein Philip, the perfidious and bloudy [sic] Author of the War and wofull miseryes [sic] that have thence ensued, was taken and slain. And God brought it to pass, chiefly by Indians themselves,….Divine Providence so disposed….The Indian who thus killed Philip did formerly belong to the Squaw-Sachim of Pocasset, ….Thus when Philip had made an end to deal treacherously, his own Subjects dealt treacherously with him…. [Philip was] taken and destroyed, and there was he cut into four quarters, and is now hanged up as a monument of revenging justice, his head being cut off and carried away to Plymouth ….

Document 6

Source: Nathaniel Bacon's Declaration, 1676

1. For having, upon specious pretenses of public works, raised great unjust taxes upon the commonalty for the advancement of private favorites and other sinister end, but no visible effects in any measure adequate; for not having, during this long time of his government, in any measure this hopeful colony either by fortifications, towns, or trade.

4. For having protected, favored, and emboldened the Indians against his Majesty's loyal subjects, never contriving, requiring, or appointing any due or proper means of satisfaction for their many invasions, robberies, and murders committed upon us.

8. For the prevention of civil mischief and ruin amongst ourselves while the barbarous enemy in all places did invade, murder, and spoil us, his Majesty's most faithful subjects.

Of this and the aforesaid articles we accuse Sir William Berkeley [royal governor] as guilty of each and every one of the same...

Document 7

Source: Poem by Anne Bradstreet from her collection, Several Poems Compiled with Great Variety of Wit and Learning, 1678, published posthumously by her family

To my Dear and Loving Husband
If ever two were one, then surely we.
If ever man were lov'd by wife, then thee.
If ever wife was happy in a man,
Compare with me, ye women, if you can.
I prize they love more than whole Mines of gold
Or all the riches that the East doth hold.
My love is such that Rivers canneot [sic] quench,
Nor ought but love from thee give recompence.
Thy love is such I can no way repay.
The heavens reward thee manifold, I pray.
Then while we live, in love let's so persever [sic]
That when we live no more, we may live ever.

Suggested Elements of an Emerging Colonial Identity

The colonists saw themselves from 1620–1680 as a people who:

- wrote down their rules of government in compacts and charters

- valued their rights as Englishmen even in the colonies

- practiced some degree of religious freedom

- were responsible to the Crown and its rules

- solved their labor problems by enslaving Africans

- felt superior to Africans and Native Americans

- justified harsh treatment of Native Americans when they resisted colonial actions

- would not accept abridgment of their rights as Englishmen

- valued marriage, family life

- saw men as superior to women in society

- accepted gender roles of women's subservience to men in colonial life

DBQ 2: WOMEN'S RIGHTS, 1848–1870

How did the strategies and supporters in the crusade for the rights of women change from 1848–1872? What factors account for this evolution in approach and personnel?

(POL-2; Continuity/Change, Historical Causation, & Analyzing Historical Evidence)

Document 1

Source: Proceedings from Woman's Rights Convention, Seneca Falls, New York, July 19-21, 1848

We hold these truths to be self-evident: all men and women are created equal; that they are endowed by their Creator with certain inalienable rights; that among these are life, liberty and the pursuit of happiness; that to secure these rights governments are instituted, deriving their just powers from the consent of the governed…The history of mankind is a history of repeated injuries and usurpations on the part of man toward woman, having in direct object the establishment of absolute tyranny over her.

Document 2

Source: Letter, Susan B. Anthony to Amelia Bloomer, August 26, 1852

Dear Mrs. Bloomer:

...I attended the great Temperance demonstration held at Albion, July 7...
I talked to them in my plain way,—told them that to merely relieve the
suffering wives and children of drunkards, and vainly labor to reform the
drunkard was no longer to be called temperance work, and showed them
that woman's temperance sentiments were not truthfully represented by
man at the Ballot Box...

...Men may prate on, but we women are beginning to know that the life
and happiness of a woman is of equal value with that of a man; and that
for a woman to sacrifice her health, happiness and perchance her earthly
existence in the hope of reclaiming a drunken, sensualized man, avails
but little ... Auxiliary Temperance Societies have been formed in very
nearly all the towns I have visited and the women are beginning to feel
that they have something to do in the Temperance Cause—that woman
may speak and act in public as well as in the home circle—and now is
the time to inscribe upon our banner, "NO UNION WITH DISTILLERS,
RUMSELLERS, AND RUMDRINKERS."

> Yours for Temperance
> without Compromise,
>
> S. B. Anthony

Document 3

Source: Cartoon of the Ninth National Woman's Rights Convention,
May 12, 1859

Document 4

Source: Address by Elizabeth Cady Stanton to the American Anti-Slavery Society, May 8, 1860

But in settling the question of negro's rights, we find out the exact limits of our own, for rights never clash or interfere; and where no individual in a community is denied his rights the mass are the more perfectly protected in theirs ... so the humblest and most ignorant citizen cannot be denied his rights without deranging the whole system of government.

I have always regarded Garrison [William Lloyd] as the great missionary of the gospel of Jesus to this guilty nation, for he has waged an uncompromising warfare with the deadly sins of both Church and State. ... In the darkness and gloom of a false theology, I was slowly sawing off the chains of my spiritual bondage, when, for the first time, I met Garrison in London; a few bold strokes from the hammer of his truth, I was free ... To Garrison we owe more than to any other man of our day...

Document 5

Source: Minutes, Women's Loyal National League Meeting, May 14, 1863

We the undersigned, Women of the United States, agree to become members of the Women's Loyal National League, ...

Resolved, That for the present this League will concentrate all its efforts upon the single object of procuring to be signed by one million women and upward, and of preparing for presentation to Congress, within the first week of its session, a petition in the following words to wit:

To the Senate and House of Representatives of the United States.

The undersigned, women of the United States about the age of 18 years, earnestly pray that your honorable body will pass, at the earliest practicable day, an act emancipating all persons of African descent held to involuntary service or labor in the United States.

Document 6

Source: Report, Eleventh National Woman's Rights Convention, May 10, 1866

Whereas, By the act of Emancipation and the Civil Rights bill, the negro and woman now hold the same civil and political status, alike needing only the ballot; and whereas the same arguments apply equally to both classes, proving all partial legislation to republican institutions, therefore...

...we have looked to State action only for the recognition of our rights; but now, by the results of the war, the whole question of suffrage reverts back to Congress and the Constitution. The duty of Congress at this moment is to declare what shall be the basis of representation in a republican form of government ... We, therefore, wish to broaden our Woman's Rights platform, and make it in name—what it ever has been in spirit—a Human Rights platform.

Document 7

Source: Speech, Frederick Douglass, American Equal Rights Convention, May 12, 1869

With us [the black man], the matter is a question of life and death, at least, in fifteen States of the Union. When women, because they are women, are hunted down through ... New York and New Orleans; when they are dragged from their houses and hung upon lampposts; when their children are torn from their arms, and their brains dashed out upon the pavement; when they are objects of insult and outrage at every turn; when they are in danger of having their homes burnt down over their heads; when their children are not allowed to enter schools; then they will have an urgency to obtain the ballot equal to our own.

Suggested Factors about Changes in Women's Rights, 1848–1870

Changing Strategy:

- held an annual meeting every year except 1857 from 1848-1861
- discussed their problems and inequalities at each convention
- joined in other reforms such as abolitionist and temperance
- during Civil War supported the union and emancipation
- after war wanted the Fifteenth Amendment to include women
- some supporters said women should wait until black men were secure in the vote
- held conventions, wrote Congress after Civil War
- formed the National Woman Suffrage Association
- formed the American Woman Suffrage Association

Supporters:

- most men did not support the women's rights movement
- exceptions were men such as William Lloyd Garrison, Frederick Douglass
- Susan B. Anthony and Elizabeth Cady Stanton wanted women included in Fifteenth Amendment (National Woman Suffrage Association)
- the drive to include women in the Fifteenth Amendment alienated former supporters such as Frederick Douglass
- some women wanted to postpone women's suffrage until black men were accepted and secure in voting (American Woman Suffrage Association)
- the women's movement split after the Civil War over this issue

DBQ 3: THE CHANGING ROLE OF GOVERNMENT, 1890–1912

Analyze the national government's changing philosophy and response to the nation's economic challenges from 1890–1912.

(POL-3; Continuity/Change, Historical Causation, & Analyzing Historical Evidence)

Document 1

Selective Categories of Employed Workers: 1880–1920

Year	Total Workers	Agriculture	Manu-facturing	Domestic Peronal Service	Government
1880	17,390,000	8,610,000	4,000,000	1,440,000	335,000
1890	23,740,000	9,990,000	6,190,000	2,160,000	360,000
1900	29,070,000	10,710,000	8,000,000	2,710,000	670,000
1910	36,730,000	11,340,000	10,530,000	3,670,000	1,140,000
1920	41,610,000	11,120,000	13,050,000	3,330,000	1,300,000

Document 2

Source: Sherman Act, 1890

Section 1. Every contract, combination in the form of trust or otherwise or conspiracy, in restraint of trade or commerce among the several States or with foreign nations, is hereby declared to be illegal...

Section 2. Every person who shall monopolize, or attempt to monopolize, or combine or conspire with any other person or persons, to monopolize any part of the trade or commerce among the several States, or with any foreign nations, shall be deemed guilty of a misdemeanor...

Document 3

Source: Henry Demarest Lloyd, Wealth Against Commonwealth, 1894

...the syndicates, trusts, combinations cry of "overproduction"—too much of everything. Holding back the riches of earth, sea and sky from their fellows who famish and freeze in the dark, they declare to them that there is too much light and warmth and food. They assert the right, for their private profit, to regulate the consumption by the people of the necessaries of life, and to control production, not by the needs of humanity, but by the desires of a few for dividends ... The coal syndicate thinks there is too much coal. There is too much iron, too much lumber, too much flour—for this or that syndicate ...

...If the tendency to combination is irresistible, control of it is imperative. Monopoly and anti-monopoly ... represent the two great tendencies of our time: monopoly, the tendency to combination; anti-monopoly, the demand for social control of it.

Document 4

Source: Jacob Coxey's proposal to Congress, June 12, 1894

1.   The Good Roads Bill—53rd Congress, 2d Session H.R. 7438, June 12, 1894.

A Bill to provide for the improvement of public roads and for other purposes.

Be enacted by the Senate and the House of Representatives ... That the Secretary of Treasury of the United States is hereby authorized and instructed to have ... printed, immediately after the passage of this bill, five hundred million dollars of Treasury notes ... and to be placed in a fund to be known as the "general country-road fund system of the United States," and to be expended solely for said purpose.

Section 2 That it shall be the duty of the Secretary of War to take charge of the construction of said general country-road system of the United States, and said construction to commerce as soon as the Secretary of Treasury shall inform the Secretary of War that the said fund is available ... it shall be the duty of the Secretary of War to inaugurate work and expend the sum of twenty millions of dollars per month pro rata with the number of miles of road in each State and Territory in the United States.

Document 5

Source: William Allen Rogers, Harper's Weekly, March 28, 1896

A GIANT STRADDLE.
Suggestion for a McKinley Poster.

Document 6

Source: *Lochner* v. *New York*, 1905

The statute necessarily interferes with the right of contract between the employer and employees, concerning the number of hours in which the latter may labor in the bakery of the employer. The general right to make a contract in relation to his business is part of the liberty of the individual protected by the Fourteenth Amendment of the Federal Constitution...

... The act ... is an illegal interference with the rights of individuals, both employers and employees, to make contracts regarding labor upon such terms as they may think best, or which they may agree upon with the other parties to such contracts. Statutes of the nature of that under review, limiting the hours in which grown and intelligent men may labor to earn their living, are mere meddlesome interferences with the rights of the individual...

Document 7

Source: Theodore Roosevelt, "The New Nationalism," 1910

I stand for the square deal. But when I say I am for the square deal, I mean not merely that I stand for fair play under the present rules of the game, but that I stand for having those rules changed so as to work for a more substantial equality of opportunity and of reward for equally good service … But I think we may go still further. The right to regulate the use of wealth in the public interest is universally admitted. Let us admit also the right to regulate the terms and conditions of labor, which is the chief element of wealth, directly in the interest of the common good. The fundamental thing to do for every man is to give him a chance to reach a place in which he will make the greatest possible contribution to the public welfare.

This New Nationalism regards the executive power [of the federal government] as the steward of the public welfare. It demands of the judiciary that it shall be interested primarily in human welfare rather than in property, just as it demands that the representative body [Congress] shall represent all the people rather than any one class or section of the people.

Suggested Ideas about the Changing Role of Government

Changing Philosophy and Causes:

* abandoned rigid *laissez-faire* and adopted a more active intervention in the economy
* the growth of big business put pressure on the government to do more
* the size of the government grew as did its workforce
* agriculture as a percentage of the workforce declined: 1880 -50%, 1910 -31%
* manufacturing became more important workforce 1880 23%, 1910 29%
* service jobs grew from 1880 (8%) to 1910 (10%)
* writers and politicians encouraged the government to adopt a more active role in the economy
* the Depression of 1893 heightened calls for more government action
* the government rejected radical programs for monetary reform (free silver)

Government Action:

* greater use of the Sherman Anti-Trust act after 1901
* more government regulation of the economy (Pure Food and Drug Act, Meat Inspection Act, etc.)
* progressive presidents (Roosevelt, Taft, Wilson) took the lead in expanding role of the government in the economy
* government action was held back by a conservative Supreme Court

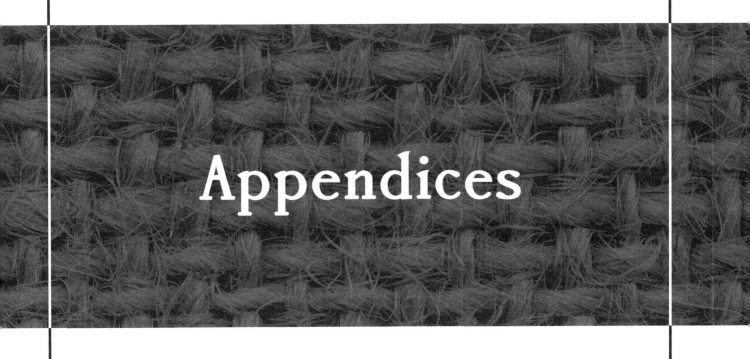

Appendices

A

LEQ Rubric Guide

First, understand the LEQ six-point scale:

A	**Thesis/Claim** (1 point)	1 point for responding to the prompt with a historically defensible thesis/claim that establishes a line of reasoning		
B	**Contextualization** (1 point)	1 point for describing a broader historical context relevant to the prompt		
C	**Evidence** (2 points)	1 point for providing specific examples of evidence relevant to the topic of the prompt	**OR**	2 points for supporting an argument in response to the prompt using specific relevant examples of evidence
D	**Analysis and Reasoning** (2 points)	1 point for using historical reasoning (e.g., Comparison, Causation, Continuity/Change over Time) to frame or structure an argument that addresses the prompt	**OR**	2 points for demonstrating a complex understanding of the historical development that is the focus of the prompt, using evidence to corroborate, qualify or modify an argument that addresses the prompt

After some practice, you should be able to use this quick scan table:
(circle the appropriate number)

Thesis	0 points	1 point	
Contextualization	0 points	1 point	
Evidence	0 points	1 point	2 points
Analysis and Reasoning	0 points	1 point	2 points
		Total Score:	

DBQ Rubric Guide

First, understand the DBQ seven-point scale:

A	Thesis/Claim (1 point)	1 point for presenting a thesis that makes a historically defensible claim and addresses all parts of the question		
B	Contextualization (1 point)	1 point for describing a broader historical context relevant to the prompt		
C	Evidence (3 points)	**Evidence *from* the Documents**		
		1 point for using the content of at least **3 documents** to address the topic of the prompt	**OR**	2 points for supporting an argument in response to the prompt using at least **6 documents**
		Evidence *beyond* the Documents		
		1 point for using at least **1 additional piece of the specific historical evidence** (beyond that found in the documents) relevant to an argument about the prompt		
D	Analysis and Reasoning (2 points)	1 point for explaining how or why a document's point of view, purpose, or historical situation, or audience is relevant to an argument—for at least **3 documents**		
		1 point for demonstrating a complex understanding of the historical development that is the focus of the prompt, using evidence to corroborate, qualify, or modify an argument that addresses the question		

After some practice, you should be able to use this quick scan table:
(circle the appropriate number)

Thesis/Claim	0 points	1 point		
Contextualization	0 points	1 point		
Evidence	0 points	1 point	2 points	3 points
Analysis and Reasoning	0 points	1 point	2 points	
			Total Score:	

Distribution of Items by Chronological Period

Time Periods	Core Chart Questions		Source Activities		LEQs & DBQs
			Multiple-Choice	Short-Answer	
1491–1607	1.1, 2, 3		1.1, 2	1.a, b, c	
1607–1754	3.3; 4.1, 2, 3;	6.1, 2	4.1, 2	4.a, b, c	LEQ 1; DBQ 1
1754–1800	3.2; 7.1, 2, 3; 8.2; 9.1, 2;	11.1; 14.1; 17.2; 19.1	3.1, 2; 7.1, 2; 8.2	3.a, b; 7.a, b, c	LEQ 3
1800–1848	2.1; 3.1; 5.3; 6.3; 8.1, 3; 12.3; 13.2;	14.2; 15.1, 2, 3; 16.1; 17.3; 20.1, 2, 3; 21.1, 2, 3; 22.3	5.1, 2; 26.1; 6.1, 2; 28.1; 11.1, 2; 31.1; 13.1, 2; 36.1, 2 15.1; 17.1, 2; 21.1, 2;	5.a, b, c; 21.a, b, c 6.a, b, c; 8.a, b, c; 11.a, b; 13.a; 14.a, b, c; 15.a, b;	LEQ 4, 7, 8, 10
1844–1877	11.2, 3; 14.3; 17.1;	19.2; 22.1, 2; 24.1, 2, 3	2.1, 2; 22.2; 14.1, 2; 24.1, 2; 19.1, 2; 33.2	2.a, b, c; 22.a, b 17.a, b; 20.a, b, c;	LEQ 6; DBQ 2
1865–1898	2.3; 5.1, 2; 9.3; 18.1;	23.1; 25.1, 2, 3; 26.1, 2, 3; 27.1, 2, 3	8.1; 25.1, 2; 9.1, 2; 26.1, 2; 12.1, 2; 27.1, 2 22.1;	12.a, b, c; 15.c; 24.a, b, c; 26.a, b	LEQ 11
1890–1945	2.2; 10.1; 13.1, 3; 16.2, 3; 18.3;	23.3; 28.1, 3; 29.1, 2, 3; 31.1, 2, 3; 32.1, 2, 3	10.2; 32.1, 2 15.2; 16.2; 29.1, 2; 30.1;	9.a, b, c; 27.a, b; 13.b; 29.a; 16.a, b, c; 31.a, b, c; 17.c; 32.a, b, c; 22.c; 36.b	LEQ 9, 12, 13, 14, 15; DBQ 3
1945–1980	10.2; 12.1, 2; 18.2; 19.3; 23.2; 28.2;	30.1, 2, 3; 33.1, 2, 3; 34.1, 2, 3; 35.1, 2, 3; 36.1, 2, 3	18.1, 2; 34.1, 2; 20.1, 2; 35.1, 2 23.1, 2; 28.2; 31.2; 33.1;	10.b; 30.a, b, c; 18.a, b, c; 33.a, b, c; 23.a, b, c; 34.a, b, c; 25.a, b, c; 35.a, b, c 28.a, b, c; 29.b;	LEQ 5, 16, 17
1980–Present	10.3;	37.1, 2, 3	10.1; 37.1, 2 30.2;	10.a; 37.a, b, c	LEQ 2, 18, 19

Distribution of Items by Learning Objective

Learning Objective	Source Activities				LEQs & DBQs
	Multiple-Choice		Short-Answer		
NAT-1	7.1, 2; 15.2; 17.1; 20.1;	22.1; 24.2	4.c; 6.a, b, c; 7.a, b, c; 13.a;	17.a; 22.b, c; 29.a	LEQ 1; DBQ 1
NAT-2	19.1; 24.1; 25.1, 2;	29.1; 33.1	25.a, b, c;	29.b	LEQ 11
NAT-3	35.1, 2;	36.2			
NAT-4			2.b;	28.c	
POL-1	3.1; 5.1, 2; 10.1, 2;	11.1, 2; 19.2; 20.2	2.c; 5.a, b, c; 10.a, b;	11.a; 15.a; 33.a, b, c	LEQ 2, 3, 4, 6
POL-2	3.2; 9.1, 2; 15.1; 21.1, 2;	22.2; 35.1, 2	3.a, b; 9.a, b; 11.b; 20.b;	21.a, b, c; 22.a; 35.a, b, c	LEQ 8, 10, 13, 14, 16, 19; DBQ 2
POL-3	2.1, 2; 8.1, 2; 14.2; 15.2; 26.2;	27.2; 29.2; 30.1, 2; 32.1, 2; 33.1	2.a; 8.a, b, c; 9.c; 14.a, b, c; 15.b, c;	24.a, b; 27.a, b; 30.a, b, c; 32.a, b, c	LEQ 2, 5, 7, 11, 12; DBQ 3
WXT-1	12.1, 2;	14.1			
WXT-2	13.2; 26.1;	27.1; 31.1, 2	12.a, b, c; 20.c;	26.a, b; 31.a, b, c	
CUL-1	4.1, 2;	6.1, 2	8.a;	20.a, b	
CUL-4	28.1, 2		28.a, b		
WOR-1	13.1		13.b;	17.a	
WOR-2	16.1, 2; 17.2; 18.1, 2; 23.1, 2;	31.1, 2; 34.1, 2; 36.1; 37.1, 2	16.a, b, c; 17.c; 18.a, b, c; 23.a, b, c;	31.a, b, c; 34.a, b, c; 36.a, b, c; 37.a, b, c	LEQ 9, 15, 17, 18

Explanation of Numbering System:

"**19.**1" refers to Lesson 19, multiple-choice question 1.

"**22.**a, c" refers to Lesson 24, short-answer question parts a and c.

Distribution of Items by Disciplinary Practice and Reasoning Skill

Category	Practice/Skill	Source Activities		LEQs & DBQs
		Multiple-Choice	Short-Answer	
AP History Disciplinary Practices	Analyzing Historical Evidence	2.1; 3.1; 5.1; 4,1; 7.1; 9.1; 13.2; 14.2; 18.1; 21.1; 22.1; 23.1; 25.2; 26.1; 28.1; 29.1	1.c; 2.a; 5.b, c; 7.a, c; 8.a, b; 10.b; 11.b; 12.a, c; 13.a; 14.a, c; 15.a, b; 16.c; 17.a; 18.a, b, c; 20.a, b, c; 21.a, c; 22.a; 25.a, c; 26.a; 27.a, c; 28.a, b; 29.a, b; 30.a, c; 31.b; 32.a, c; 33.c; 34.b, c; 35.a, c; 36.a; 37.b, c	DBQ 1, 2, 3
	Argument Development		2.c; 23.a, b	
AP History Reasoning Skills	Contextualization	7.2; 11.2; 15.1; 25.2; 31.1; 32.2; 33.2; 34.1	22.c; 23.c; 24.a; 31.c; 34.c	
	Comparison	5.2; 33.2	1.a, b; 13.b; 21.c; 30.b; 37.a	LEQ 2, 3, 10, 13, 17, 18
	Causation	1.1, 2; 2.2; 3.2; 4.2; 6.2; 9.2; 10.1; 12.1; 13.1; 15.1; 16.1, 2; 17.2; 18.2; 19.2; 20.2; 21.2; 23.2; 24.1, 2; 25.1; 26.1; 27.1, 2; 28.2; 30.2; 31.2; 32.1; 33.1; 34.1, 2; 35.2; 36.1, 2; 37.2	3.b; 4.c; 5.a; 6.a, b, c; 9.c; 11.a; 17.b; 20.c; 24.c; 28.c; 31.a, c; 33.a, b, c; 34.a; 36.b	LEQ 1, 5, 6, 7, 9, 11, 14, 16, 19; DBQ 1, 2, 3
	Continuity and Change over Time	6.1; 8.1, 2; 10.2; 11.1; 12.2; 14.1; 15.2; 17.1; 19.1; 20.1; 22.2; 24.2; 26.2; 27.2; 29.2; 30.1, 2; 31.1; 32.1, 2; 35.1; 36.1; 37.1	3.a; 8.c; 10.a; 15.c; 17.c; 22.c; 23.c; 36.c	LEQ 1, 4, 5, 6, 7, 8, 12, 14, 15; DBQ 1, 2, 3

Applying the Common Core State Standards©

The Common Core State Standards for 11th and 12th grade History and Social Studies revolve entirely around the use of primary and secondary sources, making *Threads* a useful tool for integrating the standards into your existing curriculum. The chart below identifies where each standard is directly addressed in one or more of the practice items; **boldface** indicates that the lesson as a whole addresses the standard in a larger way.

English Language Arts Standards — History and Social Studies, Grades 11–12			
Key Ideas and Details:	Lessons	**Integration of Knowledge and Ideas:**	Lessons
CCSS.ELA-LITERACY.RH.11-12.1 Cite specific textual evidence to support analysis of primary and secondary sources, connecting insights gained from specific details to an understanding of the text as a whole.	1, 2, 5, 7, 8, 13, 14, 15, 18, 20, 22, 25-35	**CCSS.ELA-LITERACY.RH.11-12.7** Integrate and evaluate multiple sources of information presented in diverse formats and media (e.g., visually, quantitatively, as well as in words) in order to address a question or solve a problem.	**17;** DBQs 1-3
CCSS.ELA-LITERACY.RH.11-12.2 Determine the central ideas or information of a primary or secondary source; provide an accurate summary that makes clear the relationships among the key details and ideas.	5, 8, 15, 17, 21, 23, 24, 28, 31, 36	**CCSS.ELA-LITERACY.RH.11-12.8** Evaluate an author's premises, claims, and evidence by corroborating or challenging them with other information.	5, 25, 29, **35**
CCSS.ELA-LITERACY.RH.11-12.3 Evaluate various explanations for actions or events and determine which explanation best accords with textual evidence, acknowledging where the text leaves matters uncertain.	3, 4, 6, 9, 17, 20, 24, 28, 31, 33, 34, 36	**CCSS.ELA-LITERACY.RH.11-12.9** Integrate information from diverse sources, both primary and secondary, into a coherent understanding of an idea or event, noting discrepancies among sources.	**17,** 20, 29; DBQs 1-3
Craft and Structure:	Lessons	**Range of Reading and Level of Text Complexity:**	Lessons
CCSS.ELA-LITERACY.RH.11-12.4 Determine the meaning of words and phrases as they are used in a text, including analyzing how an author uses and refines the meaning of a key term over the course of a text (e.g., how Madison defines *faction* in Federalist No. 10).	**9, 10,** 19, 29	**CCSS.ELA-LITERACY.RH.11-12.10** By the end of grade 12, read and comprehend history/social studies texts in the grades 11-CCR text complexity band independently and proficiently.	1-37
CCSS.ELA-LITERACY.RH.11-12.5 Analyze in detail how a complex primary source is structured, including how key sentences, paragraphs, and larger portions of the text contribute to the whole.	4, 5, 15, 17, **19,** 28, 36		
CCSS.ELA-LITERACY.RH.11-12.6 Evaluate authors' differing points of view on the same historical event or issue by assessing the authors' claims, reasoning, and evidence.	6, 11, 12, 16-18, 22, 23, 28, 32, 34, 35		

Worksheet for Document Source Analysis

Title: _____

1. Date: _____

2. Context: _____

   _____

   _____

3. Author: _____

   _____

   _____

4. Message:

   a. _____

   _____

   b. _____

   _____

   c. _____

   _____

   d. _____

   _____

Worksheet for Visual Source Analysis

Title: _____

1. Subject: _____

   _____

2. Images:

   a. _____

   b. _____

   c. _____

   d. _____

3. Points:

   a. _____

   _____

   b. _____

   _____

   c. _____

   _____

   d. _____

   _____

Worksheet for Map Analysis

Title: _____

1. Geography: _____

_____

_____

2. Event(s): _____

_____

_____

3. Benefit(s):

   a. _____

_____

   b. _____

_____

   c. _____

_____

   d. _____

_____

Short-Answer Response

The following is a chronological list of the primary source documents available in this edition of *Threads*.

Year	Type	Topic	Page #	
			Student	Teacher
1570	📄	Royal Order from the King of Spain	---	5
1600	🌐	The Atlantic Slave Trade	4	6
1644	📄	Roger Williams, "The Bloody Tenent of Persecution..."	---	24
1649	📄	Puritan Church Platform	15	25
1676	📄	Nathaniel Bacon's Manifesto	---	18
1776	📄	Loyalist view of the American Revolution (Inglis)	28	45, 46
1786	📄	George Washington on Shays' Rebellion	12	19
1801	📄	Thomas Jefferson's First Inaugural Address	21	34
1811	📄	Felix Grundy and the causes of the War of 1812	54	72
1823	📄	John Taylor's Reaction to *McCulloch v. Maryland*	63	83
1823	📄	Monroe Doctrine	148	183
1825	📄	John Quincy Adams and the role of government	45	63
1832	📄	Andrew Jackson's veto of the National Bank	32	50
1833	📄	Lydia Maria Child, "Colonization Society"	---	112
1833	📄	William Lloyd Garrison and Abolition	88	113
1835	📄	Charles Finney, "A Christian's Duty"	---	39
1841	📄	Constitution of Brook Farm	84	107
1845	📄	John O'Sullivan and Manifest Destiny	71	93
1850	📄	John C. Calhoun and the Compromise of 1850	58	77, 78
1851	✏️	The Second Great Awakening	24	40
1853	🌐	Expansion of the United States, 1783–1853	70	92
1867	📄	Thaddeus Stevens and Reconstruction	100	125
1868	📄	The Fourteenth Amendment	80	102
1873	✏️	The Granger Movement	50	68
1876	🌐	The Election of 1876	8	13
1883	📄	U.S. Civil Rights Cases	104	131

Historical Document Index

	Document		Map		Illustration/Cartoon		Photograph

Year	Type	Topic	Page #	
			Student	Teacher
1883	📄	William Graham Sumner on Social Darwinism	112	139
1888	📄	Why Great Men Are Not Chosen President	---	33
1894	📄	William "Coins" Harvey on Currency Crisis	108	135
1894	✏️	Women's Suffrage, Puck Magazine Cover	92	117
1896	📄	John Marshall Harlan's Dissenting Opion in *Plessy*	---	130
1901	📄	Theodore Roosevelt and Trusts	36	54
1905	📄	*Lochner v. U.S.*	120	149
1906	✏️	Theodore Roosevelt and the Big Stick Policy	66	88
1908	📄	*Muller v. Oregon*	120	149
1919	✏️	Rejection of the Treaty of Versailles	96	121
1935	✏️	New Deal and the Economy	132	163
1935	📄	James G. Randall, *The Civil War and Reconstruction*	---	12
1937	📄	W.E.B. DuBois, *Black Reconstruction*	---	12
1939	📄	Gerald P. Nye and Isolationism	128	158, 159
1947	✏️	Containment	140	173
1950	📄	National Security Council Paper 68 (NSC-68)	---	172
1954	📄	President Eisenhower to Ngo Dinh Diem	---	178
1956	📄	Harry Truman and the Korean War	76	98
1957	📄	President Eisenhower and Little Rock Crisis	136	167
1964	📄	Barry Goldwater's acceptance speech	40	58
1964	📄	Lyndon Johnson's War on Poverty	124	153
1964	📄	Malcolm X on Civil Rights Movement	116	144, 145
1969	📷	Vietnam Protest	144	179
2002	📄	National Security	152	187
2009	📄	War on Terror	152	187

Don't miss out on the
Teacher's Companion Website

Purchase of this Teacher Edition includes free access to the Teacher's Companion Website. In order to access the materials, you will need to register for an account using the unique ID code found on the inside front cover of this text. The following are just some of the valuable resources you'll find on the site:

- Printable and downloadable formats for the 19 Long Essay Questions and 3 Document-Based Questions, as well as answer sheet templates that simulate the exam

- H.I.P.P.O. DBQ Planning Worksheet - ready to print

- 150+ Multiple-Choice review questions with detailed answer analysis in a convenient sort and filter display; use these questions to test student comprehension in the various historical periods so you can identify areas requiring more intensive review

- Core Chart Worksheets for building students' synthesis and summarization skills

- Perhaps most importantly, critical updates to the content found in both the Student Edition and this Teacher Edition (As the College Board makes changes to the AP U.S. History curriculum, we update our content.)

Go to <ins>http://threads.sherpalearning.com</ins> to register today!

Note to Teachers and Administrators

We at Sherpa Learning hope to continue to create amazing content at sensible prices for years to come. But we're a small crew of believers with no corporate umbrella to hide under. As such, we'd ask that you consider buying a class set if you can afford it. We understand that times are tough and that sometimes you just have to do what you have to do. The students come first. But it's hard for a company like ours to survive selling one book at a time. Just keep it in mind. That's all we ask.

And if you loved this book, check out our site for other amazing resources. Don't forget to register with the site to become a contributor, stay informed about new AP resources, and be part of the leadership conversation.

www.sherpalearning.com

Made in United States
North Haven, CT
24 August 2022

23170688R00148